THE ROCK & ROLL YEARS OF A PARACHUTING MEDIC

First published in 2007 by

WOODFIELD PUBLISHING
Bognor Regis, West Sussex, England
www.woodfieldpublishing.com

ISBN 1-84683-031-1

Cover photo by Richard Maw of 'In Focus', Scarborough.

THE ROCK & ROLL YEARS OF A PARACHUTING MEDIC

Recollections of 25 years service in the Medical Branch of the RAF

MICK THOMPSON

Woodfield

With love and thanks to my wife Joan
for her support and encouragement,
and to my son Carl, who shared nineteen of my twenty five years
and six months service, with me, and is currently a serving RAF
Officer in the Engineering Branch

Contents

About The Author

The author left Bradford and enlisted in the RAF in 1957, just prior to what he envisaged would be compulsory military National Service. Whilst he initially sought to recommence a career in engineering, he was persuaded that it would suit everybody concerned much better, if he became a medical orderly ! As he had belonged to the St John Ambulance Cadets whilst still at school, he agreed to this change of direction. This turned to be a wise decision, and what was intended to be a three year engagement, eventually became a full career of 25 years and six months.

After retiring in 1982, Mick opted for a second career in the Civil Service, and the next 20 years was spent working in the Court of Criminal Appeal in Central London. There were no postings, detachments or sporting opportunities other than a day off every year for the Civil Service Cross Country Championships ! However there was more than adequate compensation with promotions, and involvement in the many interesting major appeal cases of the 1990s such as ' The Tottenham 3', 'Cardiff 3' and Judith Ward.

In 2003 he returned to Yorkshire on his final retirement, and now lives in Scarborough with his wife Joan. His son Carl was not dissuaded from an engineering career in the RAF, and is still a serving Engineering Officer. Mick remains actively involved in athletics, and still competes for Scarborough Athletic Club. This year (2007) he will be running in his 17th London Marathon.

Introduction

This is an account of my 25 years in the Medical Branch of the Royal Air Force, from post-Suez to the aftermath of the Falklands War, and includes my recollections of the popular music of the period, from Private Elvis Presley to the pacifist singer Boy George.

After leaving school at the end of 1954, I fully expected that I would be required to complete two years National Service, either at the age of 18, or later if I gained a deferment due to an approved apprenticeship. After two years as an engineering apprentice I became discontented with the low pay all apprentices had to put up with in those days. I did not wish to attend so-called Night School in order to study maths and physics etc, so I ended my apprenticeship when I was 17 and therefore had a year of freedom before call-up. It was time to earn a good wage at the many woollen mills in Bradford and enjoy the increased amount of money to spend on entertainment.

Around this time I would often meet up with conscripts who were serving in the Royal Air Force, and from their accounts, life in the RAF seemed to be much better than in the Army. After the Royal Navy, which had a limited National Service intake, the RAF was the favourite choice of most. However, entry was partly restricted for National Servicemen, particularly for those men without a trade qualification. Because of this, many opted to be become a 'regular', and enlist for a minimum of 3 years. This would ensure entry, plus greatly improved pay and a better choice of RAF trades. It often seemed that National Servicemen were placed in trades that bore little resemblance to their civilian experience. This was something I experienced in the Medical Branch, where a wide variety of tradesmen were press-ganged into nursing duties, partly because there was very few civilian male nurses in the 1950s anyway.

In addition to the favourable reports from serving airmen, I had been a member of the Air Training Corps for a short period, and had spent a week at an RAF Station in Shropshire for a Summer Camp. This was RAF Tern Hill, a unit I was to be posted to in the 1960s, and which I disliked. However when I was a young cadet, I was impressed with how the serving airmen seemed to be enjoying themselves, always laughing and joking etc., and I thought the food was very good too. So it came to pass that at the end of 1956, I made enquiries at the RAF Recruiting Office, and early the next year,

I had the required medical examination and aptitude tests, and was then accepted as a new recruit. Whilst I initially wanted to be a mechanic, the RAF decided that I might be more usefully employed in another trade. As I had also been a member of the Saint John Ambulance Brigade Cadets, I thought I would like to be a 'medic'. This was agreed and I subsequently spent the next 25 years in a wide variety of jobs in the Medical Branch and, with only a few exceptions, greatly enjoyed my contribution to the branch, which coincided with a period of great change.

Whilst decisions to withdraw from some of the British Colonies, and reduce the overseas military commitment were being discussed post Suez, a map of the world in 1957 still had quite a lot of countries shaded pink – which was used to denote our colonies! The colonies all had air bases to support the often huge military garrisons. In addition the RAF were providing numerous squadrons of aircraft, as part of the NATO presence in Germany, to guard against the threat of aggression by the Soviet Union the United Kingdom there were many RAF bases seemingly preparing for Armageddon, with the V Bomber force providing the so-called Nuclear Deterrent.

The extent of the RAF presence worldwide was extremely well illustrated in a 1960s film about the regular aeromedical (air ambulance) flights. What was often a weekly trip, started out at Hong Kong, then called at several staging posts to collect patients destined for hospital treatment in the United Kingdom Service Hospitals. First stop was Singapore, and then on to Gan in the Maldives, and from there to Aden. At Aden, other aircraft had already flown patients in from the Persian Gulf and Kenya. From Aden the aircraft proceeded to Cyprus, where again other aircraft had evacuated patients in from Libya. After Cyprus the aircraft would sometimes call at Malta, before finally arriving in the UK, where the patients would be dispersed to the various service hospitals. Sadly, in 2007 the last remaining service hospital in the United Kingdom was closed, despite widespread criticism of the alternative arrangements at civilian hospitals.

The first years of my RAF career in the late 1950s were during the National Service era, followed by the transition to an all regular force. During my twenty-five years service, I had four full overseas tours, plus three overseas detachments. Two detachments were on active service in Aden, and the other in Zambia, and which all took place during a most memorable 3-year tour of duty with the RAF Regiment Parachute Squadron – 2 Field.

After leaving the Parachute Squadron, I joined the Parachute Rescue Team in Cyprus, where I added to my tally of thirty-three descents with 2 Squadron, and subsequently completed one hundred parachute jumps, mainly training in Cyprus, but also on exercises in Iran, Turkey and the Persian Gulf.

There was also a trip to Kenya at the time of a visit by Prince Charles and Princess Anne in 1971, when I was a member of an emergency back up team.

Other pleasant diversions whilst serving in Cyprus, included a trip with a boxing team to Bahrain, representing British Forces in Cyprus as a featherweight, and also two trips back to UK for RAF Boxing Championships.

During the last few years of my service, I was employed on Aeromedical Evacuation work, both full time on a 6-month tour of Belize, and on an *ad hoc* basis for trips to Cyprus, Sardinia and Germany. My final aero medical task involved the return of injured servicemen at the end of the Falklands War, which included a trip to Ascension Island.

When I attended my farewell retirement dinner at the Sergeants Mess, the presiding Chairman described my service as being like something out of the 'Boys Own' comic. This may have been a bit of an 'over the top' description of an interesting 25 years, but one which 25 years later, has prompted me to write my story.

1. The World in 1957

On the eve of my entry to the RAF as a volunteer, I did not pause to consider either the role of the Royal Air Force, or that of the United Kingdom in World affairs. I thought that military service was something I would have to undertake at some point in the near future, although if I had been better informed, I might have considered the possibility of the end of conscription, which was subsequently decided by a 1958 Act of Parliament, less than a year after I had enlisted. This meant that some of those in my final class at school were never conscripted. I was never aware of any significant opposition by my peers to either National Service, or indeed British foreign policy, and certainly there was nothing on the same scale of opposition that was provoked by the invasion of Iraq in 2003. It was not possible to avoid conscription by claiming to be a conscientious objector. The few that made such claims were usually made to serve in non combatant units, and were often subject to equal danger if engaged on active service. It was not a popular option.

During the period I served in the RAF, British troops were deployed on active service in seven overseas theatres. At the time of my enlistment, the violent Mau Mau uprising in Kenya, was proving to be an exception to what was to be mainly a trouble free withdrawal from British colonies in Africa. This was partly due to the reluctance of the white settlers to hand over power, and the guerrilla based struggle for power was to last until a settlement in 1959 which led to independence in 1960. At the same time British troops were also engaged on active service in Cyprus. The majority of the island's population were of Greek extraction and were actively seeking a union with Greece, which was against the wishes of both the island's minority of Turkish Cypriots and the British Government. A long guerrilla campaign was waged by the EOKA 'freedom fighters' who backed the union with Greece, Enosis, continued until a settlement was finally reached, which resulted in an independent state. It is interesting that a reference is made to the troubles in Cyprus by Elvis Costello in his 1979 record of 'Oliver's Army', with the line, "It's no laughing party, when you have been on the Murder

Mile" The 'Murder Mile' was in fact the name given to Ledra Street in Nicosia, following several murders there at the height of the conflict.

The main focus for the whole of the British Armed forces in 1957 was the so called 'cold war', which described the efforts of NATO to guard against any further incursion into Western Europe by the forces of the Soviet Union. This involved a huge British military presence in West Germany, mainly in the North, whilst the United States of America maintained an even larger force in the south – which would include a certain Private Elvis Presley after 1957! This 'war' was to continue up until 1989, and the reunification of Germany, and the subsequent break up of the Soviet Union.

In addition to the theatres engaged on a war footing, either actively or passively, there was a large number of overseas bases, which were being retained for mainly strategic reasons. In the United Kingdom there was also a huge reserve of troops, which were based not only in the main garrison towns, but throughout England, Wales, Scotland and Northern Ireland. There was also a large RAF presence of fighter squadrons for the defence of the country, and bomber squadrons, many of which were based in Eastern England, and included 'V' Bombers on which the nuclear deterrence policy was based. Added to this, there was also fleets of transport aircraft, and huge training bases for aircrew and ground crew.

Those who served in the RAF during the post war period, and particularly national servicemen, will testify to the amount of overmanning that took place on many units during the National Service era. This was most obvious when conscription ended, and the manning levels of some units were scrutinized, possibly for the first time, in order to establish just how many posts were essential. There is a vast amount of anecdotal evidence regarding just how little work was carried out by many airmen, which could lead to boredom and disgruntled feelings. In my experience, I never witnessed any painting coal white for inspections, but there was never much thought given to saving time and effort. No doubt on some units, many airmen worked hard, but for most, it was a matter of passing the time away until the end of the two years. This became an art form and was known as 'skiving'. A common practice which reduced a little after the end of conscription, but remained the focus of the day for many years to come. Another practice at the time which had to drastically altered after the end of National service, was the assumption that airmen should never work unsupervised, and therefore a non commissioned officer, usually a corporal would be put 'in charge'. This led to some overmanning in Medical Centres, when there had to be two medical orderlies on duty, just in case two emergencies occurred at the same time, and of course the two had to be supervised by a corporal. After 1962, most Medical Centres found that they could manage with just one airman on duty, and for some smaller units, the reduction in staff meant that it would have been totally impossible for any more to be on standby in this way.

As I marched off to do my bit, Elvis Presley was singing his very first United Kingdom number one hit record 'All Shook Up'. His music remained in the music charts right up until I was demobbed in 1982, which was remarkably 5 years after his untimely death. In 1957 the pop charts were still somewhat dominated by Americans such as crooners, Dean Martin, Doris Day, Pat Boone Andy Williams and Johnny Ray, whilst rock and roll artists such as Bill Haley, Little Richard and Jerry Lee Lewis often joined Elvis at the top of the music charts of the time. However, the Brits were well represented by Tommy Steele who took 'Singing the Blues' to number one after Guy Mitchell had also topped the charts with the same song. Lonnie Donegan also had a number one with 'Cumberland Gap'. With some exceptions such as Cliff Richard, who topped the charts for the first time in 1959, the Americans were to dominate until the early 1960s.

2. Induction at RAF Cardington

The start of what for me was an adventure I had been looking forward to, commenced at the RAF Recruiting Office in the centre of a very sooty Bradford – years before any 'Clean Air' Acts of course. A small group of would-be recruits had assembled at the appointed hour for a final briefing, i.e. being told where to go! The oldest and most responsible looking of the party was put in charge, and was given the responsibility of exchanging an official travel warrant for rail tickets for Bedford. There we would be met by staff from RAF Cardington, the reception camp for all male new entrants, other than the potential officer and aircrew candidates. There was never any conscription for women, and separate arrangements for their induction and training at other stations were in force. I mention this here, as nowadays women undergo basic recruit training together with men, at RAF Halton, as part of the RAF, and not as a separate women's air force, WRAF.

On arrival at Bedford, we were met by RAF reception staff, and we then boarded coaches for a two mile journey to RAF Cardington. It seemed that it had been organised for all the recruits to arrive about the same time, and for some reason a fleet of coaches was always used, although there was a railway station at Cardington. On arrival at the camp we had a welcoming speech, and were then allocated accommodation. This consisted of beds in wooden huts which were strangely constructed on stilts, and entry was made via flight of steps. We then experienced our first meal, which was reasonable, and was thought to be better than we might expect once we had been sworn in and signed on the 'dotted line'. We were then free to do what we wished for the rest of the evening. The welcoming speech had advised everybody of pubs which were 'out of bounds', or best avoided due to problems with local youths. Of course for some recruits, these were the places to head for first, as they were likely to be the most lively and have the most local women present! There was entertainment laid on at the camp in the form of dances with live groups, a cinema and the Navy Army Air Force Club,(NAAFI), which included food and alcohol as the main attractions, but also a TV room, and a games room. I joined in with a group of older men, who had obviously had their call up deferred, on a trip to nearby Bedford. We opted for a pub which was seemingly full of RAF recruits, although none were in uniform. When uniform was first issued, civilian clothes had to be posted back home, and recruits were then confined to camp for the remainder of the week at Cardington. I was overjoyed that as I was obviously seen as a RAF recruit, none of the bar staff queried my age – just as well as I was still 17! The remainder of my stay at Cardington was spent on the camp enjoying the entertainment.

At the end of my first day with the RAF, I am sure I slept well, as the other occupants of the hut I was accommodated in, were mainly more mature individuals, and as such did not wish to be kept awake too long at night for no good reason. At that time the RAF enlisted a high percentage of men who had gained a deferment because of an apprenticeship, and to a lesser extent, those who had sought to delay their National Service due to a degree course at university. In addition some were married men who wanted to get the whole process of conscription over with, and high jinks was not normally on their agenda. Not surprisingly, those who were married, lived only for the time they would be allowed home on leave. In addition, it was always considered preferable to keep a low profile whilst undergoing basic training. This extended to never volunteering for anything!

On day two, the first thing on the induction programme was the medical examination. All recruits would have undergone a medical examination either soon after call up or volunteering. This examination would have been fairly cursory, and was mainly to root out anyone who would be medically unfit to serve in the forces. In some cases where illness or injury was feigned, further investigations had to be carried out. The most common form of trying to avoid National Service, was probably still the time honoured pretence of mental illness. This was no doubt difficult to evaluate, as some of those concerned were really mentally ill. Other methods involved damaging the knee joint by repeated blows to effect 'water on the knee', and deafness. I never heard of anyone pretending to be blind, but conversely there was some trickery involved for those who were short sighted and wished to enlist. At Cardington, the examination was more thorough, partly to weed out any that would not be able to cope with life in the RAF, physically or mentally, but also to record exactly what the state of health was on entry. This would reduce the amount of bogus claims that might be made on eventual discharge, in cases where a disability existed, but was one that did not rule out military service. Those with a relatively mild disability could be offered sedentary employment, and excused any heavy exercise. This was known as being on 'Light Duties'.

The next most important item on the reception programme, was a visit to the Camp Tailor, where uniforms and the greatcoat were tried on, and any necessary alterations made by the following day. No doubt in order to save money, only stocks of the most common sizes were readily available, so anyone exceedingly tall or overweight, would often have to wait for over a week or so, until the correct size was obtained. It is hard to imagine this form of stigmatising today, but those concerned in 1957 coped, or seemed to cope with their misfortune, part of which was the dreaded 'standing out'. What was often a pleasant surprise in the way that the reception staff at Cardington dealt with the hordes, did not extend to the general issue of the remainder of personal kit. This retained the stereotypical method involving a very long table, lots of shouting, and the recipients made to pass along the long table, whilst an increasing amount of kit was added to each recruits pile! It is typical of the standards of personal hygiene at the time, that for example, only three shirts were issued. This ensured that one was in use, one was in the laundry and one was spare. If the 'spare' shirt was used then you would have to wash and iron it yourself. Few did, and the shirt would be made to last the whole week, which whilst at recruit training was a full seven days. Six collars were supplied for the collar detached shirts, as these items would be the most visible. Another sign of the times in respect of uniform clothing, was that only airmen had to wear the uncomfortable stiff collars with their shirts. Officers were allowed to wear more comfortable collar attached shirts. The item of kit which always caused some mirth, was called a 'housewife'. This consisted of a small cloth container which contained needles and thread, a thimble and darning wool for any running repairs. These items were of course hardly ever used, and small repairs would be carried out by either females in the family, or by friendly willing females in the WRAF! For this reason, this item of kit lasted for the entire period of service, and I have no doubt many are still part of ex servicemen's memorabilia. The two shoe brushes that were issued, also never seemed to wear out, not even those owned by those who would always be found polishing their shoes and boots. In addition to the 'Housewife' the beret would evoke much laughter, as the brand new version looked somewhat silly. Think of Frank Spencer in 'Some Mothers Do Have Em' or a Benny Hill sketch. It was possible to make the beret look better by soaking it and shrinking the material. This was supposed to be forbidden, but almost everybody did it. Those that did not 'stood out' of course!

I do not of course recall the exact sequence of events, but an important part of the induction process, was to allocate suitable or indeed otherwise, trades to everybody before they commenced Recruit Training. Some of those who were entering the RAF as 'regulars', a phrase which signified other than National Service, would have had already been promised the trade of their choice, should they agree to sign on for at least three years, and for trades where a lot of time would be spent in training, as much as nine years. Further aptitude tests and interviews took place, and then normally everyone was allocated a trade. For those enlisting as National Servicemen, a suitable trade seemingly had a broad interpretation. There is much anecdotal evidence that many found themselves in trades which bore little if any resemblance to their previous experience in civilian life. In addition some National Servicemen opted for trades which were seen as 'cushy', which can be interpreted as not too much hard work, very little 'bull' (excessive cleaning), and possibly with the added bonus of learning a new skill. A Mechanical Transport (MT) driver, with the possibility of a HGV licence was one example. Batman or Steward as they were officially called, which involved working in the Officer's or Sergeants Mess was another similar such option.

The reception staff responsible for the allocation of trades, had one overriding aim, and that was to provide sufficient manpower in the less attractive trades, where they would rarely get sufficient volunteers. Catering was one such trade, which was seen as working long hours in what were poor conditions in the 1950s, and additionally had little job satisfaction, as often the standard was not in reality very high. Another trade which presented difficulties for recruiters was the nursing trades, as I mentioned in my Forward. There were comparatively few male nurses in the 1950s, and those that enlisted would either be of State Registered Nurse, (SRN), or State Enrolled Nurse (SEN) status. Alternatively recruits might be those without any qualifications, but who were able and willing to undergo training, which at the time was three years for SRN and two years for SEN. This ruled out training for National Service candidates. In addition there was a steady stream of would be female nurses entering the WRAF. The Ward Sister posts were invariably filled by members of the Princess Mary's Royal Air Force Nursing

Service, (PMRAFNS), which was then an all female branch of the RAF, composed of SRN qualified Commissioned Officers.

Until the late 1970s, the RAF had several large hospitals in the UK, and also a hospital at every major overseas base. In order to keep these hospitals functioning properly, or what was seen as proper at the time, meant that there was a huge demand for what was called Ward Assistants, a trade which attracted very few volunteers. In addition to the job being seen as a woman's by the majority of 1950s men, the opportunity for promotion was almost non existent, as there was little if any formal training, and therefore those selected would suffer financially. So it was not that unusual for National Service airmen from heavy industrial backgrounds, to end up doing bed baths and handing out bedpans. Many of them performed extremely well and I refer to this in chapter five.

The largest number of medical personnel were employed on RAF Stations in Medical Centres, which in the 1950s were called Station Sick Quarters, a curious use of the the word sick to mean ill and not vomit! These Sick Quarters were a mixture of a General Practitioners Surgery with a dispensary and minor treatment room, an emergency ambulance service, and some small wards for minor illnesses or injuries, mainly for those living in barracks on the station. If servicemen's families used this facility, then usually a civilian nurse would be employed, otherwise the centre would be manned by a mixture of Nursing Attendants and Medical Administrators all of whom would have started service as Nursing Attendants, which was the basic entry level trade for the Medical Branch. The Nursing Attendants would deal with minor treatments, nursing, dispensing, first aid cover, and ambulance duties, which on a station with an active airfield, (Flying Station), would include being part of the emergency crash rescue team. Unless they were to become more specialised members of the Medical Branch such as radiographers or physiotherapists, the progression from Nursing Attendant was via Medical Administration, which at that time was at the Junior Non Commissioned Officer level of Corporal. The more senior Nursing Attendants at Sick Quarters would be employed in an administrative role in the office. This was the most sought after job in Medical Centres, as most airmen wished to avoid doing any nursing duties! The trade of Nursing Attendant, was what was widely known in the services as a 'Medic', and this was the trade I signed up for.

Having now been allocated a uniform and a trade, the most important part of the induction procedure was being sworn in, or the attestation. In addition to swearing an oath of allegiance to The Queen, with the additional key phrase, 'all other officers set over me', the recruits have the meaning of the oath formally explained to them. They then sign to say that the terms of the oath, and the meaning of the oath itself has been explained to them, and also sign a written declaration of allegiance.

Another important stage in the induction process was being issued with a personal service number. This was a seven digit number that we were told had be learned by heart as soon as possible, and that failure to so would have dire consequences. To assist the process, the RAF identity card, RAF form 1250, which included the service number, was issued, also with a warning that any loss would result in 'a charge', the term used to describe the initial stage in the services disciplinary procedures. Recruits would spend time reciting the number to commit it memory. It becomes a number remembered for life, and no doubt the basis for many a 'pin' number in the present day – mine isn't by the way! It was also a custom to refer to the last three digits of the number on Pay Parades, in order to identify individuals, particularly with common surnames, but it was used for everybody regardless. The clerk accompanying the officer on such parades would shout out for example, 'Bloggs' and Aircraftsman Bloggs would respond with 'Sir 123'. A ritual that was more time honoured than anything else.

The remainder of the week at Cardington involved some talks and films on RAF life, but the most time was spent waiting for something or other. When large groups were being processed, the interests of the reception station staff were paramount, and everything was organised accordingly. For example there was no appointment system as such in place. Everybody was marched to the various offices and made to wait in a queue for their turn at whatever it was they needed. When I say 'marched' I am using the term lightly, as there was no real effort to teach drill to the recruits, which would start at the Recruit Training Camps on week two. We did however line up 'threes' – also known as 'one behind the other twice', and and then 'march' to wherever we were meant to be. This may be have been the source of the old joke about a parade with all three services present. In the joke a Sergeant Major says, ' The Army will march past, the Royal Navy will walk past, and the Royal Air Force will make it's way as best as it can'!

One of the final parts of the induction is having that very first photograph in uniform taken. So once the uniforms have been collected after any alterations, we all assemble near the giant Air Ship Hangars, one of which once housed the ill fated R101 Air Ship, and now house balloons which are used for parachute training. I did not envisage at the time, that 8 years later, I would be making my first parachute jump from a cage suspended under one of the balloons – scary stuff.

Before departure to RAF West Kirby which was is in The Wirral area of Cheshire, one final ritual has to take place, and that is for the recruits to send all their civilian clothes back home. The only items of personal belongings other than the RAF uniforms, clothing and accoutrements (a wonderful word for service equipment), which have just been issued, are just a photograph of the next of kin, and toiletry items. Recruits would have been forewarned of this procedure, and advised to restrict the amount of personal belonging that they brought with them to RAF Cardington. One reason for the restriction was because that during the whole period of Recruit Training, civilian clothes could not be worn, so they did not need not to be taken. The restriction on personal belongings was probably a form of discipline, and also because of limited space in the living accommodation at Recruit Training Camps. In the 1950s most airmen would not have considered this much of a hardship. Items such as record players and radios, were items that were not normally taken from the main home. Few recruits other than enthusiasts would have owned cameras, and items now considered essential for basic survival such as mobile phones, and Ipods were at least more than 30 years down the line. All the temporary redundant items, including the suitcases they were transported to RAF Cardington in, were wrapped in brown paper and tied with string, which followed a demonstration by a member of the reception staff. Few of the recruits were able to achieve any expertise in this task, which resulted in some very strange looking parcels, and another amusing part of a tried and tested regime.

3. Recruit Training at RAF West Kirby

At the time of my induction, RAF West Kirby was one of three remaining Recruit Training Camps, the others were RAF Wilmslow, also in Cheshire and RAF Bridgnorth in Shropshire. Everyone I know who went through the process, always claimed that their camp was the worst of the three, and could provide examples of some extreme forms of discipline that they experienced. There was also claims that National Servicemen had a harder time of it than others. The phrase 'pinch of salt' readily springs to mind. The three Recruit Training camps would have been run on exactly the same lines, and with exactly the same training programme and standards for all recruits. In addition to perceived differences between the camps, it was also claimed that some squadrons within the camps, were tougher than others. It was more likely that the *esprit de corps* engendered by the directing staff, i.e. Best intake, flight and best squadron mentality, was responsible for any differences perceived or otherwise. My account of the initial training process, will not be in any way similar to either how the French Foreign Legion operates, or how the United States Marine Corps prepared troops for the Vietnam war. It will just be about how the Royal Air Force trained its recruits in the 1950s. I am aware that events of the past can often be clouded with some fond nostalgia, and that many airmen, particularly conscripts disliked the whole process. However I am absolutely certain that the vast majority took the rough with the smooth, and coped well with everything that was served up – with perhaps the exception of the food! Those who think otherwise should now proceed to Chapter 4!

The journey from RAF Cardington to RAF West Kirby was almost 'door to door' by train, as there was, most unusually, even for the period pre Beeching Report which led to wide scale cuts in railway routes and stations, a railway station on the camp at RAF Cardington. On arrival at the small town of West Kirby, we were met by Corporal Drill instructors, known as D. I. s, who screamed and shouted at us before herding everybody into trucks, known a 'three-tonners'. This was now the preferred mode of transport for trainees. Almost as expected, and reminiscent of a scene from any British film which incorporated basic training, known as 'square bashing', when the trucks arrive inside the camp, we were again subject to more shouting and abuse, and then herded into a large hangar. Then after a roll call, we were split into flights, that is groups of around 20, and marched to our new accommodation, which was a large wooden hut that would be our home for the next 8 weeks. The next part of the arrival procedure, and would which would continue for the rest of my 25 years service, but only for junior airmen, was the issue of bedding. This was both adequate and basic, and consisted of 2 pillows and slips, 2 sheets and 3 'hairy' blankets. These items always had to be signed for, and at the end of the stay on camp, had to be returned to the Bedding Store. We were subsequently shown how to fold the blankets and sheets, and how to lay them out on the bed every morning, except Sunday, when the bed could be left with the sheets and blankets in their normal place.

The next stage in the arrival procedure was a series of talks, by an ever increasing level of rank, starting with one of the two allocated D.I.s A summary of his chat or tirade, would be that we must obey all orders, and that he was hard but fair! After this a senior and deputy man were chosen. Usually anyone with previous service experience was the first choice, then the oldest or the toughest looking! After this matter had been settled, we had a lesson in Barrack Room etiquette. This was that if a corporal or above entered the room, the senior man or his deputy, or the person nearest the door, would shout ' NCO present', at which point everybody would stop what they were doing and stand to attention. Then followed a talk by a Sergeant Drill Instructor who would be in charge of the two corporals. This was similar to the Corporal D.I. Version, but with less shouting and swearing. Next in line, was the officer in charge of several flights, a Pilot Officer, the lowest commissioned officer rank, who was often a National Serviceman. In my flight it was a very small man, who bore a resemblance to Ronnie Corbett, who was also a National Service Pilot Officer. The Pilot Officer delivered more of a pep talk, with of course no shouting or swearing.

Amidst all this activity, we were marched to the cook house or Airmen's Mess as it was known, for our first square bashing meal. I do not recall what was on offer, but it will have been a cooked meal, as all three meals, breakfast, lunch and tea were cooked, and were invariably adequate but unappetising. There were some very basic rules in the RAF catering world at the time. The first was that everybody had their own cutlery, a basic knife fork and spoon. These were washed in a huge hot water containers and rinsed in another container with cold water which were placed near the mess entrance. Another was that the only hot drink options were large urns containing tea with milk and sugar, and tea with just milk. The option of adding your own milk and sugar was generally available outside of training camps, but it was years before coffee became an option. Another oddity, especially by the standards of today, was that side plates for bread and butter were never made available. Bread and butter was only placed on a separate table, and was either then placed on the side of the dinner plate or more usually on the table – there were never any cloths of course. At the end of a meal, the plates had to be taken to a swill bin to be scraped before being placed on a rack for washing. A sensible measure for mass catering to avoid a accumulation of used plates etc. on tables, but the stench from the pig bins could be overwhelming. I feel that I should mention what is a bit of an old chestnut, that of bromide in the tea to calm sexual urges amongst men confined to camp for a few weeks. As I understand it, it is possible that bromide was added to the tea in the urns, but this was simply to make the tea which was invariably weak, taste stronger, and probably had no other effects! I can only speculate what happened to the tea saved.

So after being fed, watered and possibly calmed down with the bromide, we received instruction on how to clean the accommodation, which we were told would be inspected every morning, with dire consequences arising if it was not up to standard. This would involve the time honoured floor polishing using an instrument called a 'bumper' which is difficult to describe, but is, or was, as I am sure they were made obsolete years ago, a long handle to which a padded weight is attached. This is then dragged to and fro across the linoleum, (lino), covered floor, initially to spread the polish, and then with pads to polish and make the lino shine brightly. After the floor has been polished to a high standard, the recruits have to avoid direct contact with the floor by walking on large pads which add to the polished effect. In addition we had to carry out dusting of everywhere every day. There was also some cleaning of the toilet and ablutions area that was carried out daily. On specified evenings additional cleaning took place, such as cleaning windows, and an even greater depth of cleaning overall of the accommodation and toilets etc. These were termed 'Bull Nights' and traditionally took place on a Monday night on all stations. In the early stages of Recruit Training, Bull Nights would be much more frequent, and it would be an absolute certainty, that the recruits early attempts to achieve the imposed high standard would fail. This is of course was and is still a means of instilling discipline, and was not taken to extremes after the first week or so, when there was generally time available in the evenings for other activities.

In addition to cleaning the accommodation, and of equal or greater importance in the early stages of training, was care of the uniform, footwear and accoutrements. For the two uniforms, 'best' and 'working' blue versions, regular ironing was required to achieve neat creases etc., particularly the working blue, which in addition to being worn most days, was of a thick serge material that lost its creases very easily. The cap badge, and the buttons on the best uniform, had to be cleaned with 'Brasso' and polished regularly. Boots and shoes also had to polished to a high standard. This was achieved by a technique of mixing water, (or spit) and polish and spending a lot of time gently working mixture into the leather. In 1957, the amount of webbing issued to recruits had been reduced to a belt and a haversack, known as a 'Small Pack'. These two items had to be cleaned, and then covered with a special polish for the material called 'Blanco'. After the demonstration of cleaning techniques by the D.I. We were left to get on with it before 'lights out', which literally meant the accommodation lighting having to be switched off, and the recruits tucked up in their beds! Any airmen with previous experience of all the 'bull' were very popular in the early days of training, as those without any previous military experience sought their advice on the 'tricks of the trade' in respect of all 'bull' matters.

After describing all these seemingly awful tasks that recruits had to endure, which make somewhat depressing reading, I consider that it is worth re-iterating the remarks I made in the opening paragraph of this chapter regarding how the recruits dealt with the less salubrious aspects of recruit training. Almost all recruits coped well with the hardship, and indeed very quickly bonded together, often seeing the funny side of failed attempts to learn some military skills. If this was the purpose of the exercise, then it could be hailed as a success.

The start of the first full day of training was Reveille, (wake up call), at 6.30 a.m., which would be the same for every day except Sunday. The recruits were woken up in the traditional way by somebody walking down the line of beds shouting and bawling. I think that any lesser form of a wake up call would have been disappointing! Breakfast was at 7.a.m. Prompt, and the flight would proceed *en mass* at the appointed hour. The standard Full English Breakfast was always available, but the quality of the ingredients was poor. The eggs were the smallest and obviously the cheapest available, and were mostly overcooked and congealed due to being cooked in large batches. The bacon which would appear on alternate days rotating with sausage was always thin, streaky and very greasy. The sausages were known as 'compo', which was a form of skinless sausage, and possessed only a vague sausage taste. The 'baked beans' also had an acquired taste, as did the tinned tomatoes – no fresh variety was ever available. For those who wished to pass on the fry up, the other items on offer were of an equally unappetising variety. The porridge may have been popular with some Scottish recruits, but not with anybody else. It would have been made with the cheapest possible oats, and powdered milk, if any milk was used at all. Urns of prepared powdered milk would be available for the inevitable cheap cornflakes. For those who could not face any of this fare, thin sliced white bread and margarine was available at a separate table. Interestingly, whilst this was an extreme example of RAF Catering circa 1950s, breakfast remained an unappetising meal in Junior Ranks messes for many years. The majority of airmen would be content to miss breakfast and have some food mid morning from the NAAFI.

On return from breakfast, there was time to tidy up the barrack room for a brief inspection by the D.I.s. As expected, we were told that we had to improve our efforts, and we would be spending time cleaning once again in the evening. It is then time for our very first proper parade in uniform. This was another example of the way such rituals are similar to those portrayed in films. Seemingly sticking close to a well worn script, the D.I. Inspects each recruit in turn and engages in a familiar repartee. ' Have you polished that cap badge you 'orrible little man' etc. Few if any escape the wrath. Any former soldiers might just scrape by if they turn out is truly immaculate, with just an 'OK'. The two most popular things that attract criticism are the beret and shaving. Few will be wearing the beret correctly, and if they are, then the badge will not be clean enough. Some of the younger recruits will not have started shaving on a regular basis yet. I had not. So on that very first parade, the following exchange would take place.

'Have you shaved this morning?'

'No Corporal.'

'Why not you $%*%£!? You must shave every day, do you understand?

'Er, yes Corporal.'

'What did you say, you $%£&*!' etc.

Occasionally the completely 'over the top' remarks by the D.I.s to recruits regarding what retribution will be visited on them caused much amusement, and no doubt yet more bonding.

Having had a very graphic lesson in the intricate nature of service dress, the next stage was to learn how to salute an officer – and also how to recognise one! This reminds me of a story about another very small officer (not Ronnie Corbett), whom his Commanding Officer considered looked too much like an Air Training Corps Cadet when he wore his number two uniform with a beret. The diminutive officer was made to wear his best uniform and Service Dress hat at all times! The difference between a Warrant Officer, who is not saluted, and a commissioned officer, who must be, was also explained. However, most recruits will readily salute anybody who looks remotely like an officer, just in case. I expect that Warrant Officers on training units avoid recruits as much as possible.

It was now time to start to commence instruction in basic drill, starting with how to stand at attention, stand at ease, and stand easy. Having mastered this, the recruits had to be taught the drill movement for turning – right, left and about (a 180-degree turn). It was, of course, fairly certain that somebody would turn the wrong way, leading to the usual mixture of admonition and humour. The next stage of basic drill was how to march. This is never easy, and much time was to be spent perfecting the art in the ensuing eight weeks training before the final pass out parade. In every group of 20 or more, there will seemingly be at least one if not more people who cannot march in the usual manner of alternating arms and legs, i.e. right arm and left leg forward and then left arm and right leg forward. These individuals will march with right arm and right leg forward, then left arm and leg forward. This is slightly ungainly, and as the action bears a resemblance to a clock movement, such individuals were called 'tick-tocks'. Of course, if those so afflicted had never joined the services, they would probably have gone through their entire life without knowing that they were different to the vast majority in this somewhat strange way. Those found to be marching like 'tick-tocks', are asked to try the more conventional method of marching. If they have difficulty with this, then are handed over to another D.I. who will give them special coaching before they can join up with the rest of the flight for further drill.

Drill featured largely throughout recruit training. After the basics had been mastered, there was a progression through to rifle drill, and then parading and marching on parades with other flights, and finally marching to a military band, culminating in a final Passing Out Parade on the final day of training. I have always had some reservations regarding the time spent on drill, which even to this today seems to me to be excessive. With sufficient training, many airmen would be able to perform drill movements every bit as well as the RAF Regiment Queens Colour Squadron, who represent the RAF at many formal occasions with a Guard of Honour etc. In an age where time spent on every aspect of training is now closely monitored, the Ministry Of Defence must consider that there is a compelling argument for continuing to train all RAF personnel to a very high standard in drill, and in particular RAF officers whose training in this respect remains arguably excessive. As the RAF recruits of both sexes now train together, I assume that foul language has been toned down a little and no doubt replaced by some equally effective and colourful phrases. I note that the term' bollocking' is now known as a verbal 'beasting'!

Recruit Training camps did not have a Human Resources Department, as it would be almost a half century before anybody would have understood what the term meant! The welfare of the trainees was responsibility of the Commanding Officer, delegated down to the officers in charge. Those officers had a responsibility to ensure that any trainee, who required help or advice of a personal nature, had appropriate access at all times to the responsible officer. The most common welfare needs were requests for compassionate leave due to serious illness or death of a close relative. The 'welcome' briefings,(talks), would advise the trainees how to go about this. Whilst there would have been a specific welfare officer on the camp, the alternative to the trainee's officer in charge was The Padre. Within the first days of the recruit' s arrival, they were organised into religious groups for a informal chat with a Padre, which would include his role and availability etc. This was relatively simple in those days, with the recruits falling mainly into two groups, the Church of England, and the Roman Catholics. All other Christian religions shared a single minister. I was never aware of what arrangements if any were ever made for other religions, as it never seemed to arise. On parades which included a service or prayers, which would be Church of England, an order would be given before the service or prayers commenced, " Fall Out the Roman Catholics, and The Jews', which was amended years later to ' other dissenting personnel'. A note of every recruit's religion would be recorded, so that no Church of England trainees would take advantage to stretch their legs.

The service Padre would always be a RAF Officer, and would wear an officers uniform, but with a dog collar. He, (it was *always* a man), would be addressed as Padre rather than Sir, and could be approached direct by any recruit. Part of the training programme would include a weekly period with the Padre. This was a very relaxed period, which would take the form of a discussion about recruits non confidential problems, followed by some prayers. Roman Catholics would be encouraged to confess their sins in a confessional, which was the last time in my life I have ever done this. All those in my group also did so, probably just to please this nice man who had our welfare at heart! I trust that some similar opportunity to chat to a friendly officer was possible for 'the dissenters', but I do not know if there was. For the majority the system appeared to work well.

The welfare of the recruits, could be said to include their health care. Health was an especially important issue when recruits were living in such close proximity, often for the first time in their lives, with around 20 others. Any infectious complaint could spread like wildfire, and in addition to the suffering of those concerned, the training programme would be seriously disrupted, if the 'sausage machine' came to an abrupt and unplanned halt! In the 1950s, the concept of good health was vastly different to that of the 21st century. It was seemingly assumed that eating three good meals a day, having lots of 'fresh air' and undertaking comparatively small amounts of exercise, such as walks at the weekend, would be sufficient. Whilst a higher percentage than today were engaged in employment which required some manual labour, obesity was also much rarer amongst the population as a whole. This may have been due a very small percentage who owned cars, and the also the scarcity of labour saving devices. Whatever the reasons, it certainly was not due to only eating what nowadays would be considered healthy food. Smoking was considered normal, even for sportsmen, who might consider cutting down, but not stopping. It is hard to imagine now, what a barrack room containing 20 people who all smoked was like, or indeed how non smokers, if there were any, put up with it. Lectures on health would be almost exclusively concerned with venereal disease. These would be accompanied with an official government film, very similar to those lampooned brilliantly by Harry Enfield. The films would contain explicit shots of the grim consequences of gonorrhoea and syphilis, whether using actors or actual patients I do not know. Having scared all the recruits to death, the film and lecture would also advise recruits that free condoms were available on camp, and that there was also what was called an Early Treatment Room on every camp, usually near the main entrance. This room consisted of a urinal and a box of tubes of ointment. The ointment had to be 'inserted', between bursts of urination, after which the recruit would be expected to report sick the next day. It was stressed that the ointment was not a cure. These procedures did not survive into the 'swinging sixties' and I therefore can assume that they were at best ineffective, and at worst dangerous. At the time, as a young 17 year old, it felt good that somebody would feel it worthwhile to deliver a talk about a disease which resulted from sexual intercourse. Something of a rite of passage!

The normal method of consulting a doctor whilst on camp, was to 'report sick'. This meant packing pyjamas and toiletry in the 'small pack', then parading at a specified location, where your name was recorded, before being marched to the Station Sick Quarters. Those who required any urgent attention outside of the normal hours, would have to report to either their NCO or to the Guardroom, and explain what the urgency was. If the reason was accepted, they would be deemed to be 'special sick', and given a signed Form 624, (one of many forms that all ex servicemen never forget), to take to the sick quarters. Anyone turning up at the sick quarters without this form, would be required to supply a good reason why not. These procedures were to continue for many years after I enlisted, particularly at training camps. Once these preliminaries had been completed, recruits would see a doctor at a set time, with a queue system and never by appointment. Those requiring any bed rest or isolation, would always be admitted to the wards, because it was impractical for them to care for themselves in the barrack room. Those who did not require admission, would be supplied with what were termed Treatment Chits (an Anglo Indian word in common use throughout the services, from *chitty*), which was a form of prescription. However nothing was dispensed to recruits other than by the nursing attendants in the treatment room. Therefore, if for example, some medicine had to be taken three times a day, recruits had to attend the Station Sick Quarters treatment room to receive it, thereafter the chit would be signed. In this way, the RAF ensured that patients completed the whole of a course of treatment, and also that medicine would not be stockpiled and possibly misused in the barrack room. The time spent by recruits going to and from the sick quarters up to three times a day was of no consequence. There would have also been plenty of staff at the Sick Quarters to dispense medicine in this way. It was possible that this constant to and fro-ing to the Sick Quarters, might have deterred some recruits from consulting a doctor, but often any diversion from the main training programme was welcomed.

The schedules for basic training included physical training, (PT), but it is seemingly not the most memorable part of the recruit training schedule. I have checked on the recorded experience of others, but these are largely silent on this aspect of the 'square bashing' experience. Certainly there were sessions of the old fashioned and regimented ' feet apart place' and 'running on the spot commence' type sessions in a large hangar. There was also some basic gymnastics to build or destroy confidence, and some indoor games, but certainly no long runs or forced marches. For elite sportsmen who had been conscripted, every effort was made for their normal sports training to continue, and where necessary special leave to compete at their sport. The usual condition was that they would also represent the RAF against the other two services as required. Where at all possible, i.e., they were not unintelligent, and had no other special trade skills, they would be drafted into the Physical Education Branch, and with it, promotion to Corporal, which was a very good perk for a low paid National Serviceman.

In addition to a great deal of drill and marching on the parade ground, the recruits would receive Ground Defence Training which involved some physical activity. The most memorable part of this was a bayonet charge on a dummy! It does seem unlikely, but as we were no doubt reminded at the time, it was a secondary duty of an airman to guard and defend the camp in time of war. Therefore some military skills, (except that 'skills' was not an overused word in 1957), needed to be taught – I cannot say mastered, as we probably had just the one lesson. After being shown how to inflict severe damage on a stuffed dummy, we all had two attempts at yet another time honoured part of military training. The first attempt would always be deemed to be not aggressive enough of course, so a second attempt was required. Some recruits were reported to have imagined the dummy to be their Drill Instructor, in order to achieve the required level of mock savagery! The Ground Defence segment of training included a session on the Rifle Range using live ammunition, and ancient Lee Enfield 303 rifles. As bullets were expensive we were issued with just twelve each. The first six were for a practice, when the recruits would get used to not only firing live ammunition, but also the 'kick back' from the rifle, which would damage the shoulder if not handled firmly. The results of the second batch would be noted, and if the required standard had been achieved, a marksman's certificate and badge would be issued. Even though I had fired this rifle before as an ATC cadet, I did not qualify, for a badge, but the incentive was missing as medical personnel could not wear a marksman badge, as they were only supposed to bear arms in defence of any patients in their care. Other than on active service, medical personnel did not have any personal weapons, so they had the perk of not having to take part in any parades or guards of honour where rifles were involved. They were also excused any guard duties where any weapons at all were involved. It was seen as fair compensation for the extra duties undertaken as a medical orderly, often more than one night a week on call.

Having outlined the main aspects of my training, it is time to recall some of the good times off duty, mainly at the weekends. Recruits were initially confined to camp, but subject to attaining the set standard of dress and drill, a form of 'carrot' rather than 'stick' approach – at around the three week stage, they were then permitted to leave the camp. On the first occasion of this welcome taste of freedom, recruits were also allowed home on what was called a 36 hour pass. This was from Saturday lunchtime until 10 p.m. or 22.00 hours on Sunday. Those including myself, who opted to stay behind, were subject to the 22.00 curfew on Saturday and Sunday, otherwise we were free to leave the camp dressed in our new uniforms. Even if civilian clothes could have been worn, I would have opted for the uniform every time, and felt extremely proud to be wearing it.

For my very first outing in uniform, I joined a group of recruits on a trip to New Brighton, this being the nearest 'bright lights'. It was and still is, just a small seaside resort on the shores of The Wirral, and across the bay from the even brighter lights of Liverpool, but that was for another day. On arrival we wasted no time in heading for a pub and a pint. We did not have much time, as of course the licensing hours meant that all pubs closed at 3p.m., as all day opening was almost a half century away. If faced with a choice of pubs, a pub with music was always the first choice. In addition to the more lively atmosphere, there was also a better chance of finding young women in such pubs, as they would not be seen in the more conventional establishments of the time, which were more for the serious male drinkers making the most of the restricted opening hours! A suitable pub was soon found, and whilst of course I cannot recall exactly what it was like, there would almost certainly have been a jukebox playing at full volume. As at the time England was still coming to terms with rock and roll, most of the popular artists were from U.S.A. In 1957, those most favoured by young men, were artists such as of course Elvis who had 'All Shook Up' at the top of the charts, Jerry Lee Lewis with his 'Great Balls of Fire' and Buddy Holly with 'Oh Boy'. My all enduring memory of loud music from jukeboxes is of Little Richard, and in 1957, 'Lucille' would appear so loud and rhythmic, that the jukeboxes appeared to be lifting off! As I was now wearing uniform, I was able to drink without anyone ever querying my age again. Although I was only a few months off 18 by this time, it was a great feeling.

Having satisfied the need for a drink as a man, and no doubt also having enjoyed the music of Little Richard, what might I find to do next in New Brighton, and what did the others in my group want to do. I should add that nobody succeeded in persuading any young ladies to join us. We were not surprised at this, as no doubt we were seen and known as airmen who were 'just passing through'. We could all wait for some home leave to see if we might impress somebody in our smart new uniforms. So for the rest of the afternoon's entertainment, we went to watch some professional wrestling. This sounds like a most unlikely thing for young men to do at any time or place, but of course wrestling was a very popular sport at the time, and would remain so for decades. The promoter was no doubt hopeful of attracting a good following from the camp, and actually reduced the admission charge for men in uniform. This was very unusual which is why I recall it. Some places of entertainment that were near to RAF camps, would not always welcome servicemen in large numbers, as they could be seen as the cause of trouble between them and local youths. However at that time, everybody would eventually spend time in uniform so it was not a common problem. Places with a history of trouble were placed 'out of bounds' by the RAF, and subsequently monitored by visits by RAF police.

Before heading back to camp before the 10 p.m. curfew, there was plenty of time to have a decent meal after a few weeks of the institutionalized fare we had endured for a few weeks. I do not remember what we all had to eat, but I am certain it would have included chips, which was an item which did not appear on the menus of 1950s RAF West Kirby. I do not know why this was, but it would certainly not have been any attempt to reduce the amount of fat in the recruit's diet. I am fairly sure that in those days, only people suffering from ailments such as stomach ulcers would avoid fried food. If time and good weather permitted, we might take a stroll on the seafront to 'eye up' any likely females, otherwise we would make our way back to camp where at least the beer was cheaper, and there was always Little Richard playing on the jukebox!.

One of the 'out of bounds' establishments was a dance hall in the West Kirby area, but how this came about I do not know. Recruits had to be back on camp by 22.00 and to manage this meant that they would need to be making tracks back to camp fairly early in the evening. This would usually be on foot, as those few recruits that may have owned cars were not allowed to have them on the camp, and public transport was limited. Taxis were both expensive and also scarce in small towns in those days. Sunday afternoons was a favourite time to go down to West Kirby particularly if the weather was fine and sunny. With no entertainment on offer at the best of times in this small town, a favourite pastime for the local girls was to parade around the seafront area, a custom more typical of Paris or Rome. It therefore became a magnet for recruits to practice their 'chatting up' technique. Whilst neither I or anyone I was with, was ever successful, the expectation was not high, but it was a most enjoyable way to spend a Sunday afternoon.

As I was the almost always the youngest and least experienced at this art form, having previously only ever been out with girls I had at least known before I asked them for a date, I was often in awe at the expertise of my fellow recruits. However, the sole success I ever witnessed arose quite unexpectedly. I was walking back to camp with a very average looking recruit from Derby, who had a very broad Derbyshire accent. As we walked up a very steep hill on our way back to camp, we drew alongside a young woman, whereupon the airman from Derby came out with the most unlikely chat up line I have ever heard – which is why I still remember it. He simply said ' Stiff climb duck?' (duck is a Derbyshire term of endearment). Amazingly she responded to his concern, and he ended up getting her to agree to see him the following week. When I told the others back at camp about this success, he was given the nickname 'stiff climb' for a while, whilst he basked in the glory of it all. He certainly saw the young woman again, but I do not know if anything much came of it.

Before the end of my 8 weeks at West Kirby, I took the opportunity to visit Liverpool with a group of recruits from my Training Flight. We took the famous ferry across to river Mersey to the city. This was seven years before

Gerry and the Pacemakers had their big hit record, 'Ferry Across The Mersey' so perhaps it was not quite as famous in 1957. It was also five years before The Beatles and 'Love Me Do', which started not only their career, but the so called 'Mersey Beat' phenomenon that would last for most of the 1960s. There was however one significant event in 1957 that would have far reaching consequences in the world of pop music, and that was on July 6th when John Lennon first met Paul McCartney at Saint Peters Church garden fête.

Liverpool did have another home grown singer who was regularly topping the music charts in 1957. This was Frankie Vaughan, who had four top ten hits that year including a number one hit with 'Garden of Eden'. For some reason he was always associated with the song 'Give Me The Moonlight' and was also nicknamed 'Mr Moonlight', although this song was never a bit hit record. In common with many pop stars of that era, he tried his hand at acting, but unlike the majority, he achieved some success as an actor and subsequently appeared in a total of nine films, one of which was the 1960 film 'Lets Make Love' in which he starred opposite Marilyn Monroe. In 1957 he made a film called 'These Dangerous Years' which was more typical of the pop star – turned actor type films, and in which he played the part of a pop singer who had been called up for National Service in the Army just after making some hit records. Frankie Vaughan had also served in the army, but this was in the 1940s. My preamble about Frankie Vaughan, is partly to explain why, after a look around the centre of Liverpool, my group joined a cinema queue to see 'These Dangerous Years'! It is my main memory of this city, especially as I have never been back there since.

The final stages of training at RAF West Kirby could be summed up as just a lot more drill, inspections, physical training, Padres hours, War Office type films, and more ground defence training which culminated in a 48 hour exercise which involved camping out. This involved using a large groundsheet that doubled as a rain cape, to erect a basic form of shelter. Fortunately the weather was fine! The exercise was not very arduous and was otherwise unmemorable.

In the final weeks of my training, I was admitted to the Camp Hospital to have all my teeth extracted and replaced with a form of instant dentures. This became necessary as I had neglected my teeth for years, due to a fear of general anaesthetic following a bad experience when I was younger. When my teeth reached a state where a general anaesthetic was likely, I avoided seeking any dental treatment, and therefore I now required such a large amount of treatment, that the RAF dentist considered that what was termed a 'full clearance' was the best option. Whilst this would be done under a general anaesthetic, I decided that this was a better option than other protracted treatments. Unfortunately some complications arose, and the replacement teeth were to be severely delayed, so I had to endure looking slightly older for a while! However the good news, was that because of the treatment, I had missed several periods of rifle drill, but instead of having to spend an additional week or so with another flight to catch up, I was allowed to pass out with my original intake, and miss the final parade. As I was destined to be a medic and therefore most unlikely to do rifle drill in the future, I never did learn how to perform some of the drill movements such as 'Fix Bayonets' and 'Present Arms'!

The final evening on the training camp was spent in the time-honoured way of having a few drinks in the NAAFI. We had received the standard warnings about the dire consequences that would arise if any damage was done to either the NAAFI or the living accommodation. Probably due to the maturity of most of the recruits, who were not prepared to have to spend any longer than necessary at West Kirby, or pay for any damage that may have been caused, the only high jinks that arose, was the dismantling of somebody's bed, and reassembling it on the middle of the parade square.

On the last morning, I was allowed to watch the final Passing Out Parade from the comfort of the barrack room rather than the more traditional standing on the edge of the Parade Ground. After the usual marching and stamping around, the band struck up with the 'RAF March Past', and the recruits marched smartly off the parade, their training now at an end. There was the usual promises to keep in touch and some swapping of addresses, and then the recruits departed the camp in a much better mood than when they arrived, and headed for the railway station, and then a week's leave before reporting to their Trade Training Unit.

4. Nursing Attendant Training at RAF Freckleton

After a very enjoyable week's leave in Bradford, I travelled to RAF Freckleton in Lancashire for approximately 3 months training as a Nursing Attendant. The station was in fact a small satellite unit of nearby RAF Warton, and was situated between Preston and the genteel resort of Lytham-St-Annes, with Blackpool also nearby. On arrival at the station I reported to the Guardroom in uniform. At that time guardrooms were staffed by RAF Policemen, who also had a disciplinary role, so to justify their existence, they would often inspect the service dress of airmen arriving at the main gate. On this occasion, a corporal told me to sort out my service dress cap! After leaving West Kirby, I had made some minor changes to make it look a lot better, so I had to bend it back into the original shape at least for the time being. Everybody made changes to the cap, which was said to resemble a 'piss pot' in its original unaltered state. As civilian clothes could now be worn when proceeding off the camp, there would not be too much hassle at the guardroom in future.

After this less than welcoming start, things soon looked up a great deal. I was pleased to see that the accommodation was much better and had central heating, and that in general the camp had a much better ambiance, notably no shouting and swearing! The trainees for my course would be arriving individually from their leave addresses, so on the day of arrival, there was little to do other than to obtain the usual personal bedding and fill in lots of forms, then settle in. The most important part of settling in was to visit the mess for a meal, and I was pleased to see that both the food and facilities were a lot better than at West Kirby. This was not a total surprise, as I had a good experience of RAF catering when I visited Tern Hill as a ATC Cadet. One reason for the vast improvement was that the mess catered not only for raw recruits, but also for the permanent staff of junior ranks, and also many senior airmen who had returned to Freckleton for further training courses. Some of the more experienced airmen would attend regular meetings of what was called a Messing Committee, as representatives of their department, where complaints regarding catering, and any suggestions for improvements would be discussed. In addition to much better food, airmen were able to dine at tables for four, and even have side plates for their bread and butter. Other notable improvements were the separation of sugar from the tea urns and the occasional presence of chips on the menu!

When I made a first visit to the NAAFI club, I noticed that this was also a lot better than at recruit training. Most notably, was that there was a regular programme of entertainment. Whilst airmen at Freckleton could visit the fleshpots of Blackpool in the evenings and weekends, most would be more content to stay on camp, at least during weekdays. In fact there were few attractions locally other than Blackpool, which was not easy to get to without a car, and at the time few airmen owned one. The NAAFI club provided the usual food and drinks, plus of course the jukebox with the latest rock and roll records. There were also regular dances and what were called 'Smokers Concerts', which took the form of somebody playing a piano whilst volunteers from the audience would get up and sing. It does not sound like too much fun, but these concerts were very popular, and would usually take place on Thursdays, which was the weekly payday in those days. So all in all it looked as though I would enjoy my stay at Freckleton, which was an expectation that was to be fulfilled.

The course commenced the next morning with introductions, briefings concerning disciplinary matters, mainly delivered by the corporal instructor who would be responsible for the majority of the classroom tuition on the course. What was regarded as 'bull' was reasonably limited. We would be required to march to and from lessons, but only with a nominated 'senior man' in charge. There would be a formal weekly parade and what was called a 'Bull Night' otherwise officially known as a Domestic Evening once a week, when the living accommodation had to be thoroughly cleaned ready for an inspection the following morning. For the remainder of the week, the accommodation would be given a quick clean, by each of the occupants in turn, in accordance with a list drawn up by the Senior Man, which was called a Billet Orderly Roster. We were expected to present a smart appearance at all times, with clean and shiny shoes, well pressed uniform, a clean starched collar, short hair and a shiny hat badge. Our attention was drawn to the various orders that would be displayed on official Notice Boards around the camp, which we were responsible for reading and obeying if applicable. In practice we need never have bothered, as anything we were required to do, would invariably be brought to our attention by the corporal instructor. At the end of the opening administrative matters, we received a talk by the Commanding Officer, in which he welcomed all the trainees to the station and the Medical Branch.

Soon it was time to commence our training. There were about 20 trainees on my course, comprising of both regular and National Service airmen, and just two members of the WRAF. The course would cover basic anatomy and physiology, first aid, basic nursing, medical administration and also some basic environmental medicine, known as field hygiene in those days. There would be plenty of practical lessons in respect of first aid and nursing, but before we could learn how to dress wounds, immobilise fractures and nurse the sick, we had to spend about 2 weeks in the classroom studying anatomy and physiology. One of the very first lessons concerned mitosis or the division of human cells. I have never found this knowledge to be of any use to me, but just as years earlier at secondary school, when I learned how rubber was extracted from rubber trees, it had to be committed to memory for the rest of my life. Failure to do so might have resulted in failing of a written examination at the end of each phase of training, which carried the risk of failing the course. In addition there was also written and practical examinations at the end of the course, and failure in those might result in having to retake the exam after a short interval and some intense revision. If a trainee failed to 'pass out' as a Nursing Attendant after training, then there would be a posting to a hospital as a ward assistant. These posts did not have very much job satisfaction, and were devoid of promotion prospects, which also had financial implications, particularly for the lower paid National Servicemen. This was sufficient incentive for the trainees to spend time in the evenings revising what they had been taught during the day. However an hour of study on most evenings seemed to suffice for the majority, leaving plenty of time for recreational activities.

By today's standards the total daily hours spent under instruction seem somewhat excessive, with the working day starting at 8 a.m. and finishing at 5 p.m. However, around two hours could be deducted from the 9 hour total to account for; smoking breaks every hour, a NAAFI break every morning and afternoon when a mobile catering wagon would tour all the working areas, plus a generous lunch break. There was also a half day off every Wednesday afternoon for sport. Whilst some trainees would adapt better than others, the majority had not long left school, and the older recruits who had had their National Service deferred would have had recent experience of the learning process. It should not be overlooked that the purpose of the course was to get the maximum number of average trainees through the course and off to units to earn their pay, however low that might be in some cases.

I soon settled into the routine, and once the wonders of mitosis had been committed to memory for all time, I was more comfortable with anatomy and the cardio vascular system, which I had learned as a St John Ambulance Cadet. My cadet force in Bradford seemingly considered that it was essential for cadets to learn by heart, the Latin names of all the 206 bones in the body before embarking on the use of splints and how to stop a nose bleed! To break the monotony of the classroom in the early weeks, there were more War Office type films to help explain the many varied systems of the body, including the reproductive system of course, although we were not taught any midwifery on the course. This was probably thought at that time to be unnecessary and potentially dangerous.

Every Wednesday afternoon was deemed to be a 'sports afternoon', and this provided a welcome midweek break from the classroom. I place the phrase 'sports afternoon' in italics, as it was only sporty by a very loose interpretation. Whilst recognised and serious sportsmen, (it was extremely rare for women to participate in sport at the time), would be catered for, and suitable competition made available, usually at other units of formations, there was little if any facilities at RAF Freckleton. For example, it was not possible for any *ad hoc* games of football to take place, mainly through a lack of space on the camp. It was a rule that trainees had to state which sport they would be participating in, before they were allowed to take the afternoon off. The overwhelming favourite sport was walking. The whole of my course, which did not have any serious sportsmen, would therefore walk under the supervision of the senior man, to the village of Freckleton. We would stop at a cafe for a cup of tea, and then walk back to camp. This was an acceptable arrangement for all concerned, particularly for all of the non sporty trainees. There was no other form of mandatory organised physical exercise, which remained the case at permanent units. Sport in the RAF was greatly encouraged, and at most camps good facilities existed. Also time off work would often be allowed for competitions, and sometimes training, but there was never any direct compulsion.

Of all the social occasions on the camp, the station dances were undoubtedly the highlight. There were comparatively few females on the camp, but this was not seen as a big problem, as the opportunity existed for travel home on most weekends for many airmen, often by hitchhiking which was comparatively easy provided that uniform was worn. For others, particularly the permanent staff, there was plenty of time to become acquainted with either the females on the camp, or those either living nearby or at places like Blackpool. To address the imbalance, local women were encouraged to attend the dances by the RAF, who provided free travel by buses and free admission. Unfortunately for the airmen, the United States Air Force also held dances at nearby Burtonwood. These dances were seen as a much better option for many local women, as they undoubtedly were. This tended to result in most of the best looking local women attending the American version of camp dances, and having then become involved with the hosts, declining what the RAF at Freckleton had to offer. The dances would commence playing to an empty dance floor. The music would be provided either by what was known as a dance band, or a Traditional Jazz band. The coaches with the local women would arrive, and they would make their way to the cloakrooms and then to 'their side' of the dance hall. The jazz singer George Melly recalled this ritual in an autobiography, when he said that he often felt sorry for the RAF as he surveyed the women arriving, some of whom he said, perhaps unfairly, but amusingly, 'verged on the grotesque! The evening would then follow what was the usual pattern for that time, which was for the women to dance mainly with each other, followed by the few men who were able to do ballroom dancing at least fairly well. Only in the last hour or so would the majority of the men get up to dance, and that would often be only when the bar had closed. As I also had little knowledge of ballroom dancing, I was one of those who hung back until near the end. At one of the dances I did manage to get a dance or two with somebody, but nothing came of it. I was due to go home that weekend anyway, so I did not mind. The woman concerned did not show up at the next dance as I hoped she might. Perhaps she joined the Burtonwod crowd!

In addition to the station dances, there were some organised coach trips to Blackpool for midweek dances at the Blackpool Winter Gardens. Whilst the general pattern of reluctance by most of the men to get involved until at least the second half of the evening prevailed, these dances provided much more overall entertainment than those at RAF Freckleton. They had the very best dance bands, and whilst this was not rock and roll, it was always of a high standard, and would feature top class singers, and bands such as Ted

Heath and Johnny Dankworth. There was plenty of women to dance with, even after the main summer holiday season had ended. Perhaps most significantly, Blackpool was surely what I would regard as a RAF town. There were several large RAF bases in the surrounding area, and the American Air Force was seemingly content to keep a low profile in Blackpool. Once the Winter Garden dances had warmed up, and the men had decided to join in, the scene resembled that of a World War Two movie, because so many men were dressed in RAF uniform. As there was no compulsion to wear uniform whilst off duty, it therefore must have been seen as a good alternative to spending money on a civilian suit, (the only acceptable form of smart dress at the time), and particularly so in Blackpool, where it seemed to go down well with the local women. My own experience of the Winter Gardens experience was feeling totally out of my depth. Those in my company seemed a lot better than myself at the art of chatting up women, most of whom appeared to be a lot older than me, even though I had now passed 18. I was not unduly concerned at my inexperience and lack of success, and I enjoyed being in the company of the comparatively older airmen. I also came to realise that some of the older airmen, were in reality no great shakes at relationships. I wonder what the 1950s equivalent term for 'relationships ' might have been. Possibly something obscene!

The other most memorable form of entertainment at RAF Freckelton was the so called 'Smokers Concerts', which I referred to in my opening paragraphs of this chapter. The term 'smokers' did not in any way refer to smoking tobacco, and took the name from a description of a concert where members of the audience would be invited to step up on stage and perform, usually by singing a song, but sometimes by playing a musical instrument. In the 1950s smoking was only ever banned in schools and churches! What would elevate a seemingly boring evening for airmen, many of whom regarded only the rock and roll sounds of Elvis and co as worth listening to? It was the existence on the station of some National Service airmen with a show business background, and who were skilled entertainers. They all belonged to a department on the camp which provided fake casualties for the trainees to practice their first aid skills on. (For nursing training, blow up dummies were invariably used). The Smokers Concerts which I can easily recall, always featured a ginger haired National Service corporal on the piano. What became of him I wonder.

The remaining highlight of my time at Freckleton, was a visit to Preston North End on a Saturday afternoon. This was a good season for the Preston team, who finished the season as the First Division runners up to Wolverhampton Wanderers. It was also the year of the plane crash at Munich which decimated the Manchester United team who ended the season down in 9th place. However their match with Preston ended in a draw, before a packed house. Of course in the 1950s admission to any big match was almost always possible. You simply had just turn up and you could squeeze in somewhere. One abiding memory of this visit was not the match, but walking away from the ground through the Deepdale area of Preston, with it's industrial urban landscape, which was exactly like many northern towns of that period. Whenever I hear the football results broadcast on the radio at 5 p.m every Saturday afternoon, my mind often drifts back to 1957, and walking through the streets of Preston with its sooty houses and buildings.

Back on camp the course was progressing very well. After the early weeks of anatomy and physiology, there was a lot more practical teaching, which was a lot more interesting, often fun and did not require memorisation of endless lists of bones etc. On the discipline side, there was usually a formal monthly parade for the entire station, which was not too daunting. It was just a matter of getting a haircut if necessary, pressing the best uniform, shining the shoes and cleaning the cap badge and the uniform buttons with Brasso. As I was at Freckleton on a Remembrance Sunday, I found myself on parade at nearby Lytham, on a freezing November morning. As medics could usually avoid any formal parades, this was the only Armistice Day parade I ever took part in the whole of my service, so I recall the occasion very well, and particularly standing to attention in uniform which included a thick greatcoat, and still feeling very cold, until we eventually marched off.

There was at least one formal kit inspection, in which all RAF clothing and personal equipment had to be laid out on your bed in a set order. It also had to be extremely clean and neat which made this just about the worst aspect of training. I never had the experience of having all my kit thrown on the floor because of some minor blemish, but this undoubtedly sometimes occurred on training camps, and was also yet another favourite scene in films depicting the rigours of service life! On permanent camps, formal kit inspections would only occur once a year, if at all, and would eventually die out altogether, other than as a form of punishment at Detention Centres where it still exists.

The course drew to an end with a written examination, and if a pass mark had been obtained, those trainees took a practical examination the following day. The overall results were made known to the students at the conclusion of the second part. The same evening the students would have a celebratory drink with the corporal instructor, and the following day those who had passed both examinations would be formally presented with Medical Badges which were known as Collar Dogs, which were worn on the lapels. At the earliest opportunity, the badges would be attached to the uniform. This involved making two small holes in each lapel for which a fork suitably bent was ideal! As one of those who passed the exams, I was therefore promoted from Aircraftsman Second Class to First Class, and now had the trade of Nursing Attendant Class Two, but the 'collar dogs' were what I liked the most. The RAF never went in for lapel badges, and the only recipients were Dental personnel, and the Padres. The postings were also given out, and for me it would be RAF Innsworth near Gloucester, but only for a few months before I undertook some further training. It was now almost Christmas, so before reporting to my new unit, I would be on leave until the New Year. In the meantime, my 'collar dogs' would be on display around Bradford.

5. A Year of Training

After the 1957 Christmas, I reported for duty as a member of the permanent staff at RAF Innsworth which was just 4 miles from the centre of Gloucester. The New Years Day holiday and extended end of year break was uncommon at that time. A public holiday for New Years Day, did not commence in England until 1974. At the time Innsworth housed the staff of the RAF Records Office, which dealt with all administrative matters such as pay and postings for airmen. It was also home to Number 5 Personnel Dispersal Unit, (PDU), which processed airmen proceeding overseas in respect of clothing and inoculations etc., and also those returning to the United Kingdom for demobilisation. There was no hassle at the Guardroom this time. This was partly because I was to be a member of the permanent staff, but also as I soon discovered, most sections on a RAF camp considered it in their interest to keep on good terms with the medics – they never knew when they might be at their mercy I suppose! I was directed to the Station Sick Quarters, and there the staff looked after my initial domestic arrangements.

My living accommodation was once again wooden huts containing around 20 beds, minimal storage space and coke fires. Those fires are one of the most vivid memories of my short stay at Innsworth, which was mainly in the winter months. On my very first weekend, I woke up on the Saturday morning to a very cold billet. What I had not realised what that almost all the occupants were National Servicemen, who if they were not working at the weekend, would go home on the Friday night. I had failed to notice when I got back to the billet on the Friday after a night out, that there was nobody left to keep the fires going! For my relatively short stay at Innsworth, I also spent few weekends on camp, other than when I was on duty.

My posting to Innsworth was destined to be a short one, as I would was to be posted to RAF Hospital Nocton Hall in the spring for a Practical Nursing Course (PNC). After passing this course I had expressed an interest in becoming a Operating Room Technician (ORT), and therefore spent time in the Operating Theatre learning quite a lot about this trade, which at the time was well paid, and also led to comparatively rapid promotion on what was then a separate technicians promotion ladder. However towards the end of 1958, I was sent on a Medical Administration, (Med Admin), Course back at

Freckleton, and as I considered that this would be a much better job option than spending very long hours in an operating theatre, plus lots of 'on call' duties, I was more than content to remain in the nursing attendant trade until I was promoted to corporal which would not be too far away.

The Station Sick Quarters (SSQ), was mostly a pleasant permanent building, and unlike the barrack block it was centrally heated. It had it's own catering facilities plus a cook to cater for all the patients in several small wards. The patients were those whose condition was deemed not to to be serious enough to be transferred to a hospital, but nonetheless required in patient treatment, often because they were housed in barrack rooms. Married airmen who lived off the camp, could usually stay home in bed if necessary. The least favourite job in SSQ was working on the wards, mainly because few nursing attendant airmen had any ambition to be full time nurses. Those with such ambitions, would have been posted to hospitals to commence or await a suitable nursing course. So as the new boy, and as such the least experienced in everything, I was allocated to the wards to look after those who were suffering from minor ailments or injuries. The main duties would be to arrange for the patients to be fed and watered, give out the treatments at the prescribed times, monitoring by taking the patients temperature, pulse and respirations, (TPRs), and when on nights, for the overall supervision such as ensuring the lights went out at 22.00 and that the patients had a peaceful and restful nights sleep. During the day, a Male State Registered Nurse, (SRN), was in charge of the nursing in the Sick Quarters. Overall I enjoyed having some responsibility, and writing reports etc, but I did not wish to proceed further as a nurse. Not long after settling in, I was promoted to Leading Aircraftsman (LAC), and soon started to feel of some use after all the training received so far.

During my short stay at Innsworth, there was very little social activity on the camp. This may have been typical of many stations at that time, other than training camps with a large captive audience. There would be a cinema which would show films some time after release, but at a reduced price, and a NAAFI club which would have food and drink, television rooms, and games facilities. The senior ranks would have their own separate and exclusive facilities, in the Sergeants and Officers messes. In addition, those stations which had married quarters would often have a separate social club for service families only. For the staff at the Innsworth Sick Quarters, a night out would normally be a visit to the more lively pubs in Gloucester, particularly those which attracted women, and also had a jukebox of course. None of these pubs or the women have remained in my memory! A favourite pastime on a Sunday afternoon in the 1950s, was a visit to the cinema. I can remember going in to nearby Cheltenham to see Tommy Steele in 'The Duke Wore Jeans'. The film itself was somewhat typical of the era when pop stars often branched out into films, and was not that memorable. What I do remember was having to join a long queue at the cinema, which was not that unusual for popular films at the time, except that on this occasion a good proportion of those queuing were American servicemen from a nearby Air Force base. I expect that they would have enjoyed the comedy in the film more than the songs featured in the film, in which Tommy Steele played a dual role of a Duke and a character not unlike his own. At the time his hit record 'Nairobi' reached number 3 in the Hit parade, and was second only to his number one with 'Singing the Blues' in 1956.

As I noted in the opening paragraph of this chapter, there was a large number of National Servicemen on the staff of the Station Sick Quarters who lived on the camp, but who would all head off home at the weekend. As they were all not very well paid, even after training and some promotion, they were not able to spend much money on social activity during the week. Many National Servicemen became very thrifty, and there was a standing joke that if the much better paid regular airmen were looking for a short term loan until pay day, then the National Servicemen were the most likely to be able to oblige! One favourite means of saving money during the week was to visit Sick Quarters in the evening. The attraction was free tea and toast, (people ate a lot of toast in those days), and often at least one WRAF on duty! After just a few months I was posted to RAF Hospital Nocton Hall, and was not sorry to leave Innsworth.

Nocton is a few miles from the city of Lincoln. In 1958, the RAF Hospital, which closed in the 1980s, was a small self contained general hospital, which catered mainly for all the RAF stations in the Lincolnshire and South Yorkshire area. It was staffed by RAF, WRAF and the Princess Mary RAF Nursing Service (PMRAF) officers. The accommodation consisted of a large manor house, which was used as the Officers Mess, and permanent centrally heated buildings for the other ranks. Those below the rank of corporal were housed in large dormitory type rooms with around 20 beds, which at that time was the standard accommodation. The Practical Nursing Course (PNC) I was starting, had 12 students, nine of whom were members of the WRAF. The other two male members on the course and some of the women on the course, were hoping to be accepted for training as State Registered Nurses (SRN) at a later date. The two men had re-enlisted after previous service in the Royal Navy, with nursing training as their main ambition. I did not share their enthusiasm for nursing, and was just doing the course as I had been ordered to do it!

The PNC as the title suggested, consisted mainly of working on the wards, but there was also a classroom element involved. The course tutor was a male SRN with the rank of Sergeant. At this time, most of the SRNs at RAF Hospitals were female commissioned officers in the PMRAF. Male SRNs would start as Junior Technicians, the rank below corporal, but they had accelerated promotion to senior NCO rank. This anomaly that would exist until the 1970s. The course atmosphere was relaxed. There was no marching to and from the classroom, and once the students had been allocated to various wards, they would just report direct to the Ward Sister in charge. In addition to some nursing theory and further anatomy and physiology in the classroom, the majority of the PNC would be spent working under supervision on the different types of wards, such as surgical, orthopaedic and general medical.

However, the majority of the time spent on the wards, particularly at the start of the day was sheer drudgery. After breakfast, bed baths and bed making, the ward cleaning would commence. There was usually just one civilian cleaner employed, but their duties would be mainly confined to the ward kitchen making coffee for the ward sisters! The bulk of the cleaning would be carried out by the most junior members of the ward staff. They would be assisted by any able bodied service patients. At the time, it was the practice for patients to remain in hospital for a time as 'up patients' long after the acute phase of their treatment had passed. The routine was for the beds on one side of the ward to be moved over, and the floor swept and polished manually using bumpers, as machines had not yet entered service in the RAF. After the floor had been cleaned just about everywhere else was 'damp dusted', particularly the patients bedside lockers. The focus of all the cleaning and polishing was Matron's rounds. Late in the morning the Matron would visit every ward and carry out an inspection. If she ever found anything untoward in respect of cleanliness, the Ward Sister would be admonished and in turn the junior staff members would be 'spoken to'. All this palaver every day was certainly something that did not appeal to me. The Matron would speak to most of the patients after being briefed by the sister in charge. Remarkably she would remember what they were all suffering from and how they were progressing. e.g. 'is your back feeling any better today corporal'. Once a week the Commanding Officer of the hospital, who would normally be a doctor with the rank of Group Captain, would accompany the Matron and the Hospital Warrant Officer who was responsible for the discipline of the junior ranks, on an inspection of the hospital. This of course meant that even more time was spent cleaning and polishing, particularly the annexes such as the toilets and sluice room. Everything had to be as the saying went. 'just so'. It was a standing joke that the patients had to lie straight in the 'at attention' position. It was not that far from the truth. The patient's bed linen, would be given a further tidy up, and any 'up patients' would stand at the foot of their beds at the start of the inspection.

As I was working on the wards to gain some knowledge and experience of actual nursing procedures other than cleaning, I would get the opportunity to do things such as change dressings, and would join the party that accompanied the doctors on their rounds, but I was never minded to consider nursing as a career option. With National Service still in full swing, the RAF hospitals were partly staffed by men who had been press-ganged into nursing. They often came from occupations which were seemingly far removed from nursing, such as manual workers from heavy industry. Some of these airmen who had received no formal training, were employed as Ward Assistants, and were supposed to work only under supervision on mainly menial duties. However many of these airmen turned into excellent nurses, and were often allowed to carry out most nursing procedures. Reports of their unexpected progress in such an apparently alien environment were both legendary, and no doubt sometimes apocryphal. In my experience there was no doubt that many became so proficient and hard working members of the ward staff, that they were held in high esteem by the Nursing Sisters. They undoubtedly brought with them to the wards, the desire to do a job well, and were used to working hard, which are qualities that some may feel is lacking in some hospitals today. I do not suppose that many of them were persuaded to retrain as nurses at that time, but when the pay and conditions for male nurses improved, I would imagine that some may have been tempted. For myself I was pleased to finish the course, and especially as passing the final exam resulted in promotion to Senior Aircraftsman, with a decent pay rise. Immediately after the course, I had to work on the male surgical ward, but I was soon able to transfer to the Operating Theatre with a view to becoming a Operating Room Technician, (ORT). I was certainly not sorry to leave nursing behind for the time being anyway.

The Operating Theatre was mainly staffed with ORTs, who were responsible for the running of two operating theatres, which mostly entailed preparing and maintaining all the equipment used in operations. They would also give general assistance in the operating theatre during operations. There was also two Nursing Officers who worked as Theatre Sisters assisting the surgeons, and two Ward Assistants who acted mainly as porters. The staff were very friendly and welcoming to me, and they also worked well as a team. They would take their coffee breaks together, which for me was something new, having not socialised before with so many people much senior in rank to me. At the end of each day after the final operation had ended, all the staff would take part in the thorough cleaning of the operating theatre. Part of the routine involved washing the entire operating room using an antiseptic solution, hosepipes and plastic buckets. This procedure gave the ORTs their nickname of 'bucket chuckers'! The cleaning was often a boisterous affair accompanied by bursts of amusing tunes such as at the time, ' Hoots Mon' by Lord Rockingham's X1. It was generally avoided by the Nursing Officers who had their dignity to maintain!

With the help of all the ORTs, I soon learned enough to be on call for emergencies along with a ORT. I really enjoyed this, and looked forward to being called out. As the other ORT on call would usually have further to travel in, I would often be the first to arrive at the theatre, and would do most of the preparations for surgery, such as ensuring the necessary instruments and other equipment were ready for use. I had acquired a basic knowledge of what was required for common emergencies such as appendectomies and caesarean sections. Usually by the time the surgeon and theatre sister had arrived, I was able to go and fetch the patient from the ward. All this made me feel quite important, and was of course a step up from basic nursing. I also found the operations to be very interesting, and often when the surgeons realised that I was a new boy, they would explain to me what they were doing. Even better, was occasionally assisting in the actual operation, whilst the theatre sister had a break during a long operation. Sometimes I would also get to assist the anaesthetist by checking the patient and the anaesthetic machinery, whilst he took a break, often for a smoke. Almost everybody smoked in those days, including doctors!

I really enjoyed my time in the operating theatre, but I was hesitant about applying for a transfer. At that time promotion was quite slow compared with other trades in the medical branch, and whilst the work was interesting at the time for me, I could envisage a time when it would be less so. In addition the ORTs often worked longer hours than the other staff at hospitals, and they also had lots of 'on call' duties. There were no overtime or bonus payments for this additional work, and at the time everyone was paid only according to their rank. Towards the end of the year, I was selected to attend a Junior Trade Management course back at RAF Freckleton. This would subsequently lead to promotion to corporal in the trade of Medical Admin without any further training. I do not think I had much choice in the matter, but I was happy to leave the friendly 'bucket chuckers' and join the 'pen pushers'!

Just as at my previous posting at Innsworth, there was little social life on the camp for the junior ranks, but as it was a comparatively small unit, this was to be expected. The WRAF members of the hospital would be invited, with transport provided, to the nearby RAF stations for dances, but there was never any such entertainment at Nocton itself. There was a small NAAFI club on camp with a bar and of course a jukebox, plus a Television Room. There would often be some good evenings there, just drinking and listening to the jukebox in the company of the nurses, which I suppose would be known today as 'chilling out'. At the weekends there was always the flesh pots of down town Lincoln to experience! There was a large NAAFI club in the town that held dances at the weekend, and I would go there on occasions, but it was not a big draw for me as I still could not really dance.

Soon after arriving at the hospital, I became friends with another medic from Bradford called 'Noddy' Lighthowlers. Up until now, I have not named anyone in my book. This was not due to failing memory, but simply because nobody as yet, was a really memorable character. Noddy however was unforgettable even to this day. He modelled himself on Tommy Steele to the extent of copying the hairstyle and going round with a guitar slung round his neck. He could hardly play the guitar at all, and would just strum odd chords and beat out a rhythm with the flat of his hand on the guitar body. He never took any lessons. Whilst this seems odd now, it was an era when so called Skiffle' music was still very popular. The father of skiffle, Lonnie Donegan, and Tommy Steele, had between them a total of 9 hit records in 1958. At the time groups were being formed which utilised washboards and bass's made from tea chests. Against this background the young Noddy Lighthowlers was to a certain extent copying many others of this new breed of musicians. One of our favourite nights out, was to visit a pub in Lincoln which usually had a group playing on Saturday nights. Noddy would take his guitar along, but I do not recall him ever being invited to join in! The guitar came into play as it were, on the way back to the hospital on the bus. We would usually occupy the seats at the back of the bus, and proceed to serenade the bus with a selection of Tommy Steele and Lonnie Donegan's hit songs! Nobody seemed to mind too much, and we were never thrown off the bus. This may well have been because everybody seemed to like Noddy and his seemingly endearing ways.

Lincoln was not too far away from Bradford, so I often took the opportunity to go home for weekends as well as leave. There I would meet up with a friend from schooldays, Mick Neilan. One of our favourite haunts was a local working men's club, where all servicemen were granted honorary membership. We used to attend in our best uniforms, sometimes substituting the standard blue shirt for a smarter white one. Mick always seemed to know many young women, who knew other women etc, so visits home would have an added interest for me. Earlier in the year we went to see Buddy Holly at a cinema in Bradford. It was probably too early in Buddy's career to see him live, as he had only had three hits at that time which were, 'Peggy Sue', 'Listen to Me' and 'Rave On'. He came on at the end after all the usual back up acts, and was not on stage for too long. After singing his hits, he went on to sing some Elvis Presley songs. Given his premature death, it was still a very memorable occasion.

During my relatively short stay at Nocton Hall, I made an attempt to improve my overall fitness through my love of cycling. After a spell of leave at Bradford, I cycled back to Nocton Hall, and subsequently went for some cycle rides in the mid-week summer evenings around the flat Lincolnshire countryside. Whilst Lincolnshire is not the most scenic county in England, I found that touring could be interesting, as the area is steeped in history in respect of World War Two former airfields etc. Before I was posted away from Nocton Hall, I cycled back to Bradford. My route took me through the coal mining area of South Yorkshire. At that time, the pollution in mining areas, was even by 1950s levels excessive. I arrived home with a very sooty appearance! Other than occasional cycling, my sporting activities were limited mainly to kick around with a football outside the living accommodation. I did once take part in a mile race with an ex coal miner, which I lost, and for a very short period we would go out together for a run round the sports field.

Towards the end of 1958, I attended a Junior Trade Management Course back at MTE Freckleton. Nothing much had changed on the camp and I soon settled in once again. The course consisted mainly of SACs, but there was also some airmen who had already been promoted to corporal. There was just one WRAF and about a dozen RAF on the course. The management part of the course was mainly concerned with managing equipment, and medical administration, both of which required the memorising of a great number of RAF forms. At that time a lot of time was spent accounting for even inexpensive equipment, and required a good knowledge of the various procedures in recording the receipt and issue of equipment. There was also an emphasis on keeping medical records and reports for statistical purposes. For example, a weekly return of sickness on units had to be compiled and forwarded to Command Headquarters and the Air Ministry, as the Ministry of Defence Air was then called. A department of the Air Ministry would receive a copy of all in -patient reports and all Out Patient specialist reports, and could thus produce even more statistics on the incidence of various diseases and accidents etc. Far less time on the course was devoted to man management. We did have some lessons on how to give orders on parade and how to march a flight of airmen, plus how to inspect airmen's kit. The latter was taught by the course having to have their own kit inspection, and the former mainly by course members taking it in turns to march the course to and from the classroom! I assume that it was not considered necessary to teach management theory, as everybody simply had to obey orders – or else!

After a few weeks, I completed the course successfully. The examinations all took place at the end of each phase of the course, so once the final phase and examination had taken place, there was nothing further to do other than the usual 'clearing' the unit. This involved handing back bedding, getting paid and filling in leave forms. For the second year in a row, my course ended at Christmas time, so I had a few days leave at home before returning to Nocton Hall.

On return to Nocton Hall, I found out that I was to be posted to RAF Hospital Bahrain in February. This was very short notice, as normally airmen were given about 6 months warning of an overseas posting. This was known as Preliminary Warning Roster, (PWR), however I had volunteered to serve abroad, and was required to replace somebody who had been withdrawn for compassionate reasons – his wife had just given birth to twins. Why he had not been replaced sooner and why his replacement was not somebody already on the PWR, I was not told, but I was pleased to be going abroad, even though I knew nothing at all about Bahrain, or even initially where it was.

In the meantime I was to work in what was called the Hospital Medical Inspection Room, (MI Room), which was the name given to the small department that dealt with the medical needs of the staff. It was in effect a General Practitioners surgery. I would act as the manager, assisting the doctor by arranging appointments, looking after the medical records of the staff, and of course compiling statistics. As this was a hospital, I was never required to provide any treatment or dispense any drugs, it was just pen pushing. There was nobody else required in this small department, other than the doctor, who would hold a morning surgery, and carry out routine medical examinations at other times in the day, so I was left to work mainly on my own. A friendly Warrant Officer who was in charge of all the Medical Administration for the hospital, would occasionally call in the MI Room to ask if I had any problems, and I would sometimes seek his advice on administrative procedures, otherwise I had a free rein, and was certainly what was known as a 'cushy number'. The staff doctor was, unusually for that time, a female Squadron Leader. She had a pleasant disposition and was very easy to work with. Possibly she was very easy to get on with, as I had agreed to carry out a completely unofficial and additional duty for her every afternoon. No it was not what you might be thinking, it was to take her dog for a walk! This was a great way to spend some time on an afternoon, and I am surprised that I was allowed to do this, and that everybody just accepted that she would bring her dog into the M.I Room every afternoon, so I could take it for a walk!. Alas this halcyon existence would soon come to an end when I left the hospital en route to Bahrain after less than two months.

In 1959, all airmen posted abroad went to RAF Innsworth to be 'prepared'. This would involve mainly the supply of tropical uniforms and having the necessary inoculations and vaccinations. There was also an element of herding, in that all those destined for a particular posting, would be brought together, processed together, and subsequently transported together. At some point in time, some genius came up with the idea, that the supply of tropical uniforms etc. could all be done at the airmen's station from whence they were posted, therefore making the role of RAF Innsworth redundant. After being kitted out with so called Khaki Drill uniforms which were of poor quality and design, and after receiving any necessary injections we were ready to travel. However instead of proceeding to Heathrow for the direct flight to Bahrain by a civilian charter aircraft, we travelled to RAF Hendon for an overnight stop. At the time many airmen posted to the Middle East and the Far East still travelled by troopships which were still in use, so the detour to Hendon was nothing in comparison, and indeed gave me an opportunity to see a little of London at night for the first time. This was just before the 1959 Street Offences Act had become law, so the first people I saw on leaving the Underground was the 'ladies of the night' plying their trade. At the time I was with a small group of airmen who were also posted to the RAF Hospital at Bahrain. None of us were tempted, and at the time I did not even realise what was being offered here, as I was unfamiliar with their euphemisms for sexual activity such as 'good time' etc. Perhaps this was just as well, as 45 years later, by coincidence, I found myself living just a few doors away from one of the group. He was then SAC Jim Henstock, who had recently married, and still is to this day, to Rita. Eventually we all arrived safely at Bahrain, which was for me the start of two very interesting and mostly very enjoyable two years.

6. RAF Bahrain

On arrival at Bahrain in February, I found that it was pleasantly warm during the day, but cold at night. The climate resembles that of southern Europe for a few months in the winter, so myself and the new arrivals were spared having to wear our tropical uniforms for a couple of months. Approximately 20 RAF medical personnel accompanied me on the flight, and they would be mainly replacing staff of a Field Hospital, who were returning to the United Kingdom. The Field Hospital was set up in late 1958 following the withdrawal of British forces from Iraq after the 1958 revolution. Tensions in the Persian Gulf had now eased, but an RAF base with a more permanent hospital, would subsequently remain at Muharraq, and indeed did so until a final withdrawal of British Forces in late1971, when the Protectorate status of this small constitutional monarchy state finally ended by mutual consent. However since 1971, the RAF has been allowed to use the airfield at Muharraq to support operations in Eastern Europe and elsewhere, and 30 years after I left Bahrain, my son Carl was to spend time there as an engineering officer detached from RAF Brize Norton.

The hospital which replaced the tented Field Hospital, consisted of a former school building, with some added out buildings. It was somewhat makeshift to say the least. It had just two main wards which could accommodate around 30 patients, but mainly those with less serious conditions requiring in- patient treatment. It could also cope with major cases pending their removal by air to the RAF Hospital at Aden or to the United Kingdom. The nursing element consisted of four male SRNs, (there were no female servicewomen on the station), the senior of which acted as the Hospital Matron. The SRNs were supported by Nursing Attendants, one of whom was yours truly, so my pen pushing days were on hold for several months until a vacancy arose in one of the hospital offices. However the nursing experience was not like that at Nocton Hall for several reasons. Firstly local Arab cleaners were employed as cleaners, so they did most of this under supervision. Secondly, the patients were mostly not ill enough to be classed as 'strict bed', so bed baths and bedpans were rarely required. Finally with such a small all male staff who worked closely together, there was no tedious daily rounds of inspection. The Commanding Officer of the Hospital was a Squadron

Leader who doubled up as an anaesthetist. He was supported by two Flight Lieutenant medical officers, one of whom was a general surgeon, and the other acted as the Unit Medical Officer, in effect the General Practitioner for the station. There was also some back up given by a Royal Army Medical Corps medical officer who was based at a nearby military base. In addition there was another Medical Officer at the hospital, but his was the mainly Administrative post of Senior Medical Officer Persian Gulf, who was responsible for the medical cover for several small units in the Persian Gulf.

Because most of the hospital staff had arrived at the same time as myself, the social side of my life got off to a very slow start, as I discovered what life was like on a RAF station in a foreign country. The social element was certainly different from that of a RAF station in the United Kingdom. The hospital staff's accommodation was better than most on the camp, as many would be working shifts. It consisted of small rooms, which could accommodate up to 4 airmen. This turned out to be a mixed blessing, as living so close to others in this way, frequently led to rows and then some chopping and changing of rooms. The normal working hours which remained the same all year round, were from 7 a.m to 1.30 p.m every day except Sunday, so there was plenty of time for leisure activities, once I had settled in. However many of those who arrived with me, were married men who would soon be joined by their families, and in the meantime, they were seemingly content to spend the interim period lounging about in their rooms, writing letters, listening to the radio and playing endless games of whist and 'Hunt the Queen'! To help pass the time, we could purchase duty free cigarettes at the NAAFI in packs of 200s, which almost everybody did. During the early part of my tour, the food in the airman's mess was very unappetizing. Some airmen would not eat it at all, and preferred to exist on food purchased from the NAAFI, and occasional meals at the civil air terminal which was attached to the station. The blame for the poor food was blamed on the presence of the resident Army detachment, which at that time was the Royal Fusiliers who recruited mainly from the London area. It was said that they would eat anything and never complain. When they were replaced by the Inniskilling Fusiliers, the food did get a little better!

The small NAAFI shop sold duty free goods, mainly cigarettes and spirits, although single airmen could not purchase spirits other than in the bar by the glass. The club part of the NAAFI was extremely spartan and consisted of a counter for snacks and a bar, all in one large room. There was little entertainment other than darts matches, and of course some drinking. In addition to airmen's birthdays, there were always parties to celebrate things such as the end of the tour at Bahrain, coupled with demob in many cases. The favourite tipple was tins of lager – there was nothing at all on draught. There was much more entertainment in the Corporals Club, Sergeants and Officers messes, but the other ranks were not very well catered for on the camp. The main pastime for everybody on the camp was the open air cinema. This had a change of programme about twice a week. The open air facility was good for the warm weather, but somewhat chilly in the winter. Everybody took a blanket to keep warm. I can still recall the first time I went to this cinema. It was to see 'South Pacific' which was about troops stationed on a island with very few women around!

The main sport on camp during the winter months was football. Although I was not a good player, I organised a hospital team, and we subsequently managed to play a game about once a week on one of the pitches just outside the camp. These matches were mainly against teams from the units and sections on the camp, but also some local civilian teams. There was never a problem mixing with the local population, who were normally friendly towards the service population. There was an open air swimming pool on the camp, but unfortunately it was closed in the winter. Some members of the hospital staff often went fishing both on the camp which had it's own beach, and also off the camp at the sailing club. I tried fishing and also sailing just the once, but I started to use the Sailing Club for its social activities later on in my tour. Other sports such as Rugby and Hockey were limited to a station team, which played matches against other units on the island. Tennis was even more limited, as the only court on the camp was part of the Officers Mess, so unless any of the junior ranks were part of the station team, it was not possible for them to play on this court. However at that time, very few airmen played tennis players. There was one exception which was a SAC National Serviceman whom I knew. He was too good to be excluded from a station team which otherwise consisted of officers, but he was not allowed to enter the main part of the Officers Mess for any drinks after a match, which he told me, caused some embarrassment to the other team members!

In 1959, Bahrain was not the wealthy state it has become today, and the capital city of Manama did not hold many attractions for servicemen. There was just a few shops selling western style goods, plus the souks with their traditional goods such as gold and silver jewellery. This was not a big hardship at the time, as most airmen's main purchases were seemingly limited to a Rolex watch, a transistor radio and a new suit! The island was 'dry', so there was no pubs other than on the military bases and at the British owned B P Oil Refinery at Awali. The refinery was about twenty miles away, and had some good social facilities, one of which was an air-conditioned cinema, which some of the hospital staff would visit on a Saturday night, sharing a taxi for the journey. Taxis were inexpensive due to cheap fuel, and were used for most journeys off the camp. Other than the cinema, the other social facilities at Awali were not generally open to servicemen. However sporting teams would usually gain admission after a match, which led to frequent visits by official and *ad hoc* service teams in a variety of sports. I played in a hockey team there once even though I had hardly ever played the game before. Whilst my two year tour got off to a quiet start both socially and at work, as the tour progressed, both improved a good deal.

On the music scene, there was no British Forces Broadcasting station at Bahrain, but there was an American Forces Broadcasting station nearby on the Saudia Arabian mainland at Dharhan, which of course broadcast a lot of music. As this was a few years before the so called 'British Invasion' of America by numerous British groups led by The Beatles, almost all the music played on air was American. However at this time, American artists such as Elvis, Buddy Holly, Bobby Darin and The Platters had all UK number one hits. Elvis with two number ones, 'One Night/I Got Stung' and 'A Fool Such As I/Need Your Love Tonight'. stayed at the top of the UK charts, a lot longer that the solitary week in the USA charts with 'A Big Hunk of Hove'. We would only get to hear artists such as Cliff Richard and Russ Conway on records which might have been on sale at the NAAFI, or else brought out by recent arrivals on the station, or airmen returning from leave in UK. I must add that only married airmen whose wives were not accompanying them in Bahrain were allowed UK leave. One such airman returned from leave in the UK with the late Adam Faith's number one record of 'What do you Want'. We all found it hard to believe it was ever number one, having never heard of Adam Faith, and therefore not being familiar with his odd singing voice. His follow up record of 'Poor Me' was to be his only other number one before he concentrated more on acting.

In the period when I had a nursing hat on, I had some trips in light aircraft such as the Pembroke and the Pioneer, to evacuate patients from small

RAF stations in the Persian Gulf. Those whom I collected, were those who were too ill to travel as normal passengers, and required only basic nursing on a stretcher. I greatly enjoyed this role, but after 1959, it would be another 21 years before I became involved in any aeromedical evacuation work again, and then only after a proper training course at RAF Brize Norton. One of my first trips was to RAF Sharjah, and after arrival, there was a delay before we could take off. I was amazed at the isolation of the camp, and it's airstrip of packed sand. At the time, the normal tour of duty there was two years, and all the airmen were unaccompanied. It was reduced to 12 months later in 1959. However as airmen always tended to do, they made the best of things. I was told that the RAF medical officer, who was a National Serviceman, and the Sergeant in charge of the medical centre had formed a music group, and that they had some good parties on Saturday nights! Shades of 'South Pacific' again. On another occasion I stopped at an even smaller and remote airfield at a place called Firq. Under a windsock someone had spelt out Firq in small white stones, and underneath had added 'U 2'! It seemed perfect for this lonely outpost.

Whilst Bahrain was far from being anything like the RAF Stations in the Persian Gulf, there was a definite shortage of girlfriend material. No female servicewomen were stationed on the island (although three PMRAF nursing officers would arrive later in 1959) and whilst there was a limited amount of socializing with some of the Arab population, this never extended to the women, who were never seen in public without the traditional purdah form of dress. There was some limited contact with British women, and quite a lot of time was spent making the most of this. The main contact was with the service families, some of whom might even have grown-up daughters, although this was rare, with many older children opting to stay in the UK and attend boarding schools, spending only summer and Christmas holidays with their parents (the flights were paid for by the services). In addition, other than mainly senior airmen, most married servicemen were too young to have older children. There would often be parties to attend at the homes of the married members of the hospital staff, which afforded some female company, and I am sure these occasions were enjoyed equally by the wives as they were by the lonely airmen. I am not sure about the husbands! At one such party I attended, the host, a corporal from the hospital, had somehow managed to find a solitary single woman, a Chief Petty Officer's daughter. Bees and a honey-pot would be a good analogy. I managed to get to take her home in a taxi, but sadly for me that was about all. Still, it made me happy for weeks afterwards!

As my first year progressed, I became a member of a Sailing Club at nearby Jufair, and attended social events there, which included not only families, but also British civilians working in the capital. As far as meeting single women was concerned, it was on a par with hospital staff family's parties, but that did not deter some of my friends and myself from attending. There was also some enjoyment to be had with the mixed bathing in the sea on many an afternoon! The swimming pool on the camp opened in the spring, and was a popular pastime, and would combine with sun bathing. There was never any concerns about skin cancer in those days of course. Sun bathing was also a very popular pastime, and those who had only recently arrived from the UK, were often mocked and called 'moonies'. Airmen who were due to go home at the end of their tour, spent as much time as they could sunbathing, so they would have a good tan to show off when they got back home. Those concerned would be said to be 'panic tanning'! At the railway station at Gloucester, airmen from overseas units who were proceeding home via nearby RAF Innsworth, would often be seen waiting for trains with their new suits and sun tans. The service families also used the swimming pool on the camp. However the wives and older children were spared from any undue lechery, by having exclusive use at separate times. However one of my friends discovered that there was to be a life saving course to be at the camp pool which would include women. After learning of this, he told me and another friend, and so we both then enrolled for the course! There was as we hoped, a couple of women on the course, the best looking of which was an officers daughter, and therefore somebody we would not really be able to ask out etc. However we all loved getting to know her, so much so that when the course ended, and we found that she had enrolled a more advanced course, we all did too. I used to list the life savings qualifications obtained when asked, but otherwise have never had to use these skills – obtained for all the wrong reasons! The only other contact with women was achieved by visiting the civilian airport restaurant run by the British Airways Overseas Corporation (BOAC). We would go to this facility which was on the edge of the camp, usually just for coffee, but occasionally for a meal. There we would get to see all the transiting Air Hostesses as they were then called. In the 1950s they were always young and very attractive. We never went to any extreme lengths, such as checking on aircraft arrival times, and it was really just a pleasant diversion and change from visits to the NAAFI club.

Towards the end of my first year at Bahrain, which was by far the longest period of time I had spent on the same RAF camp, I began to grow in confidence, both at work and also in my social life, even though I was still younger than the average airman, particularly the older National Servicemen. Whilst I was also comparatively younger than those employed as Nursing Attendants at the hospital, I had already qualified for promotion to the rank of Corporal, which carried with it an automatic transfer to the trade of Medical Administrator, (Med Admin), so when a vacancy arose in the administrative department of the Hospital, my full time nursing career came to an end. I say 'full time' as the RAF would continue to utilise my nursing training, limited that it undoubtedly was, but never again as my main duties. The Hospital Administrative Department, was just a large room with an additional small office for the Chief Clerk. My first job, was to arrange specialist out patient clinics at the hospital for the resident surgeon, and also for visiting specialists from Aden and occasionally from the UK. It was not a very demanding job, and required some skill to eke out the time in the office. Trips to a soft drinks seller at the back of the hospital, and also to headquarters and other sections on the camp department all helped to pass the time. Whilst not of the same extent as at United Kingdom units, there was still a fair amount of over staffing, which was to continue until after the end of National Service. In addition to their normal duties, the junior airmen and NCOs were on a roster to provide emergency medical cover during after duty hours. A corporal and an airman would stay in the hospital and respond to any emergency situations on the station, either by attending the scene in an ambulance, or at the hospital by assisting the standby Duty Medical Officer. Throughout my tour there were very few serious accidents on the camp, and the out of hours duty care was usually limited to treating minor injuries, and referring anybody who otherwise required urgent treatment to the duty doctor. On one occasion during my tour, an airman came to the hospital to request some sleeping tablets, as he was unable to sleep due to worry about going prematurely bald. When the request for sleeping tablets was denied, he insisted and the Medical Officer was then summoned. The doctor told the airman that he was indeed fortunate that a specialist was visiting the hospital the very next day, and that he would arrange for him to be seen. The next morning the airman was to spend time asking another doctor if his baldness could be cured, and seemingly failing to notice that the doctor he was consulting was himself completely bald!

Things improved a great deal on the social side, particularly towards the end of the year when I was able to take a holiday in Mombasa For single airmen, leave in the United Kingdom, was not permitted, but free trips to Kenya were granted in lieu. For those on a two year tour, it was possible to take two holidays either at a service holiday camp, or at other accommodation of your choice.

Around November time, I set off with a friend, SAC John Hart from London who was also a nursing attendant at the hospital, first to Aden where we had some additional days holiday waiting to catch the plane to Mombasa In 1959 there was a large British service presence in the colony of Aden, which included two RAF stations and also an Army garrison. We stayed on the large RAF station at Khormaksar, which had all the usual entertainment facilities, and also spent some time visiting the base at Steamer Point, which had in addition both WRAF and Women's Royal Army Corps, (WRAC), plus a large number of service families. There was no terrorism in the Colony at that time, so we were able to travel round freely to the various beaches and service clubs, which seemed like paradise to us. The climate was hot, but not as humid as in Bahrain, and was generally pleasant when not exerting yourself. We also visited the town of Crater which had a large number of shops selling duty free goods, which were sold only after some bartering took place. This was something that never appealed to me, partly because I always suspected that I would always spend more than I might have for something I had settled for, but it was also very time consuming if the bartering process was engaged in at different shops for the same item. John Hart managed to buy a Rolex Oyster watch for a bargain price, but I settled for a cheap fake watch, which lasted years!

A lasting memory of Aden in late 1959 is of the British Forces Broadcasting Service, (BFBS), which broadcast over the two main bases. It was greatly appreciated, as the only alternative was the sporadic broadcasts of the BBC World Service Radio, with the familiar signature tune of 'Lily Bolero'. As Aden had a predominantly young audience of service personnel and families, pop music occupied the most airtime, which included many request programmes. At the time, transistor radios had become very popular and in the Duty-Free shops of Aden were very affordable. The concept of noise nuisance was not something that seemingly troubled anybody at the time, so it was not at all unusual to witness people walking around with the radio switched on, belting out the latest hits being played on BFBS. In addition radios on the bases, would all be playing the same song, which would therefore reverberate around the working areas. This was very well portrayed in the film 'Good Morning Vietnam' with James Brown's ' I Feel Good' serenading the American troops on a base in Vietnam during the war. In 1959 Aden, it would more than likely have been Elvis, or Cliff Richard with his number one hit 'Travelling Light'. What this must have been like for anyone who disliked pop music I cannot imagine, but nobody seemed to mind.

So after a few enjoyable days in Aden, John and myself finally flew to Mombasa in a civilian aircraft of Aden Airways, which was a subsidiary of BOAC. After clearing the airport at Mombasa, it was a return to the more traditional form of transport for airmen, a truck in which we drove into the town. Those who are staying at hotels were dropped off first at their hotel and the remainder stayed on the truck to the holiday camp. I suspect that by now some would have been wondering if they made the right choice. Certainly the camp was a cheaper option but John and myself had no wish to spend a holiday on service run premises, even a holiday camp. We soon checked into a hotel that was moderately priced, probably because it welcomed Kenyan Asians whereas the more expensive hotels did not – Kenya was still a British Colony at the time. We had a really good meal, particularly as we appreciated even basic items such as proper cows milk. It was then time to have a look round the town. It was perfectly safe to walk round at night in those days, so we strolled around until we came across the sound of what can best be described as African Rock and Roll coming from the upper floor of a building. We went up to investigate, and I recall that the intention was not to stay too long as we must have been tired after the flight. As we entered the room with the band, we spotted somebody we knew from Bahrain. He was sat down with a bottle of Tusker beer, in between two young women, and was looking pleased with himself. We thought we ought to join him. It was many hours later before we eventually left the premises. So the pattern was well and truly set for two weeks hedonism. During our stay in Mombasa, we discovered many other similar places with great music and young women, who were always happy to be in our company. In the afternoons, we would visit some great beaches with the soft white sand, for a swim and sunbathing. This would also serve to conserve our energy for the evenings. On this holiday we did not venture on any Safari's, having decided that we would do so on the next Kenyan holiday, mainly so we could say we had done so whilst in Kenya, and thereby avoid relating what we did get up to!

John and myself arrived back at Bahrain, about the time that plans for Christmas celebrations were being formulated. For the airmen living on the camp this mainly concerned the building of bars in the barrack rooms. For Christmas and Boxing day, bars were permitted exceptionally in the living accommodation. These bars were often of a very elaborate construction, and the different billets competed against each other for the best design. The bars would be built with materials that had been mainly 'written off', (scrapped), such as for example items of wood etc. Other essential things such as paint could be scrounged from workshops. The most important task for the bar builders was to obtain sufficient stocks of beer and other drinks. This was achieved partly by donations from married airmen living off camp, senior officers and other money raising schemes such as sweepstakes. The goal was for free drink to be available for the two days that the bars were open. The construction of the bars and the fund-raising was undoubtedly made successful by utilising the civilian talents of the many National Servicemen still serving in the RAF. There was always somebody with under utilised artistic talents, decorating skills, and also very many who were good at 'acquiring' things!

Over the Christmas holiday period, the bars were the main focus of entertainment, and this was regarded as quite normal. Other entertainment was limited to a comic football match, some *ad hoc* live music, and the usual Christmas Dinner served by the officers on the camp. To get into the spirit of Christmas, I went with some friends to a midnight mass on Christmas Eve. This was almost certainly the very last time I have attended such a service. Perhaps the fact that the Hospital Commanding Officer, who was a Roman Catholic, was laying on some drinks at his house after the service, and a desire to create a good impression, may well have influenced our decision to attend Mass! On my first Christmas Day away from home, I was on duty at the hospital along with other volunteers from amongst the hospital staff's single airmen. This enabled the married members of staff to spend time with their families. It was also seen as important to keep well in with the married airmen who lived off camp, for reasons I will explain later in this chapter.

New Year was fairly uneventful, as celebrations were not as widespread as today, other than mainly in Scotland, which did have a public holiday. So my first year at Bahrain came to a quiet end. With it the start of the 'Swinging 60s' and the increased popularity of British pop music and culture. At the new year of 1960, a British record, 'What do you want to make those eyes at me for' by Emile Ford and the Checkmates had taken over from Adam Faith at number. In 1960, only four USA records would make number one. As Bob Dylan was to sing later in the decade, 'The times are a changing'

They certainly were!

Two of the most significant events that occurred during my time in Bahrain, occurred in 1960. On the work front, I was promoted to Corporal, and was subsequently moved to a new post in the Station's Medical Centre, which was in reality just another part of the camp hospital. My new duties were similar to those at Nocton Hall, but this time they were shared with another corporal. This meant that except for after hours cover, when I would be in charge of an Senior Aircraftsman for the period of the duty, I would not be burdened with too much man management! Additionally I was required to perform the duties of the Station Orderly Corporal on a roster basis. This was also not too demanding, and the main duty was to ensure that the NAAFI club bar was closed and locked up on time. This could occasionally be tricky, but persuasion would usually work wonders! On the social side, after joining a small team of 4 boxers on the station, I became very friendly with two of them. They were Tom Mulholland and John Morley, who were two SACs who worked in the Accounts section. Their *raison d'etre* was seemingly to do all that they could to enjoy life at RAF Bahrain. As mentioned earlier, sport could open some social doors, and boxing was seen as just another opportunity. In this particular instance, it resulted in a trip to Aden for the four of us, and apart from just a small amount of training whilst we were based at Steamer Point for over a week, it was an extra weeks holiday – on a RAF Camp with plenty of WRAF and WRAC servicewomen! Our trainer at Bahrain, was none other than the CO of the hospital, a Squadron Leader Mulrooney, who was partly responsible for getting me interested in boxing, as I had never even considered this sport before. In Chapter 11, I will cover my amateur boxing career which was to last up to January 1973.

In addition to joining the station boxing team, John and Tom were active in several other sports on the station, all of which had a good social element. John who was a National Serviceman, had previously played professional Rugby League for Saint Helens, but was permitted under the governing rules to play in the amateur game during his National Service, so he took the opportunity to play for RAF Bahrain. This involved some touring and of course extra time off work. Tom had played Hockey before, and was part of a team that played a limited amount of games on the island. There was insufficient interest in the sport at Bahrain for a league to be formed at the time, and so RAF Bahrain struggled to field a team. This led to Tom persuading me to take up the sport, with the inducement of away fixtures at the BP refinery at Awali, and the after match hospitality. Both John and Tom also played water polo, but this was not a sport that I would be tempted to try, partly because whilst I was a competent swimmer, I had never mastered a fast crawl. In addition, and as far as I could see there was little if any social side to this 'cinderella' sport. All three of us were members of the Sailing Club, but like myself, John and Tom would just use the club for mixed bathing and the many social functions. John would also get me out for a run of an afternoon as part of general fitness training, but neither of us took part in organised athletics, which was almost non existent on the island. It would be almost twenty years before I started to participate in athletics.

During the second part of my tour, both John and Tom, plus some other friends decided to arrange their own Saturday night parties, sometimes using the flats of friends who were married and living in the capital Manama, but on at least one occasion, using a private swimming pool complex belonging to a rich local resident who was probably connected to the ruling Royal Family. The main problem in organising any party on Bahrain for single airmen, was that of obtaining alcoholic drinks. The island was officially 'dry' other than on the bases and significantly private houses. On the bases, single airmen could buy alcoholic drinks but not in sealed containers. This restriction could be circumvented by the NAAFI barmen making just a minute hole in the can – there was no draught beers available. Married airmen living off the camp, all held a liquor licence, which enabled them to purchase sealed tins of beer and most importantly bottles of spirit. Those organising a party would first of all collect some money from the single airmen who wished to attend. Most of those invited would be happy to donate, as they would in turn be organising their own parties. The next step was to issue an invitation to all those in the party organiser's section who were married and held a liquor licence. Those married airmen who were invited, would usually enquire if the organisers had been able to obtain enough alcohol. The answer was always no, would you mind buying x number of cases of beer and a bottle of spirits for the party, (the allowance for bottles of spirits was limited), here is the money. The next stage is perhaps best left to the imagination, but by some astute dealing, sufficient drink was eventually acquired, and any surplus after the party went to a good cause or should I say causes! A further spin off from these deals was to be able to hire one of those classic 1950s American saloon cars, which were very popular on Bahrain, at a minimum cost.

When I automatically became a member of the Corporal's club on promotion, I was able to join in some more social activities. These took the form of occasional dances on Saturday nights, and darts matches. The dances were well attended, but there were rarely any single women. However, it was nice to have some female company, and especially those whom you knew well. Perhaps you worked with their spouses, or else got to know them from other functions. As John and Tom were not members, I was not a regular at Corporals Club functions. The Darts matches could provide a good night out either at the Oil Refinery Social Club, or at other service units on the island. It was not necessary to be in the team, as supporters were always welcome. I particularly recall a darts match at the Royal Navy base at Jufair, which at the same time was entertaining a party of sailors from a United States ship. The United States Navy does not permit any alcohol on board ship, so when their sailors come ashore they tended to make up for lost drinking time. Some were drinking cans of lager together with glasses of vodka. They seemed able to cope well with it, perhaps a reflection on the strict discipline on board ship. It certainly was a jolly night, ending with lots of jokes and of course singing lewd songs and some patriotic anthems. However in the midst of all the jollity, a huge figure of a sailor started to shout at another across the room. The second sailor responded with threats, which were repeated by the first sailor, and became more and more menacing. Eventually the pair go out of the bar, followed by a large number of spectators who thought they were about to witness something like Ali v Frazier. After some squaring up and another exchange of threats, one of the pair approached the other and gave him a very delicate slap on the face. In seconds it became obvious that they had fooled everyone – again seemingly. With plenty of social and sporting activity, the year seemed to fly by. It was soon time to visit Kenya again, and see some big game this time!

My second spell of leave in Kenya was preceded by a visit to the RAF Hospital in Aden at Steamer Point, in order to have some specialist dental treatment. I was not admitted and simply had a consultation appointment and then some treatment a day or so later, so I stayed in staff accommodation at Steamer Point. This was almost as good as an extra weeks holiday. Even though I was on my own this time, I knew some of the staff from Nocton Hall, and in addition to some afternoons at the beach, I had a few pleasant nights at the hospital social club, which was frequented by some of the WRAF nursing and administrative staff. My plan for the Kenyan holiday this time was to spend a few days in Mombasa each side of a week on a farm in Moshi, a town over the border in Tanganyika, now Tanzania. On arrival at Mombasa I settled for some basic accommodation, but I mostly ate out at superior hotels or restaurants. Whilst the food provided by the RAF at Bahrain had improved slightly in 1960, a decent meal remained a much sought after ingredient of a holiday. My idea of a good meal in those days was; tomato soup, steak and chips and apple pie. These choices were to stay much the same for years to come! With the experience of a recent Mombasa holiday to go by, I visited the two bars in town that I had liked best, which were The Rainbow and The New Bristol. After a repeat of the earlier hedonistic days in Mombasa, I headed out of town for Moshi three days later, camera at the ready.

I made the trip to Moshi by bus, and it was certainly a memorable journey. There was a first and second class on the bus, with the first class consisting of a few seats at the back of the bus, which were marginally more comfortable. I had been told not to bother paying the extra for first class, which was used almost exclusively by the more affluent Kenyan Asians. The white settler types used their own transport of course. I was not too surprised when the bus occasionally stopped – seemingly in the middle of nowhere, for passengers to board or leave the bus, as I had already been told about this phenomenon. I had also heard about the other common practice of passengers carrying some live poultry. You never knew just what would be on the seat next to you! Around the half way stage in the journey, the bus made a rest stop, and the passengers left the bus for refreshments at a couple of stalls set up under the shade of a tree. Just as soon I had got off the bus, I saw the bus driving off with the first class passengers, to what I later found out was a small hotel! As I wanted to enjoy the rest of my holiday, I stuck to a bottle of coca cola, as not only was the food on sale unfamiliar to me, it was covered with flies. After I arrived safely in Moshi, the owner of the farm collected me in a land rover, no doubt amazed at my mode of travel. The farm was partly a working agricultural farm and partly a holiday centre managed by a married couple. The husband looked after the working farm, whilst his wife ran the holiday side of the enterprise. She organised things such as safari trips, treks up the lower slopes of Kilimanjaro, water skiing, and some social activities with the white settlers. Most of her holiday guests were servicemen and women, from the Persian Gulf, Aden and also from British bases in Kenya, such as RAF Eastleigh which was outside the capital, Nairobi.

I had a very enjoyable and interesting week at Moshi. The highlight was day in Tsavo National Park when I got to see all the major types of wild animals in their natural environment, including the Tsavo 'Big Five', namely Elephant, Lion, Rhino, Water Buffalo, and right at the end of the safari, a leopard. The Kilimanjaro trek was also memorable, not only for the views of the snow capped mountain, but also the lunch break by the side a pool containing piranha fish. The fish rapidly disposed of the remains of our chicken salad with deadly efficiency! On another day out, to a nearby lake, I had my one and only experience of water skiing, which I enjoyed, but even to this day, this is something which I have not done since. The evenings were mainly spent lingering over the meal, followed sometimes by games of Scrabble! There was no television, and the only English radio was the World Service. With the other servicemen guests, I went to a Saturday night dance at Moshi which was an all white settler affair. We were made very welcome, but after Mombasa, the settlers and their fox trots seemed just a little tame. After a memorable, interesting and enjoyable week, I headed back to Mombasa. This time a farmer offered those heading back to Mombasa a lift on the back of a lorry. We made ourselves very comfortable, and enjoyed the slip-stream which cooled us down. However when we arrived at Mombasa we were covered in red dust from the roads. I still had a couple of days left before flying back to Aden, so I was able to visit what were by now old haunts for the last time. I was destined to visit Kenya, albeit just briefly on two more occasions in 1971, on service business, but to date this was last time I would ever see Mombasa.

Not long after returning to Bahrain, I joined up with John Morley, Tom Mulholland and another boxer on a trip to Aden for a boxing tournament at Steamer Point, in which we represented RAF Bahrain. It was in effect another week's holiday. We went for a couple of morning runs along a beach road, and had some light sparring sessions in the gym, otherwise we just enjoyed the beach club and some shopping in Crater. None of us did too well at the tournament, but we were not disgraced either. I lost my first ever bout, mainly because I was outclassed, and so the referee decided to end the bout towards the end of the second round. However I was not too discouraged and continued to box on return to England, and as mentioned earlier, I will be devoting Chapter 10 of my story to my boxing career. Soon after returning to Bahrain, I celebrated my twenty first birthday, which of course was a more significant event back in 1961. On the actual day, I had a meal at the BOAC restaurant with John and Tom, and on the following Saturday, I had a joint birthday party with John Morley on the roof of Mike Gouge's house in Manama. The party was a great success, at least as far as John and myself were concerned. Together with our mutual friend Tom, we conspired to have a big party, and managed to end up in profit. I still have an invitation card, on the back of which John Morley had worked out the profit, which we shared between us!

Christmas and the New Year was much the same as the previous year, but this time I avoided being on duty on Christmas Day, and opted to work on Boxing day instead. By now my thoughts were very much on the end of my time in Bahrain, and after what in effect was two recent holidays, I was not exactly hell bent on seeking any social events. I did attend a News Years Eve party this year with Tom and John, and recall that our first words after Midnight was ' We go home this year!' After New Years day, the days were too cold to seriously sun bathe, so I just had to hope that the some normal exposure to the winter sun would maintain my suntan. There was time to get a new suit made, and I managed to get a three piece suit made by a tailor in Manama from a picture in an American magazine – 'Playboy' I think it was! It was in a dark grey material, and I thought that therefore it would not look like those suits that regularly appeared on the platforms of Gloucester Railway Station, usually in sky blue! The average suit made by the Arab tailors on the camp, were very good value for money, but not really suitable for the smoky and grimy streets of 1961 Bradford. I did however get a smart navy blue blazer made by the camp tailor, which lasted for years. The final act of preparation for the return home was to buy some souvenir presents. Fancy musical boxes were a favourite choice, followed by carved animals, usually elephants, purchased from roadside vendors in Kenya. A bottle of *Chanel Number 5* was the only type of duty free perfume that anybody bought, and indeed stayed the number one choice for many years. For the only time during the tour, airmen were allowed to purchase a single bottle of spirits from the NAAFI to take back to UK. This would always be scotch whiskey.

In February, I bade farewell to Bahrain and looked forward to life back in England, where it transpired I would spend the next four and a half years before my next spell of overseas service. Overall it had been a successful two years. I had gained a lot of experience in my job, achieved promotion to corporal, and had the experience of service overseas in a volatile area, which led to the award of a General Service Medal (GSM) with the 'Arabian Peninsular' clasp. Thanks mainly to people like John and Tom, I learned how to make the most of life in places like Bahrain. What could have been a dull social life for a young single man, was more than compensated for with holidays in Kenya and some new sporting activities.

Soon after arriving back in Bradford for 6 weeks leave, I started driving lessons, and also went to a ballroom dancing class, mainly to improve my social life now that I was back home. I subsequently failed the driving test, and did not get to grips with the slow foxtrot, but I did learn how to drive and passed the driving test at a later date. Alas, I never did master the art of ballroom dancing! When I found myself at a loose end during the daytime, I took a job in a woollen mill for a few weeks, and really enjoyed the hard work knowing that I would be well paid for it, and that it would only be for about a month. I met up again with Mick Neilan, and started going out with a friend of his current girl friend for a while, until we split up at Easter. In addition to cinema going, dances and even on one occasion a play, 'Pygmalion' at Saint Georges Hall in Bradford, the favourite pastime was visiting pubs with a loud juke box, particularly on a Sunday night. At the time there was a ban on music in pubs on a Sunday in Bradford, but a bus ride just beyond the city boundaries, took myself, Mick Neilan and our girl friends to a pub in the Queensbury area that was unaffected by the ban. In the first part of 1961, chances were that Elvis would have been played a lot on jukeboxes. He had four number one hits that year. During my leave in Bradford, 'Are you lonesome tonight' and Wooden Heart' were at number one. The charts were becoming more British, but artists such as The Everley Brothers' and Del Shannon certainly bucked the trend for that year. After a great six weeks leave, I travelled to my new posting at RAF Henlow, which was in Bedfordshire, but just five miles from Hitchin in Hertfordshire.

7. Home Units

Four years after arriving at RAF Cardington, I alighted at a railway station just a few miles down the line, called Henlow Camp. As the name suggested, it was right next to RAF Henlow. The RAF station housed the RAF Officer Technical Training College, (Tech Coll), which included the training of officer cadets destined for the Engineering Branch, and the Radio Engineering Unit (REU). The REU was the base unit for aerial erectors, who would spend most of their service detached away from Henlow, servicing and erecting radio masts on RAF stations in the UK. I was to work at the Station Sick Quarters, (SSQ), which was one of the administrative sections that came under Tech Coll, but was used by both units on the station. SSQ consisted of a large building with two wards of 12 beds and two small wards of two beds – mainly for officers and officer cadets, consulting rooms, treatment rooms, a dispensary and medical stores, and several offices. Emergency ambulance cover was provided for the station, using the Nursing Attendants on the staff. There were two unit medical officers, a Squadron Leader Gilbert for the Tech Coll, and a Doctor Crowley, a retired Medical Branch Group Captain for the REU. There was also a serving Group Captain who was the medical advisor to the Commandant of the Tech College. He had a mainly administrative role, but also saw a limited number of patients. In addition to providing medical services to all the RAF Personnel at Henlow, families who lived in quarters on the camp, could register with the two unit medical officers, and almost all did so. Two female civilian nurses were employed for the care of the service families, otherwise the staff was all RAF males. There was no WRAF stationed at RAF Henlow at that time. SSQ was managed by a Flight Sergeant, who was a World War Two veteran, and a dour Scot. Most of the junior staff were National Service airmen, many of whom had been successful in gaining a deferred call up to complete apprenticeships or higher education. They were now in their early twenties. As National Service was drawing to a close, they were less than pleased about having the honour of being the last group to have their lives disrupted in this way, but they never let their feelings interfere with their work or how they related to the regular airmen like myself. In much the same way as the SSQ at RAF

Innsworth, 3 years earlier, the section was over manned, which could not have helped with the morale of the National Service element.

As I was now a corporal Med Admin, a slot in the office was found for me. I therefore avoided having to spend an initial period of time working on the wards, where I could have been employed in a supervisory capacity. My first job was to deal with officers and airmen who were unable to return to the station for medical reasons, following leave at home. The job consisted of receiving the medical certificates, then writing to the the person concerned to remind them of all the rules and regulations, such as having to supply a fresh certificate every 7 days, and to return to the unit as soon as they were fit to travel, and not just when they were fit and well. A letter was also sent to the Doctor concerned, offering assistance in transferring their patient to a nearby SSQ or RAF Hospital. The medical certificate was supposed to certify unfitness to travel and not just unfitness for work, but some common sense was usually applied. There was another rule to be observed, which was that if somebody was absent from the station for medical reasons over 28 days, then Command Headquarters had to be informed of all the circumstances, including what steps had been taken to arrange a transfer back to RAF care. I therefore had to do what was necessary to prevent such an occurrence. Although proforma type letters were used, there could be quite a lot time spent doing the the paperwork for each instance. On return to the unit, the patient had to be seen by the Unit Medical Officer, and a record of the sick absence made, plus statistics compiled. The periods after Christmas was naturally particularly busy for the 'Sick at Home' clerk. My other main task was to act as the Duty Corporal in SSQ about once a week and one weekend in five. This entailed supervising two SACs who in turn looked after any in-patients, and dealt with any emergency situations that may arise on the unit. This would involve attending any accidents on the station, providing cover for any urgent medical matter by liaising with the duty medical officer, and subsequently carrying out any necessary treatment and dispensing medicine as prescribed. It was often the case, particularly at weekends, that there was no in-patients and very few out patients, so there was very little to do other than watch the television and drink mugs of tea. By 1964, when National Service had ended, there was just one airman on duty after hours.

The accommodation and amenities on the camp were poor even by the standards of 1961. At least this was the last time I would be housed in the standard pattern wooden hut, complete with coke fires and up to 20 airmen sharing the same room. There was just one individual room, but as this already was occupied by another corporal from SSQ, I settled down in the main room. At least winter had ended, so I would not be left alone to stoke the fires at the weekend, when the mainly National Service occupants went home as at Innsworth 3 years earlier. My fellow room mates all worked in SSQ, and were mainly Nursing Attendants, but included a clerk/typist and a corporal pharmacist. They were a mainly good humoured bunch, who lived for the weekend when they could go home. Most came from South East of England and could easily manage the weekly journey. Some would also go home on Wednesday afternoon, which at the time was a free afternoon for sporting pursuits, but there was no compulsion to take part, so many took the opportunity to have an extra night at home and return for duty on Thursday morning. This arrangement meant that they would only sleep on camp three nights a week, one of which would be whilst doing a night duty in SSQ. Although some airmen were happy to hitch hike home, and this was fairly easy if dressed in RAF uniform, some preferred to take the train. Whatever the means of transport, this meant that they did not wish to spend much money on entertainment during the week, as even in the later months of National Service they were poorly paid. Only those from a wealthy background tended to go out much during the week.

Most likely because of the close proximity of Hitchin, 5 miles and Bedford 12 miles, and also amenities such as a cafe, shops and a pub at Henlow camp, there was not a great demand for facilities and entertainment at the two small NAAFIs on the camp, one of which was directly opposite to the SSQ hut, the other at the far side of the camp where the REU personnel were housed. The usual snacks and drinks were on sale for a limited period of an evening, but during my 18 months stay on the camp, I cannot recall anyone from SSQ going there for anything stronger than a cup of tea. In addition to the pub at Henlow Camp, on the other side of the road from the SSQ hut, was a small dog racing track, which on race days was somewhat lax in enforcing the standard licensing hours! My social life at Henlow got off to a slow start whilst I made friends with many of the SSQ staff, but particularly with those that did go out on the town a fair bit. However, it is often the case that men will chose to spend most of their time with their girl friends, so I had to bide my time a little, plus up until Easter I had a girl friend at home in Bradford.

After Easter, I was fancy free again and to assist my social life, I was persuaded to buy a Rover saloon car from a corporal at the medical centre who was posted abroad. It was a great car to have, at least until I came to the conclusion, just a few months later, that I could not afford to run it and pay the hire purchase on it, so I surrendered it back to the financiers. As at that time servicemen were seen as poor credit risks, I agreed to a condition of the loan that if I failed to keep up payments, the car would be resold and I would be responsible for any loss. Not surprisingly, there was quite a difference in the amount I paid and the amount the car was sold for. I obtained some legal advice and achieved a slight reduction in the amount owed, but it took a while until I had paid off the debt, and many more years before I was able to buy another car. A harsh lesson learned. In the late spring I started to go out a fair bit during the week with a SAC from Oxford called Chris Perry. Chris used to always go home to Oxford every weekend, for the football in the winter – he supported Oxford United, and in the summer as he played cricket in a local Oxford League. We spent most of our off-duty time in Hitchin, and just occasionally went to Bedford. In Hitchin it was the Trad Jazz club on a Monday night, and the Rock and Roll night on the Wednesday. In 1961 Trad Jazz was still very popular, and the venue in Hitchin attracted a larger crowd than did the Rock and Roll night did. We both preferred the Trad Night, which always featured the very best at the time such as Chris Barber, Humphrey Littleton, Kenny Ball and Acker Bilk. The Monday night crowd was slightly older and included many students, whilst the Rock and Roll night attracted a much younger audience, and what was generally regarded as 'jail bait'! For a short period – nothing in my life lasted long around this time, I went to to other venues on what was known as the North London Jazz Circuit, and got to know other devotees fairly well, including a young woman who I never did manage to see except at jazz concerts! For a while I started to go to a dance hall in Bedford with Chris, but we stopped going for quite different reasons. In Chris's case it was because he wanted to distance himself from someone there who he no longer fancied, and in my case it was because I failed to find anyone who fancied me, although the choice tended to be limited to whoever was with the woman Chris picked up. Chris was very good at 'chatting up', and whilst he was not exceptionally handsome, he was always immaculately dressed, and he would spend more time than was the average for this period on personal grooming. The other venue in Bedford that we would visit was the Conservative Club. This was by no means because of any political reasons, but because there used to be a really good dance night to records – it was not called a disco as this term was not then in use. A lot of the music was American, and so were many of those attending the dances, as there was an American base at nearby Chicksands. I heard the Chubby Checker record 'Lets Twist Again' which reached number 2 in August 61 at the club. It was incidentally denied the top slot by Helen Shapiro's 'You Don't Know'. It was at this venue that I saw somebody dancing The Twist for the first time. We were of course aware, that those who attended these dances, probably did so in order to meet Americans and not the RAF, so our visits were not surprisingly infrequent.

After being told how it was possible to have a inexpensive holiday on the continent, by hitch hiking and staying at hostel type accommodation, I decided to try this out in August of 1961. I took a ferry from Dover to Ostend, and started hitch hiking to the North of Germany, and once there, decided to continue as far as Copenhagen. I had been told that a Union Jack stitched onto the back of a rucksack would ensure sufficient lifts, but not with British holidaymakers, who would often have a fully loaded car, but many Dutch and German people seemingly liked to practice their English language on hitch hikers. This advice turned out to be accurate, and whilst I did not have too much trouble getting lifts, few were given by Brits. However my very first lift, which was just outside the Ferry Port, was almost a disaster. A Flemish motorcyclist offered me a lift to Ghent which I readily accepted, but there was a couple of problems. Firstly I had never ridden on a motor cycle before, and secondly neither of us could speak the other's language. When we went into a bend, I naturally leaned completely the wrong way. After a short while, the motorcyclist had to stop and explain, mainly in sign language, what I ought to be doing on bends. Thankfully there were no further sharp bends to test my new found skills! I arrived in Ghent, booked into a hostel, and then headed for the Town Square for a drink and some Belgian *pomme frites*. From the start I loved the atmosphere of towns like Ghent, and as is most peoples experience, I enjoyed sitting watching the world go by, on what was a lovely summer's evening. The next day I headed for Hamburg where I stayed for the weekend. On the Saturday night, I visited the famous Reeperbahn, but only for the music! This was the area of Hamburg where The Beatles learned their trade around this time. I do not recall seeing them, but as they were unknown to me and not well known at that time, I was not looking for them. From Hamburg I travelled up to Eisberg in

Denmark and spent a couple of night in a hostel there. This was quite a contrast to Hamburg, but I enjoyed my visit to this seaport, which was comparatively quiet in the early sixties. As I was slightly short of money, I sold my wristwatch to a young Dane, and then headed to Copenhagen, for what would turn out to be the first of six visits to date. It follows that I like the country. However, this time I was limited in the amount of leave I had left, and also by my diminishing amount of spending money, so I headed back home, this time via Holland. I had teamed up with a man from the Hook of Holland, and we hitch-hiked back together. I picked up some tips on how to travel cheaply, such as sleeping out in the open, and living on food such as bread soaked in condensed milk. When we arrived at the Hook of Holland, I was invited to spend the night at his parent's house which I readily accepted. I have no doubt that being a member of RAF, went a long way towards their hospitality, as the German occupation had only ended 17 years earlier.

Having enjoyed the European tour so much, I repeated it in mid September. The mode of travel and destination was the same, although when I arrived at Copenhagen I went on to Sweden this time. Another difference to my travel arrangements, was that I had by then joined the Youth Hostel Association and was able to stay at hostels throughout Europe. The contrast between hostels and countries was amazing. In Germany I stayed in one hostel, which was miles away from even a small village, and whilst scrupulously clean and tidy, it was very Spartan. When I checked in to the Youth Hostel in Copenhagen, I noticed that the guests could partake of something stronger than a mug of cocoa, and which was brewed in the City by Carlsberg! There was a very cosmopolitan crowd staying there, comprising of some young Americans and Australians on a sort of Gap Year, but of course it was not so named then. After swapping experiences with some Australians, I was told that if I travelled over to Sweden, I could get a casual job, earn some money and generally have a good time. This sounded like a good idea, so I took the ferry to Malmo, and went straight away to the Employment Exchange – somebody had written the Swedish name for it – *arbetsformedlingen* on a piece of paper for me. I have always remembered it! The reason why, is that I came up against an impasse. In order to get a job you needed to obtain a work permit, and to get the work permit you needed to have a job. This was too difficult to unravel on a brief holiday, but as luck would have it, I met an American student who told me that hotels would probably overlook the paperwork in order to fill short term vacancies. He suggested a hotel in Halsingborg, which was further up the coast, where I was subsequently was hired to work in the kitchens cleaning pots and pans. I got at least two cooked meals every day, and stayed at the Youth Hostel. Any ideas I had about Swedish women, proved to be somewhat false, and those I encountered seemed shy by British standards. What they may have been like after they had known you for more that a few days, I never found out of course. At the hotel, I did not even get to mix with the waitresses, (they were the only female catering staff), as they never mixed with the kitchen staff, not even the cooks and certainly not with the skivvies! I got on well with the cooks, one of whom had worked in England and had some fond memories of his time there. After an interesting week, when I collected my wages, I was told that there had been a check made by the Swedish Police on the hotel's employees. I therefore had to go to the police station, but was told that I need not worry about it. They might fill in some forms but as I was leaving Sweden, they would probably not bother to even do that. However, I was interviewed and asked why I had been working at the hotel. I explained that I wanted to earn some extra holiday money. This was a concept that was seemingly not fully understood. Perhaps there was may well have been a problem with interpretation of my English to Swedish. An impasse similar to the employment rules therefore took place. e.g. 'You are in the Royal Air Force, so why were you working in a hotel in Sweden?. This was a question to which no suitable answer could be found. I was eventually allowed to leave the Police Station and Sweden, perhaps after Interpol had been alerted! My final memory of this trip, was meeting up with a group of Australians in Copenhagen, and then again at a Youth Hostel in Belgium the day before I caught the ferry back to Dover. One of the group looked like Judith Durham of 'The Seekers', and I would certainly have liked to see her again! They were all living in the Earls Court area of London, which even back then was a Aussie colony. I did get a general invite to look them up when I got back, but somehow I never did. Such is life!

My desire to have new sporting experiences, was quite strong in 1961. In the summer, I went on a weekend course based at a Youth Hostel in Shrewsbury, which on the first day I was taught how to built a canoe from scratch, and on day two to float and paddle it, and I also learned how to roll over' in it. This was another skill which I have never found useful! In the early Autumn, a long distance walk between Halton and Henlow took place. This was at a time when long distance walking was something of a craze in the Kennedy era in America. For a while it caught on in UK, at least it did in the RAF, so along with a few hundred others, I walked from the RAF Hospital Halton over the Dunstable Downs to RAF Henlow. I found that this was reasonably easy, even though I had not done any training for it, other than some short runs as part of boxing training. I even managed to jog some of the course, as I wanted to finish near the front. I was very stiff the next day, but otherwise OK. The joys of being young! When I recommenced my boxing training, I became friendly with Karl Barton, a sprint cyclist who was a National Serviceman and Nursing Attendant at SSQ. Karl was a top class cyclist and represented Great Britain at the Commonwealth Games in 1962. We would sometimes do some gym work together, but Karl was also responsible for an improvement to my diet. He had a friend who was a cook on the camp, who would cook us both special meals such as steak, but only at night when the mess was closed!

In between holidays abroad, and various sporting activities, I continued to work in the office at SSQ, and was beginning to discover that life in the RAF could consist of a very familiar routine for long periods of time between postings. I was stationed at Henlow for 3 years and my work routine stayed much the same for all that time. When the National Servicemen started to leave and were not replaced, there was an increase in the amount of work that most of the staff were required to undertake, but there was so much spare capacity that it was not onerous. A reminder that I was in the armed forces came in December 1961, when large numbers of servicemen were deployed to American Air Force bases in England to guard against an invasion by members of the Campaign for Nuclear Disarmament, (CND). CND were protesting about the deployment of American Aircraft armed with nuclear weapons, and planned to infiltrate the bases as a form of protest. The government were rightly concerned at the possible outcome if CND supporters were confronted by armed American servicemen on the base. A decision was made to send hundreds of RAF personnel to these bases to guard the perimeter fence. If any CND members were able to entry the base, then they would be arrested by Ministry of Defence Police who seemingly had the responsibility for security. All American Air Force bases were and still are, classed as RAF stations, and had a token RAF presence of a 'Commanding Officer' and a couple of airmen. I was sent to RAF Whethersfield in Essex, not to do guard duty, but to set up a first aid facility. In the end, whilst the CND turned up at the camp, there was only a token attempt to enter the base before the members dispersed, threatening to come back again at Christmas. They subsequently announced that for the sake of the British servicemen who would have to spend time guarding the base again, that they had cancelled any further plans to invade bases. No doubt they were satisfied with the tremendous amount of publicity they achieved, and no doubt support from the many National Servicemen who would now be able to spend Christmas at home and not at Wethersfield.

In 1962, my social life changed when I met my first wife Jenny at the end of 1961. Jenny worked as a nurse at a hospital in Hitchin, and much of my time was then spent in her company in that town. In September we got married and went to live in Bedford, where we mainly stayed for the rest of my time at Henlow. My routine then became more like that of a civilian, as I commuted to Henlow each day, but as it was also a new experience, I was content with it. In September 1963, my son Carl was born which added to my feeling of married civilian. However a reminder that I was in the RAF came soon after Carl's birth when I was posted to RAF Tern Hill in April of 1964.

During the last two years of my posting at Henlow, all the National Servicemen were demobbed and returned to civilian life, known as 'civvy street'. Those with whom I worked with seemed to leave fairly quietly. There would be a few drinks at the local pub, but no wild parties. One young Scottish National Serviceman at SSQ, ensured that the retired Group Captain Crowley, who seemingly disliked National Servicemen, was left in doubt what he thought of him and National Service, but this sort of thing was rare. I am certain that overall many conscripts made a valuable contribution to the armed forces in the post war years, and that in spite of all the hardships some will have enjoyed the experience. However for those airmen who were called up right at the end of the National Service era, and who served in the United Kingdom, there must have been some resentment of their plight. It was to their credit, that it did not usually affect the way they conducted themselves at work, or with the regular airmen, who they often called 'thick'!

In the spring of 1964, I arrived at RAF Tern Hill for the second time, the first being 10 years earlier as a ATC Cadet. The station had two roles. The main one was the training of pilots and other aircrew on helicopters, and the other was a training centre which ran a senior management course for junior officers in the zone for promotion to Squadron Leader. It was a comparatively small station in both size and number of staff, as was the Station Sick Quarters. As this was what was known as a Flying Station, there was an emergency operating theatre which doubled as a treatment room, and two small wards for minor conditions. There was also the usual dispensary and stores, plus one large room used as an office and reception room. The staff consisted of one Medical Officer, a Squadron Leader Pallister with whom I had worked with at Bahrain, a Sergeant in charge of the administration, two corporals and three SACs. There was also a civilian nurse employed mainly for service families who were registered for General Practitioner services, but also to oversee the treatment of both in and out patients generally.

My main job was to look after the medical records of servicemen and families, including receipt and despatch of the medical records of ever changing camp population, and to operate a Kardex system which indicated when medical examinations, inoculations and vaccinations, and specialist appointments were due and therefore had to be arranged. There were numerous other smaller tasks to be carried out, such as a daily appointments system for a doctors surgery and medical examinations, arranging transport for hospital appointments, and dealing with telephone and other enquiries. The administration and smooth running of SSQ was the responsibility of a sergeant, who was an Irishman who seemed to lack the usual charm of his race, and was very difficult to get on with. He was a stickler for doing everything 'by the book', had little sense of humour, and seemingly only enjoyed the company of other Senior NCOs in the Sergeants Mess where he would spend most of his leisure time. As we worked together in the same office, he therefore overlooked everything that I and another corporal and SAC did, all the time. Whilst this was something that was not ideal, once I had got used to his ways it was not too bad. He helped me to pass a trade promotion examination, which meant that I got a small pay rise, and I also was able to deputise for him in his absence which was good experience.

What I disliked the most was the system and amount of duties. Even with a full complement of staff, there was one mid week duty which involved staying in the SSQ all night, albeit as a sleeping duty, mainly to act as the contact point for any emergencies that may arise on the station. When flying was taking place, an ambulance and attendant was necessary, and when there were in patients there was a definite need to have SSQ manned to care for them, but otherwise there was not. Even worse was the weekend duty every 5 weeks, often more frequently, which involved being on duty from Friday morning to Monday night. Whilst a 4-day weekend the following week was granted to compensate, I disliked the system, and started to consider the possibilities of a move. The Medical Officer, Squadron Leader Pallister, was aware of the tedium of both the work in the office and the time spent in SSQ in after duty hours, and started to organise some training with the station's helicopters. He considered that if there was any emergency landings or crashes involving helicopters, he and and a nursing attendant could accompany the crew in a rescue helicopter, so we therefore received some basic crew training, and had some training flights in helicopters. This could be a bit scary, (there was a fatal crash the week before I arrived at the station), but anything was better than office work, at least as experienced at Tern Hill! Whilst not directly connected to my job, I started to get some mountain walking experience, and then took parties of visiting ATC cadets up Snowdon.

The half day off for sport on a Wednesday afternoons, seemed to end with National Service, but anyone representing the station at an official sport would be allowed to take time off. I did not take part in any official team sports whilst at Tern Hill, but half way through my year there, I started to do some running, and even took part in a 3 mile race on Station Sports Day, coming 2nd of 3 starters! The reason for starting to run was mainly to improve my fitness, as I had heard about a vacancy on the RAF Regiment Parachute Squadron, (Number 2 Field Squadron), at RAF Colerne. The other corporal in SSQ, called Gerry who was from Liverpool, had also heard about this vacancy, which offered the possibility of getting away from Tern Hill, plus an extra £2.50 per week parachute pay, which was a fair sum in 1965. Early in 1965 he went down to Colerne, but failed the basic two day selection for entry onto the Pre Parachute course proper which lasted for about 5 weeks. From what he said about the selection, I thought that I would at least like to try it, and put my name forward. At this time my daughter Linda was born, and it was agreed that I could attend the selection course at a later date.

During my year at Ten Hill I had very little social life, partly as I did not have a car, and partly because money was a little tight. There was a limited amount of entertainment in the NAAFI such as Bingo and occasional dances, but very little else. The nearest town was Market Drayton, but I never went there at all in the evening. The nearest large town was Shrewsbury, but the bus services were infrequent and almost non existent in the evening. It was perhaps just a time for staying home and enjoying the television. One programme which I always looked forward to was 'Top of the Pops' which had started in 1964 and was broadcast at 7 p.m. on a Thursday. At that time there was no countdown of the top 20, the programme started with the Number One record. The announcer would say, 'It's Number One, It's Top of the Pops' and then the number one record would commence. In my opinion this was the best way to present the show. In 1964, it would have been a British number one for all but two weeks of the year, when The Supremes had a number one hit with 'Baby Love'. In 1965, British records continued to dominate the charts, notably The Beatles and The Hollies each with two number one hits, whilst The Rolling Stones had three. After a rare blank year in 1964, Elvis Presley was back with two number ones. There were great debut number ones for Sonny and Cher with 'I Got You Babe' and The Byrds with 'Mr Tambourine Man'. Bob Dylan first appeared in the UK charts that year with arguably his best ever two hits, 'The Times They are A Changing' and 'Subterranean Homesick Blues'. In amongst all the early hippy songs was Ken Dodd who remarkably also had a number one with 'Tears'!

Around mid August I left Tern Hill to attend the two day pre selection testing at Colerne. It was something I never regretted doing, and brought down the curtain on spending long periods of time spent on duty in the SSQ engaged in extremely tedious work, at least for over 11 years.

8. RAF Regiment Parachute Squadron: Training

My very first sight of the airfield at RAF Colerne in August of 1965 was somewhat disconcerting. Many of the two resident squadrons of Hastings Aircraft were stood on the tarmac outside the aircraft hangars, as they had all been grounded, and there was obviously no room in the hangars to house all the aircraft. All the aircraft had had their tail unit removed. This bizarre sight was due to a fatal accident the previous month which occurred at RAF Abingdon. A Hastings Aircraft which was transporting parachutists to the Drop Zone, (DZ), at nearby RAF Weston on The Green crashed soon after take off. The suspected cause of the accident was metal fatigue in the tail unit. All 41 people on board, who in addition to the crew, were mainly army paratroopers, were killed. There was however one RAF trainee parachutist, who I later found out had once applied to join the RAF Regiment paras, but had failed the selection course. There was an irony in this, as whilst his failure to successfully complete the selection course meant that he could not proceed to RAF Abingdon for the full airborne parachute course, he could apply for a basic course which consisted of just 4 parachute descents, and on completion would result in a badge bearing a parachute but no wings, and would not attract parachute pay. It was called 'The Light bulb Course'. The irony of the situation was enhanced by the fact that when it became known that he had applied for the 'Light Bulb' course, the RAF Regiment tried to block his application on the basis that it would not appear fair to others, that after proving unsuitable once, he could then apply again, albeit for a much less demanding and prestigious course. However it was decided that he could do the course, which was to result in his death. He was destined to be my predecessor, and as there were no others who passed both the Pre Para selection and the subsequent full airborne para course, if I passed the course I would be the first fully qualified medical orderly on the squadron, which had commenced conversion to the parachute role in 1962 with just 12 volunteers. This was generally more in my thoughts than any problems with Hastings aircraft.

On what should have been the first day of testing, the Squadron was deployed to Hankley Common, a DZ in Surrey, to undertake some parachute descents from a balloon – presumably because of the absence of the Hastings Aircraft. The tests were therefore postponed for 24 hours, and so myself and the other 6 volunteers went along to watch. I, and I am fairly certain all the others, thought that parachuting was something we still wanted to do after watching members of the Squadron jump from the cage suspended underneath the Air Balloon. After a day spent lazing in the sun, watching the parachuting, it already seemed that I was a long way from sitting in a SSQ office, and hopefully would remain so for a long time to come.

The tests commenced the following day back at Colerne. To start with I was slightly concerned that the other volunteers might have superior physical fitness, as they had joined the RAF Regiment in the past year whilst still in their late teens. I considered myself to be much older at 26, and as I was a corporal whilst they were all junior airmen, also made me feel a lot older. However as the tests progressed and I got to know the other volunteers better, I ceased to worry about this as I considered that I would hold my own on the physical front. The tests commenced with some confidence tests, none of which were too daunting, at least they did not seem so at the time. There was a rope swing where you had to let go on the word of command and land in a safety net. Usually there was what was known as a 'death slide', but this contraption which involved ropes and a pulley to slide down a hill, was out of commission at the time. The next test was a walk across a type of scaffolding erection at height, which involved negotiating a joint in the bars half way across. After that was a circuit of an assault course which required a mixture of strength, stamina and confidence. Whilst no time limit was set on this occasion, the trainees were vigorously encouraged not to dawdle by the instructors! A further and final confidence test took place at the swimming pool, where it was necessary for all the volunteers to jump from the top board whether or not they could swim. For those who could not swim, a couple of swimmers waited in the water to grab them and stop them sinking! The final test was a mile and a half road run in boots, which included a long hill. This was timed, but the main object was to keep running and not stop and walk. Having passed the tests, I started the Pre Para course the following day, along with the other five who had done the tests, and another airman who had been withdrawn from a previous course with an injury.

RAF Colerne was on the Wiltshire and Somerset border, about a mile from the Wiltshire village of the same name. The nearest town was Chippenham about 7 miles away, but the much larger town of Bath which was slightly further away, provided the main rail link. It was also, even then, a popular tourist centre, with much better shopping and entertainment facilities than Chippenham. In the mid 1960s, few airmen owned cars, but there was a regular bus service from the camp to Bath, which continued into the late evening, so this town was favoured over Chippenham. In addition to the RAF Regiment Parachute Squadron, or Number 2 Field Squadron, (2 Field), as it was called, the camp was the home base for two squadrons of Hastings aircraft, which at that time, and until 1967 were the 'workhouse' transport aircraft of the RAF, alongside the massive Beverley aircraft, and to a lesser extent the Argosys. The camp had some good social facilities which included a cinema and a recently built NAAFI club, which during my stay attracted some top groups for dances. The accommodation remained dormitory style for airmen, but in relatively modern centrally heated buildings. There was also three small estates of married quarters on the camp, and the increased camp population resulted in more than average social and sports facilities. For the period of my course, I was living on the camp, and was pleased to discover that the food in the airmen's mess had continued to improve, and that it was no longer necessary to bring your own cutlery at meal times. The improved ambiance added to the enjoyment of the cuisine. Because of the intense physical nature of course, none of my fellow course members went out very much in the evening, other than for snacks or just the odd pint in the NAAFI club.

In addition to the favourable impression I gained of the camp, soon after the course started, I enjoyed the experience of spending the working day engaged in physical activity, and with it the increased physical fitness and stamina. With hindsight, I think that the training had much more of an effect on stamina and endurance than physical fitness, as I had continued to smoke, and I just cut down on the amount smoked when sitting in an office. For just over two weeks the daily routine involved a 'warm up' session in the large hangar which served as a gym. This would include games such as 5 a side football and English Bulldog. After a NAAFI break, we would have a much tougher session of exercise such as circuit training. In the afternoon, there would typically be a longer single session such as a march or a run, with the working day often ending about 4 p.m. so we had plenty of time to bathe and change before teatime. Much of what I was now spending my day doing, I would have gladly done as part of training for sport, and I was therefore able to cope well with periods of intense training. Mentally I may have had an advantage over others on the course who had come to the course after basic training, and overall our comparative fitness levels levelled out. One disadvantage I suffered however, was being unused to wearing boots for large parts of the day. This resulted in some blisters mainly on my heels. At the end of the first week of the course, I exchanged the boots I was issued with at Colerne, for a pair I bought that were lighter and fitted better. I also developed a method of treating blisters using orthopaedic felt which was effective. On one occasion whilst on an exercise, when I did not have access to this felt, which was in short supply as it was expensive, I constructed a replacement using a cigarette packet. It worked and everybody was suitably impressed!

After about two weeks the course had a 48 hour exercise on Salisbury Plain called 'Hard Push', and which as the name suggests involved pushing, and was indeed hard. The first part of what is a test of endurance and spirit, involved pushing a heavy trailer over Salisbury Plain, which included some hills. On the level ground we were made to get some speed up and run with the trailer. This was by far the hardest part of the course so far, but we seemed to cope well with it. In the evening we were sent out on patrols with some objectives. I was put in charge of one of the patrols, just because I was a corporal and the others in the patrol were SACs! I was therefore grateful to the young gunners on the course for letting me have the benefit of their experience on a subject of which I knew nothing of course. Whilst it had been a long tiring day, I have to confess that I did get some enjoyment out of being on patrol armed with an SLR. It was like a adult version of 'Cowboys and Indians' to me. Over the period of the exercise, I learned some useful things such as the art of making 'compo' meals at least edible if not appetising. I also learned how to construct a decent form of shelter. The second day involved more pushing and running with the trailer, and in the evening a tough test which involved locating an ammunition box hidden a few miles away at a given map reference. When the box was located it had to be brought back to our camp site. The box was filled with gravel and had been locked to prevent the removal of the contents. It was clearly too heavy for an individual to carry, and even two men would have struggled to carry it very far. We experimented by attaching ropes to the box so that the weight could be shared between four people, but this proved cumbersome and slowed us down too much. In the end we attached several ropes and just dragged the box along behind us. This worked better, but the route back to camp was partly on roads, so that the effect of all the dragging was to wear out the box. We just made it back to the camp before holes started to appear in the box and the contents leaked out. Nothing was said about the state of the box, either as the wear was not noticed or the instructors were too bemused by our method of transporting it back to comment. After a few hours sleep we had an early breakfast, and then a march out of the area to our transport back to Colerne and the end of the first part of the course.

The second half of the course was a mixture of continued fitness training and the time-honoured Airborne Soldier tests. These remain part of the final selection process to this day for both would-be RAF Regiment and the Army paratroopers. The confidence tests were much the same as the initial selection, but slightly harder. For example, the walk on the high scaffolding was increased in distance and the swimming pool test was now a somersault off the top board. Everybody managed these tests, but our course number was reduced by one, as the gunner who had picked up an injury on an earlier course, sustained another injury in the fitness training part of the course. The remaining six men on the course, proceeded to one of the big tests, which was called 'milling'. This was when two men both don 16-ounce gloves for safety, and then proceed to attack each other in a boxing ring. The object is to test aggression, and boxing skills are not required, and indeed are forbidden. For one minute, the aim is to connect with as many punches as possible, and thus the description of 'milling'. I was matched with a young gunner called 'Brummie', and for a somewhat painful 60 seconds we swapped punches in about equal measure to satisfy the instructors. In between further fitness and strength training, two very hard tests were undertaken by the course. First there was the 'Stretcher Race', but as there were now insufficient men for more than one team, it was a race against time only. The test involved four men running with a stretcher with a 'patient' on board, over rough, hilly terrain at speed, and in this case, a rotation of the extra two men. It was imperative to keep going and anyone 'dropping off' the stretcher, would be declared unsuitable – the word 'fail' was never used. The final test at Colerne before the concluding exercise in Snowdonia was the 'Log Race'. This involved all the course members carrying a 'log' the size of a telegraph pole, to which they have attached ropes to lift the log at arms length, over a set distance, and also in a target time based on the number of left on the course. These two tests were the hardest on the entire course, and required a very great degree of strength, stamina and extreme determination to complete the test. One course member had not satisfactorily completed a crucial part of the course but he still joined in with the final phase at Snowdonia, even though he could not now pass the course.

The morning after the Log Race, we set off for the final set of tests in Snowdonia, by the standard mode of travel – in the back of a 'three tonner'. We arrived at our Welsh destination on a damp and misty afternoon, and were made to decamp and get our packs on as quickly as possible. We then started a march at speed. It was not called a 'tab' in those days, but this is what it was. After a few miles of a hard effort over the some hilly countryside, we had what was undoubtedly a stroke of luck. One of the two instructors, a Corporal Jobson sustained a strained leg muscle, and was forced to slow down the pace. We marched on and completed the march in the early evening, and we then had to find our own site to shelter, feed ourselves, and rest for a short period. The instructors would stay with the exercise vehicles, a Land Rover and the Three Tonner. Whilst looking round for a suitable site, one of course members discovered a shed which was unlocked. We soon got inside and started preparing a meal and hot drink. Later that night we had an unsupervised march to a village a few miles away, where we had to make notes and then answer questions about features of the village such as the name of the church. That was the end of day one.

The next day started with another unsupervised march to the base of Snowdon, where we met up with another instructor, a Sergeant Roberts, who would be leading us up to the summit of Snowdon. The course member who would be unable to pass the course, was allowed to stay behind so as not to hinder the progress of the others on the course. It became obvious that the plan was for the younger and fitter Corporal Jobson to lead the march, but he was now unable to march at all due to his injury. It was also soon apparent that Sergeant Roberts was not as familiar with the various routes to the summit, and we ended up on the most difficult route, the Snowdon Horsehoe. However this route could not be negotiated at speed, so overall it was relatively easier, and thus our luck continued. When we reached the summit we had a tea break, and a Scotsman on the course, SAC Jock Sandison, celebrated the climb in the more traditional manner with a whisky! We now were required to make our own way down the mountain to our transport at

Llanberis. This was the high point of the course for me. I was feeling strong and started to get ahead of the others. When I caught sight of the rendezvous point in the distance, I broke into a jog, and complete with my pack and rifle, continued on down the mountain to the waiting vehicles, well in advance of the others. As I smoked a welcome cigarette, I felt euphoric at the thought of what I had achieved already. After returning to our camp and a meal, we were driven to Anglesey from where we had to walk back to camp, a distance of about 12 miles. This was to be the final part of the selection course, as the usual final stretcher race was cancelled for some reason. The remaining four left on the course were confident that they had passed, but it was very late when we arrived back at Colerne, we had to wait until the next morning and an individual interview with the Commanding Officer of the Squadron, a Squadron Leader Dicker for this to be confirmed. In three days time we started our parachute training at RAF Abingdon, which we were assured we would be a much easier course. It did not involve any hard exercise, and once the nerves had been settled after the first descents, it was actually enjoyable!

In mid September 1965, I travelled to RAF Abingdon with the other three successful members of my course. The three were 'Jock' Sandison, 'Curly Legge' and Tony Reynolds who were all young RAF Regiment gunners. We were billeted together and were all on the same course, Number 626, which had a Sergeant Granados as our instructor. The other members of the course were mainly members of regiments other than the Parachute Regiment, such as the Royal Electrical and Mechanical Engineers, (REME), who had also gone through the Pre Para course to qualify for the course. Members of the Parachute Regiment made up another course which was running alongside ours.

As usual the course started with introductory talks by an ever increasing rank structure, who all assured us, that if we obeyed all the rules, we would have no trouble completing the course, and would enjoy it. The course was the Basic Airborne Parachute Course, which consisted of a total of eight parachute descents or 'jumps' as they are usually called. The first two were from a balloon, then the remaing six were from a aircraft, with one taking place after dark, and two final jumps with equipment. Much of the very first week was spent learning and practising aircraft drills and landings. The drills involved practising the movements in the aircraft prior to and immediately after exiting, so that all the procedures necessary for a safe exit would become automatic. Landing practice was necessary, as there was not usually total control of the landing. In the usual event of any breeze, the parachutist would land at speed forwards, sideways or backwards, and an appropriate rolling technique was required to avoid injury. To start with, a gentle roll from a static position was undertaken, and then there was a gradual build up to running jump up a ramp and assorted rolls – to the right and left, forward, backward and to the side at speed. There was also a scary exercise called 'The Fan'. This involved jumping from a platform thirty feet from the ground, and around half way the 'fan' cut in, so that a parachute roll could be carried out safely when the feet touched the ground. There was also plenty of time spent suspended in a harness, practising steering and control of the parachute, and also the employing of the reserve parachute, should problems arise with the main parachute.

All too soon it was time to make the first jump at RAF Weston on the Green, which was just a few miles away from Abingdon. The trainees jumped from a cage structure, which was suspended under a barrage balloon, at 800 feet. So on the 28 September, I boarded the cage along with four others plus the instructor. The balloon ascended to the required height in deadly silence, and soon the big moment had arrived. We had been made ready to jump before we left the ground. Our parachutes had been 'hooked up' so that after exit from the balloon, the parachute would start to deploy immediately. The safety bar across the entrance to the cage was removed, and the first to jump took up a position at the edge. After a final check of the parachute equipment, the instructor gave the firm command 'go', and thankfully the first recruit jumped out automatically, just as he has been trained to do over the past week. If he had hesitated or refused to jump, he would have been made to wait until last, and then given a final chance to jump. Refusal would result in a withdrawal from the course. I understand that most courses would have somebody, who even after all the hardships of the Pre Para and the intensive training at Abingdon, could not bring himself to jump out of a balloon. Some trainees might refuse to jump from an aircraft, but this was much rarer, as the aircraft phase came after two previous jumps from balloons. I was the second to go, and tried my best to just concentrate on the drill aspect, and was soon floating safely at the end of the parachute. An instructor on the ground gave instructions via a loud hailer such as 'hard right' indicating a need to pull down hard on the parachute cords to the right side to slow down a drift to the left side. There was also reminders to get into a proper landing position before the ground was reached. Many of the reminders were to no avail, as the excitement of completing the very first jump, tended to overrule everything else, so there were many bumpy landings. It was a great feeling to have made this first jump, and myself and the other three returned to RAF Abingdon talking about nothing else for hours! The next jump was scheduled for the next day, so we avoided any great alcoholic celebrations, as indeed we did until the end of the course.

I have to confess that my memory of the parachute course, is greatly assisted by a small red book, which bears the inscription, 'Log Book – Parachute Descents with British Airborne Forces'. The book records details of all my 100 jumps, including the first 8 on the initial course at RAF Abingdon. On the following afternoon, I joined 4 other trainees in a cage under the balloon for the second parachute jump. This was by no means the same nervous experience as the previous day, and the instructor fed on this by reminding all 5 of us in the cage that this time we could and indeed should, all be concentrating a lot more on the technique of the initial exit, the flight to the ground or 'Drop Zone,(DZ), and a good landing. On this occasion there was even a little light conversation, mainly nervous jokes, during the ascent to the normal 'drop' height of 800 operating height. There was a variation to the exit on this occasion, which was for the trainees to exit the balloon cage via a large trap door. When the balloon stopped ascending, we all had our parachutes checked, and then after the instructor had satisfied himself that we were all 'hooked up' and ready to jump, the large trap door in the centre of the cage was opened, and for those who looked down into the hole, there was a view of the DZ, 800 feet below! It was in effect a final test of confidence before the parachuting from aircraft commenced. The instructor undoubtedly made this second test of courage easier by advising the would be parachutists to concentrate on the exit technique. This entailed jumping just enough to clear the edge of the aperture, but not forcibly which might result in a very painful collision on the far side of the aperture, and a loss of front teeth! For this second jump, my Log Book records that I was the 4th of 5 to jump. I have no doubt that my landing technique was severely criticised, but was at least proficient to enable me to proceed to the final 6 descents from aircraft.

The aircraft descent phase commenced the next day. My first aircraft jump was from the massive Beverley aircraft, which was taking the place of the Hastings, which had not yet been cleared to fly after the recent fatal crash. At the start of the course, all the trainees had been asked if they had ever flown in any aircraft previously. Those who had never previously flown in an aircraft, were given a trip in an RAF aircraft so that they would not have to endure both the anxiety of a first flight, followed by a parachute descent at the same time. There were tales, possibly apocryphal, of airborne soldiers who had flown many times, but had never actually landed in the aircraft! This was a period when holidays abroad by air was not yet common, and not long after troop ships had ceased to be the mode of travel for servicemen. The Beverley aircraft was almost certainly the most comfortable aircraft for parachuting of all times. There was 3 modes of exit. The one used by trainees was via the side doors of the huge main frame. There was also the possibility of an exit from the so called passenger extension at the tail of the aircraft, and in addition, an exit from the rear of the aircraft ramp, usually restricted to Free Fall parachutists of the Special Forces or the RAF Falcons Free Fall Display team. In addition to the three possible modes of exit, the total amount of parachutists exiting the aircraft in the same descent sequence, required an increased degree of skill and practice.

So at midday on the 30th of September, I boarded the Beverley at Abingdon and was soon airborne en route to the DZ at Weston on the Green. The arrival at the DZ was first signalled by a noticeable change in the noise of the aircraft engines, as they reduced their speed to around 100 knots. This was followed by the preparation procedure drills, which commenced with the command to 'Stand Up'. The parachutists would stand, and then the order to 'check equipment' would be given. They would then check their own equipment, and then the equipment of the parachutist stood behind them. A verbal confirmation of the check would be shouted out, and then the parachutists would be ordered to 'stand in the door'. The dispatcher would then open the aircraft door, and a signal would be given both by the red light above the door and the command, 'Red On, Standby', followed soon after by a green light, and the command 'Green On, Go!' The parachutists would then jump out forcibly into the slipstream, to avoid colliding with the side of the aircraft, and what was known as a 'rivet inspection'! The parachute would be deployed whilst in the slipstream, so there was not the dropping sensation associated with descents from a balloon My very first aircraft jump, involved just two others exiting with, but before me from the port side of the Beverley aircraft. We all landed safely, and another stage in training had been completed successfully The very next day I had my 4th jump. This involved 6 trainees jumping in groups of three from each side of the aircraft. This is a procedure described as 'Sims', meaning simultaneous exits from both sides of the aircraft – the normal mode of exit. This jump went well, and with half of the jumps had now been completed, I hitch-hiked home for the weekend. Of course I had to wear my parachute jacket or smock as it was called, overlooking the obvious fact that a camouflaged jacket was not an ideal garment for hitch-hiking in the dark. I reverted to my normal RAF uniform for future trips home!

After two aircraft jumps, and a lot more ground training, three days later I completed a jump with 15 others all exiting the Beverley at the same time. This was achieved with 8 parachutists jumping from each side of the aircraft. I was 8th on the port side, which was the furthest back in the line or 'stick' as it was called. When the green light goes on the command 'go' was given, and the stick moved down the aircraft to the door in an odd shuffle movement, which was achieved my moving the rear foot first. This was designed to prevent anybody slipping and falling in the stick, which would cause chaos and if near the door, some danger if the exit was affected. Due to some very windy weather, the next jump was delayed until three days later. This was the night decent, but what was to make this a nervous occasion, was that the Hastings aircraft had returned to service. One of my memories of the occasion was of the afternoon, when there was no ground training, so a group of us went into Abingdon town to kill time. There was constant speculation as to whether the weather had improved sufficiently for the jump to take place. We spent time in a cafe, and on the radio, Barry Maguire's hit record 'Eve of Destruction' was playing. This was not the record I needed to hear right then! Just after darkness fell, we boarded the Hastings like condemned men, with the usual wry humour about whether the tail plane was properly attached etc. Of course all was well with the aircraft and the jump, which was a comparatively simple 6 at a time from the Port side. I was the 6th and last in the stick this time.

There was now just two more jumps to complete for our parachute wings. These were both from Hastings aircraft, and were to be made whilst carrying equipment. The procedure employed, was for the equipment pack to be strapped to the parachute harness for the exit from the aircraft, and then once clear and the parachute has inflated, the pack was released to dangle on a rope several feet below the body. Before the final two jumps were made, we all handed in our uniform jackets, so that the camp tailor could sew on the parachute wings in time for the final parade after the 8th and final jump. The first of the two equipment jumps, was just 5 at a time jumping from the Port side. On this occasion I was the first in the stick, so as I waited for the green light, I watched the Oxfordshire countryside below for a minute or so. The jump was completed satisfactorily, and the very next day the final jump took place. This time there was 28 jumping all at the same time, 14 out of both the Starboard and Port doors. This was the culmination of two months hard work, and it was a great feeling, when as soon as I had landed, I realized that I had now qualified as a para medic. The job description of a paramedic was of course somewhat different in 1965 to what it is in 2007, and the use of the term to describe an airborne medical orderly, is not included in the 'Collins 21st Century English Dictionary'!

In the evening the course went to the local pub for the traditional end of course drinks with the instructor, Sergeant Granados. This was a midweek evening, and the pubs then shut at 10.30, and as the instructor was a rather quiet sort, my first night out with paratroopers was fairly quiet. The course ended the next morning with a formal parade. This included taking the paratroopers oath. This took the form of a formal warning that from now on, we would have to jump when ordered to do so, unless we were to withdraw from the course there and then. This final opportunity is declined by all the students, so the parade continued with individual congratulations from the Commanding Officer of the Parachute Training School, and presentation of the red berets. Unfortunately the RAF did not agree to any airmen wearing any other colour beret than blue, so I had to be satisfied with wearing wings. I was indeed more than satisfied and was overjoyed when I returned to Tern Hill to 'clear' the station. The clearing process involved visiting various sections on the camp, to return any equipment out on loan, and collect any documents required for the new unit. I hoped that everybody would notice my 'wings' in the process. I was very pleased to be leaving Tern Hill, even though in less than two months, I would be detached to RAF Khormaksar in Aden for just over 5 months.

9. RAF Regiment Parachute Squadron: Tour of Duty

Soon after I returned to Colerne, I was summoned to a chat with the Commanding Officer of the Squadron, a Squadron Leader Dicker. He welcomed me to the Squadron said that he hoped that I would enjoy my tour of duty with the RAF Regiment. He also explained that he considered it necessary to talk to members of the Squadron who did not belong to the RAF Regiment, about the need for greater discipline than I may have experienced in the past in the RAF. He explained, giving examples, why it might be essential that an order was obeyed without question. I accepted all what he said, but pondered whether he had a true picture of the relative state of discipline vis-a-vis the RAF and the RAF Regiment. Was it necessarily a lot better in the RAF Regiment than the RAF I wondered. There was an amusing saying about the differences in respect of 'orders' between the three services. This is that in The Army, an order is an order; in the Royal Navy an order is a request, and in the RAF an order is the starting point of a debate! It was very good that the CO should take time to talk to me about this, when this could have been delegated to somebody else, or left for me to find out for myself, possibly after a charge for transgressing orders.

I was welcomed to the Squadron by the members of Headquarters Flight, to which the RAF members of the Squadron belonged to. They were generally referred to as 'penguins' by RAF Regiment personnel, and on the Squadron as Tradesmen – presumably the trade of Regiment Gunner was not considered a 'trade'! In turn, the tradesmen referred to the gunners as 'rocks' which was an abbreviation of 'rockapes', the accepted description of RAF regiment personnel. All the tradesmen had mostly passed the Pre Para course and the Parachute Course at Abingdon. There was 3 cooks, 2 wireless mechanic/fitters, 3 mechanical transport, (MT), mechanic/fitters, an armament fitter and a storeman. Whilst we tended to bond together as a flight, we also developed many friendships with the 'rocks', and 40 years on, many of the tradesmen still attend annual reunions with them at Colerne, and there is also a five yearly reunion at the current base at RAF Honington. Some of the Headquarters Flight's tradesmen were good standard sportsmen. These included two cooks who were boxers, one of whom was 'open class' and had also been the RAF Champion Race Walker. A clerk who was a good standard track athlete, and another who was an accomplished rugby player. Many of the others tradesmen kept themselves very fit throughout their tour, so that they could and indeed did, hold their own with the 'rocks'.

Whilst I now belonged to 2 Field Squadron, it was not practical for me to work independently of the existing medical facilities at Colerne, or any RAF station where the Squadron was based. I was therefore based in the Station Sick Quarters, and where possible I would assist with the normal running, and also be on the Duty Roster. However, the medical administration I was involved with, mainly concerned with the 150 members of the Squadron. For example, it was my responsibility to ensure that all of the Squadron was 100% up to date with inoculations and vaccinations, so that they could proceed abroad at short notice. I also kept the relevant certificates to avoid possible problems if these were mislaid by those concerned! As at the Squadron, I was made most welcome at SSQ by the Senior Medical Officer, Squadron Leader Jolly. As he was a jovial Yorkshireman with a pint pot mug on his desk, he was well named! He decided that as I would shortly be away from home for nearly six months, I would not have to do any weekend duties, so that I could go back to Tern Hill at the weekends where my family remained for the time being. This was a thoughtful act which I fully appreciated.

In the few weeks left before the Squadron left for Aden, I spent most of my working day in SSQ, as there was no parachuting, or any other exercises requiring my attendance with the Squadron. For the remainder of my 3 years with the Squadron, I would likewise spend periods of time just working in SSQ on basic medical administration duties. However, unlike my two previous RAF units, particularly Tern Hill, I would avoid excessive paperwork by joining the Squadron for parachuting and other exercises. When Norrie Chapman took over as the Squadron Warrant Officer, I was also able to take time out during the day, to go on training runs with him, and other members of HQ Flight. I got on well with the staff in SSQ both at work and socially, and I would happily contribute to the day to day work of SSQ, when not engaged with Squadron matters. In the few weeks before Aden, I seemingly encouraged some of the SSQ staff to take more exercise, as occasionally some of the staff would join me for a long walks in the evening to faraway pubs and back! Other than these jaunts, it was a quiet time socially on camp during the week, and the weekends were spent back at Tern Hill. On 12 November, together with the main part of the Squadron, I departed from RAF Lyneham for Aden via a three stage journey in Britannia aircraft. For obscure political reasons, which also required that we travelled in civilian clothes, the ageing Britannia aircraft was routed via Cyprus and Bahrain. We finally landed at RAF Khormaksar about 24 hours later to start our tour of duty in Aden.

2 Field Squadron's role in Aden was that of Internal Security (I.S.) duties at RAF Khormaksar, which in addition to the airfield, encompassed one of the largest overseas RAF bases at that time, with a large technical and domestic area, plus many married quarters. The I.S. duties were shared with another RAF Regiment Squadron, at the time 37 Squadron, who were detached from Cyprus. The Squadron operated mobile patrols around the RAF Khormaksar, whilst airmen on the camp provided most of the static guards, as an additional duty, assisted by locally employed security guards, and the RAF Police. Since 1964, a State of Emergency for the colony was in place, following the onset of a terrorist campaign against the British, by those seeking the formation of Socialist Republic either before or after the planned British withdrawal in 1968. Whilst there was a steady stream of terrorist attacks, and the level was such that movement outside the bases was restricted, but it was still possible to travel between bases and to the beaches. The need for caution was demonstrated a few days after the Squadron's arrival, when a gunner of 37 Squadron was shot and killed whilst travelling on a local bus. If not at that time, transport around Aden was then restricted to service transport which would include an armed guard.

The normal tour length of duty for Aden was two years, which partly reflected the amount of leisure activities, which were much better than those at Bahrain, and far superior to stations in the Persian Gulf where the normal tour had been reduced to 12 months. For married airmen whose families had joined them in Aden, and were living in married quarters, the tour was seen as a pleasant two years in the sun, with an opportunity to save money due to additional allowances and duty free goods. For single airmen, the lack of single women and separation from their family for two years, was a undoubtedly a hardship. To compensate there was the possibility of one free flight back to UK, and also one flight to Kenya for a holiday. Contact with women was mainly limited to the comparatively small number of servicewomen at the nearby base at Steamer Point, which housed both WRAF and

WRAC servicewomen. With a very strict night curfew in force, and also single living accommodation being out of bounds to the opposite sex, the so called 'swinging 60s' had not and never did reach Aden! There was no social contact with the local Arab population, at least not at airman level, particularly in view of the security situation. Some airmen became extremely depressed with their situation, and the daily 'sick parades' would invariably include airmen who proceeded from the Doctor's surgery to the SSQ dispensary with a prescription for anti-depressants in their hand. There was a resident RAF psychiatrist at the RAF Hospital, and it was generally considered that if the medical officer was to refer somebody for an opinion, then invariably the end result would be a return to the UK on medical grounds. The reason for this was that firstly, medical officers would only refer those whom they were very concerned about, and secondly, it would be at least the safest option for a psychiatrist to recommend the return to UK for such patients. With the current state of emergency and the resulting widespread carrying of loaded weapons by airmen, a misjudgement might have had dire consequences. Those who succeeded in obtaining an early return to UK on medical grounds, were described as 'working their ticket'!

For the members of 2 Field, all were in the same boat in respect of the separation from their families, which was better than most sections on the camp, where some married personnel went home to their wives and family every day, and the remainder who only saw their families and girl friends, just once during the 2 year tour. Other than the designated days of 24 hour patrols, the normal working day ended at 1.30 p.m. which gave everyone the opportunity to enjoy the sporting facilities on the camp and around Aden. The two most popular pastimes being football and swimming. The weather was never too hot for football for most of the time the squadron was based in Aden. Matches would normally take place late afternoon when the sun was going down, but there was also floodlit facilities for evening games at Steamer Point. Midweek, there was swimming at several pools, and also or especially, at the services beach club at Steamer Point which had mixed bathing! On Sundays, it was possible to swim at other guarded beaches in the colony, which had the added excitement of an occasional stingray that had somehow managed to somehow get through the safety net. In the evenings there was the usual NAAFI clubs on camp, which held weekly dances, open air cinemas showing fairly up to date films, and numerous social clubs for organisations such as the Buffaloes and Church groups. All places of entertainment would close early, well before the midnight curfew. This together with the early morning start to the day of 7 a.m., limited excessive drinking – for most anyway! Many airmen would be content to stay in their living accommodation, and spend time writing letters home, whilst listening to their own music, or to the BFBS radio, There was a local Television station which broadcast mostly in Arabic, but occasionally showed films which retained the English language and had Arabic sub titles. There was also some English football matches shown, usually weeks old, but which still had some interest for many. This was to be the general pattern of off- duty life for the next 6 months for the Squadron, and as usual it was a case of making the very best of things, which we all sought to do, although in my case, 'the best' would not possibly not equal that of Bahrain, but I was now a much older family man!

As at Colerne, I worked in SSQ for most of the tour, escaping whenever possible for duties with 2 Field squadron. SSQ was an extremely busy place, which dealt with around 5,000 airmen on the base, plus families who lived in the married quarters. There was several wards for minor conditions, and a large compliment of nursing and administrative staff supporting 6 medical officers. Most of the staff were young single airmen who lived on the camp. There was a Flight Sergeant in charge, and a Sergeant as his deputy. Neither appeared to have very much in common with those under their command. The Flight Sergeant lived in married quarters and the Sergeant lived in the mess, and both enjoyed a much better all round life style. The airmen in the SSQ offices, worked very hard using systems that struggled to cope with the huge amount of paperwork which resulted from the strength of the station. Even with modern day computers, the amount of administration would have been daunting. For example, every morning there was a Sick Parade' which consisted of everybody who wanted to see a doctor attending before 7 a. m. An appointment system was deemed unworkable, so those attending were divided between 4 Medical Officers. Then all the relevant medical documents then had to be quickly located, which was invariably an awful job, given the amount of movement, and the manual system of recording movement of documents. There was often problems caused by misfiling, as the medical documents, (Form Med 4), were filed using the last 3 digits of service numbers. Whilst this was generally better than a strict alphabetical filing system, if a document was misfiled it was more difficult to locate, especially when a large number of Form Med 4s was involved. After the daily sick parade and the associated administration had been completed, the office staff worked with a Kardex system which involved a lot of manual checking on things such as when inoculations and vaccinations, and routine medical examinations were due. This then subsequently involved compiling lists, sending out a very amount of memos, and further checks on what remained outstanding. The staff also had to cope with a big turn round of station personnel, and the resulting receipt and despatch of the F Med 4s, plus the regular flow of medical records to and from hospitals. It was another case of drudgery, with little job satisfaction as the junior staff performed seemingly endless, tedious repetitive tasks day in day out. There was very little rotation of work, other than when somebody was replaced at the end of their tour, and during my 6 months stay, no staff meetings ever took place.

Discipline was partly imposed by the threat of having to work in the adjoining clinic for locally employed workers on the station. An Arab orderly looked after the clinic, but when he took annual leave, a replacement from the RAF staff was assigned. The problem with working at the clinic, was that there was frequent disorder, arising when an Arab employee was denied things such as X Rays, which it was believed would result in a cure, and the police often had to called to deal with any resultant disturbances. When it became known that the Arab Medical Orderly was about to take leave, nobody turned up late for work, everybody smartened up, and did not do anything that might have resulted in a spell at the clinic.

I undertook my share of after hours duties, which were reasonably easy. The After Duty roster had a corporal and an airmen on duty at the same time, and there was also a Medical Officer present in SSQ at all times. Sometimes the afternoons would be busy, but any call outs were dealt with by the SAC. We would tend to take it in turns to deal with anyone attending for emergency treatment, and likewise the telephone calls. We had no dealings with in-patients, who were cared for by a separate nursing staff. There were however some perks. Firstly, the duty staff ate in SSQ, and the food which was cooked in SSQ was much better than in the airmen's mess on camp. Secondly, at around midnight, and the curfew, I could retire to a duty bunk to sleep and was rarely disturbed, but still had the following day off regardless.

Along with another medic who was attached to 37 Squadron, I mainly took care of the F Med 4s of the squadron members, and assisted with the morning sick parade. After this we both dealt with the documentation and the running of the Families Clinic. This was a comparatively easy task, mainly because we were not dealing with such large numbers of patients at the same time, and the movement of files was not great. There was no apparent resentment of my comparatively easier workload, probably because of my rank and the apparent basis of the higher the rank the less the work, and also my absences on Regiment Squadron duties, appeared to add to my work load. For convenience, I was billeted with the SSQ staff, and spent some of my off duty time socialising with them. The living accommodation was a large air conditioned room, which had the services of a 'Bearer'. The bearer would do all the cleaning, look after the laundry for a small fee, and would also supply tea and rolls for a modest fee. There was never any room inspections, at least none that required any action by the occupants. The phrase 'clouds and silver lining' springs to mind!

Shortly after settling in, I took the opportunity to do a night patrol with the Squadron. This was something I asked to do, so that I would get to know what was involved, and also get some experience of radio communications. I learned the international phonetic language of Alpha Bravo etc so well, I have never forgotten it. It can still come in useful spelling things out on the phone, providing the recipient realises exactly what you are doing when you say 'Charlie – Alpha – Tango' for cat! I also took the opportunity to practice driving as I did not own a car at the time.

There was at least one interesting task I undertook at SSQ during my tour. This was accompany a Medical Officer on a visit to Crater. At the time service families had been withdrawn from this town, but some civilians working for the services and some UK based British Government employees still lived there. They were no doubt reluctant to vacate their guarded properties which were of a high standard, and which had superb views of the bay at Aden. On this occasion, the RAF Medical Officer had agreed, most unusually, to make a home visit to a civilian worker who was not able to attend the normal surgery at Khormaksar. Travel to Crater for such visits were made by an RAF ambulance, and an armed attendant was required to accompany it. For some reason, it was not a simple procedure for SSQ staff to draw a weapon from the armoury, so to save time I volunteered, as I knew that I would be able to obtain my own personal weapon, a Sterling sub machine gun comparatively quickly. I also wanted to see Crater again, having been there five years earlier in more peaceful times. As we drove through the centre of Crater, we stopped at a road junction traffic lights. As we waited for the lights to change, I spotted a young Arab boy approaching the ambulance. As he raised his arm to seemingly throw something, I froze for a second and then saw that what he throwing was simply a cigarette packet. I had of course momentarily forgotten that I had a loaded SMG in my hand, as I had not been trained to react to what may well have been a grenade. At that time, the terrorists often used children as grenade throwers, although they were often unsuccessful. As it turned out, my inexperience was both fortunate for the boy and indeed myself.

My first parachute jump with the squadron was on 21 December 1965. This was a drop at first light at Falaise which was out in the desert at Little Aden. At around 4 a.m. I was feeling somewhat apprehensive about the occasion, and I am sure that the others in the squadron were at least slightly nervous, as they had not done any parachuting for a few months in the build up to the detachment. As we lined up at the parachute section to draw our equipment, the mood was lightened when Jimmy Sinclair, a Scottish SAC and one of the squadron 'characters' removed his boots, and commenced to 'walk' the boots on the huge counter, singing 'These Boots are Made for Walking', which was soon to be a number one hit for Nancy Sinatra. After this rendition we boarded a Beverley aircraft in a better mood, and were soon airborne heading for the DZ at Falaise. The jump formation was Sim 9s, and my log book confirms that I was back at number 7 on the starboard side. Everybody landed safely, and after leaving the DZ we were able to relax with mugs of tea as somebody had arranged for a large tea urn to be available. After the tea and of course a cigarette, as most of the squadron smoked in those days, we drove back to Khormaksar in high spirits. For me this was a great start to my parachuting with the squadron.

Four days after my first parachute jump with the squadron it was Christmas Day. It was fairly low key due the internal security situation, and there had to be a balance between a reasonable amount of traditional celebration and widespread drunkenness. There were no bars in the living accommodation, but nobody seemed to mind about too much to some alcohol being consumed there on Christmas Day. I joined the squadron for the Christmas Day lunch, which was served in the airmen's mess and as tradition dictated, by the officers. This was more of a jolly occasion rather than a riotous assembly, as whilst beer was served with the meal, this was severely rationed to one tin! After the lunch I joined several others, who thought that it would be a good idea to go to the swimming pool and have a swim and fool around until darkness fell at tea time. After tea, I returned to the medics billet and listened to a Forces Record Request programme on BFBS which had been pre recorded in UK and flown out to Aden for the day. There was no live link at that time. I remember that none of squadron were lucky enough to have a record played on the programme. I cannot recall what records were played, but one would almost certainly have been either 'Day Tripper' or 'We Can Work It Out' which was a double 'A' side number one hit by The Beatles. Christmas Day ended quietly with probably many airmen including myself feeling a little homesick. There was just a little more drinking, but nothing excessive. I think that the NAAFI was closed, but if not, nobody bothered to go there. It was certainly a memorable Christmas Day, but not so much a merry one.

The new year of 1966 dawned, and as it usually did in the 1960s, very quietly, and New Year or Hogmany was mainly observed by Scottish airmen, who would often celebrate the New Year firstly at midnight in country they were serving in, and then also at what would be midnight back in Scotland, which in Aden was 4 in the morning. This was confined to somebody wishing everybody a Happy New Year – again, following which we would go back to sleep! In the colony of Aden, sporadic and often unsuccessful terrorist attacks against British troops continued, but working and social life remained unchanged. On the 20th and 21st of January the squadron jumped on both days at Falaise again, this time from an Argosy. This was my first jump from this aircraft which was very good aircraft for parachuting. On the first day, I was due to jump with what was called an 'airborne stretcher'. This was basically a normal sized stretcher that had been modified with hinges so that the length was reduced, and therefore making it capable of being strapped to me body for the exit from the aircraft. However the dispatcher had some grave doubts about this piece of kit, and when I had stood up with it strapped on, he decided that it would be unsafe for me to jump with it. Perhaps as I was only 5 feet 5 inches tall had a bearing on the decision. The stretcher remained on the aircraft on this occasion. Both of these two jumps were uneventful, and my confidence regarding parachuting continued to increase. Two more jumps took place in February, both were with equipment and from a Beverley aircraft. Whilst they were successful for myself, one member of the squadron had a harder than normal landing after having to deploy his reserve parachute, when his main parachute developed a problem with its rigging lines after opening. He was taken to the hospital by myself for x rays of his spine, but he suffered mainly just severe bruising, and was soon back to normal fitness.

Around this time, I did not actively participate in any organized sport. Members of the squadron played lots of football, mainly in leagues on the camp, but occasionally at night under floodlights against some good military teams at Steamer Point, and I often went along to support them. There was also a boxing tournament during the tour, but I had not done any boxing training or had any contests for over 3 years, so I did not consider taking part this time, but I thought about taking it up again when we returned to UK, and in October 1966, I was back in ring action. Meantime I heard about a race which took place up the so called 'Barren Rocks of Aden', overlooking Crater, which was called the Sham Sham race after the name of one of the mounts. There was a saying that if you completed the race, which included some tough climbing at the top, then you would never return to Aden. Whether or not the medics at SSQ were inspired by my contrasting lifestyle I know not, but I did manage to persuade 3 or 4 to join me in a team for the race. Having a target to aim for, I started to go for runs around the camp, sometimes with the others from SSQ and sometimes on my own. In hind-sight, my training was totally unstructured, and after the initial enthusiasm had died down, probably irregular, but it was at least a pleasant diversion, and everybody stuck to it. On a typical hot afternoon, the race started on a flat section, and along with most of the field, I probably went off too fast, as when the hilly part was reached, I was starting to really feel the heat and was sweating profusely even though I was thoroughly acclimatised. The severity of some of the sections, resulted in a slow down of the pace, which probably enabled me and the rest of the SSQ team to finish the race at the top of Sham Sham, where troughs of water were provided for rehydration. Lemonade powder had been added to the water, no doubt to make the local water taste a bit better, but even though I was very thirsty it tasted vile! We all made our way back down the mountain to seek out a more pleasant tasting form of hydration, with the thought that if the saying was correct, we would never return again to Aden. Of course as the British were due to withdraw in two years time, this was more than a likely scenario for most. Alas for 2 Field Squadron, we were to return again at the end of 1967, and as it turned out, for an earlier than first planned British withdrawal from the colony.

Back on the squadron, I had three days on a live firing range in the desert at Little Aden. I was attending in only in a first aid capacity, but I was given the opportunity to fire both 2 and 3 inch mortars The 3 inch version was both exciting and scary, as I practised the necessary procedure required to load and duck in one smooth movement. This was necessary to prevent, as Clint Eastwood once famously said, 'having your head blown clean off', and in this case also travelling a long way from the trunk! The squadron also fired a Karl Gustav missile, but whether it was because of the cost of this missile, or my previous performance with the mortars, I was not allowed to try this out. As I was required to attend with different flights on three consecutive days, and spend a large part of the day in the sun, I developed the sort of tan that would be considered a health hazard these days. However at the time I loved it, and was disappointed when I started to lose it as my skin peeled a little. On 3 March, I did my last jump in Aden, this time in an Argosy. The DZ was once again at Falaise and took place at first light. We jumped as Sim 10s, and I was number 10 and last on the Port Side, and was allowed to use a include with my equipment pack, a further modified stretcher. There were no injuries, and I found that the stretcher was a convenient way for myself and the MT fitter, Sergeant Mick Tobin, to carry off both our equipment and parachutes. The stretcher was never used again for a parachute jump, at least not during my tour. When a parachute drop took place, a manned ambulance would be present on the DZ. If an active service drop were to take place, one small stretcher with just one para medic would severely restrict the usefulness of it. This was my 6th jump in Aden and was the highest total achieved of the squadron in the colony during the tour of duty.

As March progressed, everybody on the squadron started to look forward to April and a return to Colerne. The permanent single airmen at SSQ could only anticipate a spell of leave either in UK or in Kenya during what must have seemed a long two year tour. For many, the two things that were regularly enjoyed, was the camp cinema and Sundays at the beaches. The cinema showed fairly up to date films with a regular change of programmes. Before the audience settled down for the film, there was always a cartoon, and as most were seemingly directed by a Fred Quimby, as soon as his name appeared on the credits, there would be a shout of 'Good Old Fred'! Following the cartoon would be a Pathe Newsreel. This was invariably greeted with cat calls, and whistling at any women featured in the news. Occasionally there would be also be cat calls during a film, particularly a war film such as 'Zulu', but generally quiet ensued for the main feature. One slightly disconcerting feature of a cinema visit, was the system in use whereby those on call for emergencies would be alerted by a notice appearing on the screen. Depending on the level of the emergency, the amount of personnel being summoned would steadily grow, so that everybody was left wondering what was happening. Some would leave to return to duty as soon as the alerts commenced.

Because of the internal security situation, some of the medical officers who lived in married quarters would ask the SSQ airmen to baby sit, even if the children concerned were about old enough to be left alone. The carrot, (there was no stick at all of course), was the possibility of cooking yourself a good meal and having a few beers. There was always the invitation to bring along somebody else for company, but this invitation was usually declined, as not many were that interested in babysitting anyway, meal or no meal. I volunteered a few times, and can recall a couple of amusing occasions when I did some baby sitting. On one occasion two couples met up for a drink before they set out for a meal. They were drinking mainly whiskey sours and the like, and these were going down nicely,including with myself who had joined them. The drink and resulting conversation continued to flow freely into the night, until they realized that it was too late to go out for a meal because of the early curfew. The most sober of the four had to drive me back to my billet! On another occasion I took up the offer of bringing a friend, and after raiding the medical officer's food supplies for a jolly good fry up, we proceeded to take up the invitation to help ourselves to some beer. We did our best to hide some of the many empty cans, but I was never asked to baby sit again by this family.

At the end of April, the Squadron flew back to England via Bahrain and Cyprus at the end of the detachment. The primary task of the internal security at RAF Khormaksar has been a total success. With the exception of just one gunner who had been returned to UK on medical grounds, unconnected with the detachment, all the squadron returned safely, and were subsequently awarded the new pattern General Service Medal, (GSM), with the South Arabia Clasp. As I already had an old pattern GSM with the Arabian Peninsular Clasp, I now had two medals, which often resulted in being spoken to by Inspecting Officers on formal parades! It was now time to take some long overdue leave, and then to start enjoying the second half of the so called 'swinging 60s'. For airmen living on a RAF base in Wiltshire, perhaps the most notable and immediate changes that the decade brought, was the 60s pop music. For the past three years, British pop music led by The Beatles and The Rolling Stones had dominated the pop charts. In 1966, 14 of the 20 number one hit records were British. The exceptions were the artists of the stature of Frank Sinatra and the very popular Beach Boys. Changes in civilian clothing were more gradual. Suits and ties were still being worn, but the shirt could now be pink – like the one I bought with a matching polka dot pink tie! The birth control pill was now available, but its use had not yet become widespread. The poet Phillip Larkin observed that 'sexual intercourse began in 1963', but the sexual revolution took a little longer to reach some parts of the country outside of Chelsea!

After my leave I returned to my dual role of work in SSQ and the squadron. In SSQ, there was now a new Flight Sergeant by the name of Pitman. I got on fairly well with him, but he disliked the RAF Regiment gunners. He probably considered that overall they caused more work for the SSQ staff with their requirements for ambulance cover, and slightly higher accident rate due to the nature of their employment. I continued to deal mainly with the medical administration of the squadron personnel, and generally filled in. I joined the After Duty Hours roster, but this was not much of a burden. A week of night night duty was worked. This was a sleeping duty, which lasted from 5 pm. to 8 a.m the next morning, and there was time off during the day except at the weekend. A long weekend the following week was granted in lieu of the weekend worked. The section also had sufficient staff not only for the daily workload, but also for the weeks duty to only come round every 6 weeks. There were sometimes in-patients with minor complaints to feed and care for, but otherwise very little to do other than keep in contact with the Duty Doctor who was on call for emergencies, and be prepared to render first aid as required for any emergency arising after hours on the camp.

Parachuting commenced on 16 June with a series of three jumps all from Hastings aircraft on Salisbury Plain at Everleigh DZ. All were with equipment and for the first drop I was number 1 on the Port Side, thus having the chance of a good view of Salisbury Plain before the green light came on, and I jumped onto it. The second jump was a night jump which was my first night jump with equipment. The Hastings took off near sunset and flew over the Bristol Channel on a beautiful summer evening with a picturesque sunset, before turning round to fly over Salisbury Plain. Whenever I pass by the camp area off the M4, I am reminded of that evening. The jump went well as did the third jump of the series four days later.

Before I had chance to get bored at SSQ, I joined the squadron at Sennybrige in Wales in July of 1966, for a 'live firing' camp. I spent about 10 days in a tented camp, during which three batches of gunners were rotated from Colerne. My job was to render first aid in the event of any accidents. The only casualty was a sheep which had strayed into the line of fire and was accidentally shot. There were quite a lot of sheep roaming around, and they would scatter at the sound of gunfire. Unfortunately after a group of sheep had passed by and the firing had recommenced, a lone sheep ran after the others and was hit by a round from a gunner's SLR. I was then asked my opinion as to whether the sheep was dead as it appeared so, but was still twitching. I was unsure, so it was decided that the best course of action would be to shoot the sheep again to put it out of its agony. Nobody wanted to do this at first, but eventually the sheep was shot again. There was more conjecture as to whether it was dead, until somebody ended the speculation by cutting its throat. The sheep was carried back to camp, and one of the squadron cooks, Mick Nolan made a stew out of it. It tasted awful! The first weekend at the camp coincided with an England football game against Mexico in the World Cup. We watched this at a local pub, and I can remember even the Welsh locals cheering when Bobby Charlton scored the first of two winning goals in what had been a boring match up to this point. The following weekend, we went into Builth Wells for a drink, and came across a dance in the town. A group of us were hesitant about whether we would go in, partly as we were in field uniforms with boots. The doorman then suggested that we might like to go in, because he said that there was still plenty of food left to eat in the hall. He considered that our dress would not be a problem as nobody at the dance was dressed up. We dived in and had a good feed, and our presence was hardly noticed by the many beatniks at the dance. We even managed to dance with some of them!

Before the training at Sennybridge, the Commandant General of the RAF Regiment paid an informal visit to the Squadron at Colerne. As I sat waiting with the rest of the squadron to listen to what he had to say to us all, one of the gunners said to me that it would not be good news, and it was likely that he would tell us that we had to go to Zambia, even though we had only recently returned from six months in Aden. The gunner was spot on, we would be going to Zambia for a three month detachment starting in early

August. The RAF had been supporting the air defence of Zambia following the Unilateral Declaration of Independence by neighbouring Southern Rhodesia, and in addition was assisting with an oil airlift from Dar-es-Salaam and Loepoldville to supplement Zambia's stocks. 29 Squadron equipped with Gloster Javelin fighter aircraft was deployed to Ndola, whilst two Britannia aircraft squadrons from RAF Lyneham were rotating at Lusaka. So in August, the squadron made the long round about journey to Zambia via Cyprus, Bahrain and Aden, then on to Lusaka. Some of the squadron then continued the long journey to Ndola, and a small party travelled to the border at Livingston. I stayed at the capital Lusaka, and worked from a small medical centre on the temporary base, which was the site of a former agricultural show ground on the outskirts of the capital.

Most of the accommodation at Lusaka was very basic. One large building housed most of the beds, and space was very limited. Storage for personal items was almost non existent, and even after 9 months of the RAF Detachment, the camp remained not much better than a camp site. I had no hesitation of joining three medical staff in their accommodation adjoining the medical centre, which was a room with just 4 beds. My daily work routine was extremely light for the length of my stay. The working day consisted of attending a morning sick parade carried out by a RAF Medical Officer, which often had hardly any patients at all. Whether this was because Lusaka was a very healthy place to be, or that the camp housed just a small number of fit young men, who were seemingly not too discontent, I know not. After the morning surgery, I drove down to a military hospital to deliver any specimens for the Pathology department, and collect any reports. Very occasionally, I would take a patient to the Out Patients Department. I then went to fill up the land rover ambulance with petrol at the adjoining Zambian Army barracks. These journeys were something I did because I was qualified to drive service vehicles and the other medical staff, other than the medical officer were not, but mainly because it was convenient and gave me something to do. I would invariably arrive back at camp just before midday, and that would be the end of my working day, unless it was my turn to be on call for emergencies. This entailed just remaining on call at the camp. If anything urgent arose, either the medical officer would be contacted, or if necessary the patient would be driven to the hospital. During my stay no emergencies ever arose, and other than for a brief period in the morning, I never saw the medical officer for the rest of the day. I have no memory of his name or even what he looked like, as I saw so little of him during my 6 weeks working for him at the Medical Centre! I do recall that the Medical Centre was in a building with a large sign above the entrance, which had the initials NPC. This stood for Ndola Packing Company, but NPC in service circles stood for Neuro Psychiatric Centre, which cause much amusement.

Not very long after arriving in Zambia, we learned that our stay would be much less than expected, and in the end we spent only around six weeks in the country. Any military threat to Zambia from neighboring Rhodesia was always remote, and with the British demonstrating their firm support for Zambia over almost 9 months, it was non existent. This left only the lifting of sanctions by both the British and Rhodesians, which were expected to end very soon. There was therefore little time to explore all the social possibilities of Lusaka. We were made welcome by both the native Zambians and the white settler types who still appeared to be the ruling classes in this newly independent country. On the first weekend at Lusaka, we were invited to attend a horse race meeting, which was at a race track next to our camp, free of charge. There was of course bars for those without too much interest in horse racing, and many members of the squadron enjoyed what was in those days, the novelty of drinking on a Sunday afternoon.

We were also invited to various clubs, whose members seemed to be mainly the settler types. However, many airmen including myself, soon tired of this company which we felt had little in common with us as far as race relations was concerned. By the standards of today, we might have been considered racist, but we regarded the black airmen on the squadron as not only equal, but also as comrades and often close friends. It was perhaps the case that the white middle class managerial types living in Zambia at that time, may have held illusions of superiority by living in what was a poor developing country. However, it often seemed to be the case, that those with the most prejudicial views, were often those who whilst they had prospered in Zambia, we considered would have not have done so well in the UK. There was more of a racial mix in the bars in Lusaka, but they mostly lacked the happy atmosphere of similar places in Kenya a few years earlier, so they were not frequented regularly by airmen. The RAF medical staff did have contact with some of the nurses at the military hospital, but as far as I know no 'relationships' resulted from occasional parties and dances at the hospital social club. The white nurses were seemingly on a much higher social plain that humble nursing attendants. The Medical Officer might have fared a lot better!

I passed some of the time in the afternoons by going on long speed walks, as I did not run in those days. This I hoped would keep me fit, and top up my tan. In the evenings there was a small club on the camp which sold food and drinks. It had limited opening hours, but these were just about sufficient. There was a memorable final night at the club before the camp closed for good, when the officer in charge, an Army officer in the Royal Army Ordnance Corps, (RAOC), decided to give away all the remaining stocks of cans of beer, as the cost of transporting it back to UK would exceed its value. Whenever I hear about the so called 'binge drinking' of today, my thoughts go back to that night in Lusaka and I smile. Soon after this final night in Zambia, we flew back home in a Britannia via Aden, Bahrain and Cyprus. There would be no medals awarded for this detachment, which was by far the strangest mission ever undertaken by the RAF Regiment.

After some leave, it was back to work at SSQ and the Squadron. So that I did not become too bored with the SSQ routine, I started to do some boxing training, initially with a cook on the squadron called Mick Nolan, who was a good standard middleweight. He was also a very good race walker and had won RAF Championships at this sport. As the main championships in each sport were at the same time, he organized his training around both sports. As a part of my overall training I used to run alongside him when he went for walks of about 7 miles around RAF Colerne. As I got fitter, I joined in with some other boxers on the station, and carried out the normal boxing training. On 12 October I made my return to the ring at RAF Lyneham. This was followed at the end of the month, by a week at RAF Cosford for a novice championship, and in December two weeks of boxing training and the RAF Inter Command Championships at RAF Halton. As mentioned previously, I will deal separately with my boxing career in Chapter 12.

There was even more time off work for sport the following January, when after some coaching by Mick Nolan, who was helping me to train for boxing, I was persuaded to enter the RAF Walking Championships at RAF Thorney Island. I did reasonably well, but was never tempted to take up this sport. Mick however won the race and the RAF Championship. On a previous occasion he came close to achieving a unique double championship on the same day. He had won through to the final of the boxing which took place the same day as the race walking championship. Having won the race in the afternoon, he was in the ring later in the evening for the middleweight final. He had no great expectation of victory as his opponent had beaten him on previous occasions. However, this time he found that the bout was going very well, and he was definitely winning. He told me that when things were going his way, he started to think how good he was to win both championships, especially on the same day. He thinks that his mind started to wander as he pondered this, with the sad result that he found himself on the canvas listening to referee counting him out!

When I was not engaged in sporting activities, I made 3 more parachute jumps with the squadron. The first of these was very memorable, as it was part of a rehearsal by both squadrons of Hastings for a major airborne exercise. To simulate a mass drop, all available members of 2 Field were distributed between all available aircraft from the two Hastings Squadrons at Colerne. I ended up in one Hastings with SAC Ken Prout. This caused some amusement as he was even smaller than I was. At one time he had boxed as a flyweight, and we could have fitted on the same aircraft seat. We pretended to argue as to who would jump first. In the end I went first, and made a successful 18th jump with equipment onto the Everleigh DZ on Salisbury Plain. Three days later, I made my 19th jump on my 27th birthday, and once again from a Hastings at Everleigh, but this time with 19 others in a con 10 stick. This was the final jump of the year, and as it transpired the last for over 4 months. In between my parachuting and absences for boxing, I continued to work at SSQ. My frequent absences ensured that whilst I would normally be able to take my turn on the After Duty roster, it would have been difficult to allocate very much of the routine work. I continued to do what I could to assist when I was there, as I knew that the Flight Sergeant in charge would have a big input into my annual assessments. At the time I wanted to sign on for 22 years, and this was by no means easy at the time, unless at least satisfactory annual reports were filed. As it turned out I was first allowed to sign on for 15 years, and then less than a year later for 22 years. As 28 days leave was due for each re-engagement, I therefore ended up with an extra 56 days leave, a good part of which I took in 1967.

1966 ended on a happy note back at Colerne with no imminent attachments overseas. Due to my dual role, I was able to attend two work Christmas parties. The SSQ one was just a staff only evening at a country pub. We played a form of skittles, and then had an evening's food and drink for ten shillings. Those were the days! The Squadron Christmas do consisted of a dance with a group from Bristol called The Wurzels, or at the time, Adge Cutler and the Wurzels. They broke into the charts in 1967 with 'Drink up Thy Zider' and then had a number 1 in 1976 with 'The Combine Harvester (Brand New Key), which came back in a remix version in 2001, so the Squadron was ahead of time in respect of pop music.

At the start of 1967, I continued with my boxing with a civilian contest at nearby Bristol, and then another appearance for Transport Command, which involved some time away from work to travel up north to RAF Leconfield near Driffield. As I now live in nearby Scarborough, I often drive past what is now an army barracks. In March I joined the squadron for an annual airborne exercise in Libya. We flew out to RAF El Adam, which was the main base in Libya, in Hastings aircraft. This entailed a refuelling stop at Nice. I remember being surprised at how pleasantly warm the weather was at Nice in March. It was slightly warmer in Libya, and a pleasant change from the English climate. Our stay in Libya was restricted to the RAF camp, and no excursions into the surrounding countryside were made. I think that the feeling was that there was nothing there that would interest us, or perhaps anything that could be arranged in the short time we spent there. As the squadron went to Libya annually if they were not otherwise engaged overseas, I assume that we did not miss very much. The normal tour length at that time was two years, and it seemed obvious that this was not somewhere than the single airmen would experience very much normal social life. When we visited the NAAFI club, the place was always packed, and every night, there seemed to be a party involving a vast consumption of tinned lager. The normal procedure was for somebody in a group to go to the bar and buy a case of 24 cans to save queuing. Nobody bothered to clear away the cans, with the result that the bar was a real mess as the evening progressed, with empty cans everywhere. Groups at a table would stack the empties as high as they could before somebody at another table demolished them. One evening we inquired of a group, what the occasion was that they were seemingly celebrating. Was it someone going home? No, it was for two airmen who were facing a Court Martial the next day for taking without consent, a service landrover and driving off into the desert, then getting lost and having to be rescued. It seemed to be an awful place to spend two years. Perhaps there was things to do in the evening other than drink, but these were not obvious.

During the day, the squadron spent time doing parachute ground training, and organised sporting activities. Due to weather which affected the exercise as far as the aircraft was concerned, we made just the one parachute jump into the desert at the DZ at Raz el Eleba. The area was prone to outbreaks of a very strong wind, known as *shamaal*. Because of the adverse weather, we jumped without equipment. The drop was uneventful and that was the end of the exercise and the detachment. We then flew back to RAF Colerne in the Hastings. For some reason some of the squadron members thought that the Customs and Excise check on landing would be cursory as it had been before. They therefore brought back a lot more than the duty free allowance would permit. Whilst some of the squadron passed through the checks without being searched, one plane load was subjected to a search. After the customs discovered cigarettes and spirits way above the allowances, the officer in charge of the party read the riot act, and told everybody to declare all of what they were attempting to bring in. The result was that a large amount of contraband was declared and subsequently confiscated, but other than a reprimand, that was the end of the matter. We never landed at RAF Colerne again, as the Hastings fleet were soon to be replaced by Hercules operating out of RAF Lyneham. There would be some more flights in the Hastings, but the landings would be by parachute on Salisbury plain with no customs involved.

The next detachment with the Squadron came in June, when along with every available RAF Regiment Squadron in the UK, 2 Squadron went to RAF Catterick to prepare for a visit by The Queen, who was presenting new Colours to the RAF Regiment. There was to be a big formal parade, plus a large show depicting the role of the RAF Regiment. We were there for about 10 days, and because of the huge influx of airmen, 2 Squadron was accommodated in the barracks of the Royal Irish Rangers at the nearby Catterick Garrison. On the very first day at RAF Catterick there was a massive parade of all the Squadrons, for a briefing and pep talk by Warrant Officer Danny Gaud, who was the Depot Warrant Officer and a living legend. After the briefing, a signal was given to a fleet of NAAFI vans waiting in the distance for the parade to be adjourned for a tea break. The vans then moved in a sort of procession towards the parade area, whereupon the order to 'Fall Out' was given, and the tea break commenced. During this break, all the tradesmen learned that their presence on the parade was not required. It was obvious that Danny Gaud would not wish to have his moment of glory in front of

Her Majesty ruined by what he would undoubtedly have considered to be sloppy tradesmen. As none of the tradesmen were all that keen on parades, and particularly any under the control of Warrant Officer Gaud, we bore this rejection stoically! The decision meant that there was a lots of cooks, medics, clerks, various mechanics and fitters from all the Regiment Squadrons without anything planned work for 10 days. At first some of us went to the appropriate section on the camp, e.g. the cooks to the Catering Section and myself to the SSQ. However these sections were already prepared for the influx of airmen on the camp, and we were therefore superfluous to requirements. In the SSQ there was very little spare space for any extra staff to work in even if work could be found. Eventually we were found some work connected with static displays etc. for the Royal visit.

The summer of 1967 was the 'Summer of Love'. As I was not that young and was also married, I cannot speak from experience as to what affect this period may have had on the lives of those who were young and fancy free. However it did seem that there was much more sexual freedom than before, and that things had certainly changed a lot since the more oppressed 1950s. There was the growth in the numbers of women taking the birth control pill, and a more relaxed feel to life in general, even for those living in a very structured society such as the armed forces. I think the mood of the summer of 1967 was evoked by the Procol Harem's number one hit, 'A Whiter Shade Of Pale' which was in the charts for 15 weeks. The lyrics were indisputably nonsense, but the song has endured to the present day. The Beatles took over the top slot in the charts for three weeks, and stayed in the charts for 16 weeks, with 'All You Need Is Love'. This song had lyrics which spelt out the Beatles' ideology, and as they were the most influential pop group of the 1960s, their views would have been shared with many people, particularly the young. The mood of the period continued in the charts, when Scott McKenzie took over from The Beatles with 'San Francisco'.

In the summer of 1967, a much more significant event took place which affected millions of people, and would soon have an effect on myself and 2 Squadron. This was the war between Israel and Egypt, the so called 'Six Day War'. The Israeli victory led to a backlash effect in the colony of Aden. With the imminent withdrawal of the British which was planned for January 1968, there was an intense power struggle between the rival factions, the Federation for the Liberation of Occupied South Yemen, (FLOSY) backed by Egypt, and the National Liberation Front, (NLF), backed by North Yemen. The

British originally had hopes of handing over power to a Federation backed by local Sheiks, but this plan was eventually abandoned. After the 6 Day War, the British Forces in Aden were subject to constant attack by both opposing groups, and maintaining law and order was becoming increasingly difficult,. As casualties began to rise, the British electorate fuelled by the popular press, wanted a swift withdrawal to save British lives. The withdrawal was subsequently rescheduled for a secret date in November, and 2 Squadron was to cover the final stages of the withdrawal from the Colony and in particularly, RAF Khormaksar starting from 11 October to the penultimate day of British Occupation. The last British troops to leave would be Royal Marines based on an off shore aircraft carrier. In the meanwhile 2 Squadron had the remainder of the 'summer of love' to enjoy, as they returned to RAF Colerne after the Queen's visit to RAF Catterick.

After what was a somewhat boring Catterick experience, I had a much more exciting 4 parachutes jumps in the following month of July, the first of which was momentarily very scary for me. As the Squadron had not had any parachuting activity for four months, we all spent a day doing parachute jumps from a balloon at RAF Hullavington. After a total of 20 previous jumps including the very first two from a balloon, this should have been a piece of cake for me. However jumping from the static cage below a huge barrage type balloon can be slightly disconcerting. There is a greater sensation of a drop than there is when exiting an aircraft, when the parachute is mostly deployed whilst in a slipstream. Jumping from a balloon involves a r free drop until the parachute deploys. To avoid any gut wrenching sensation, you just need to look up towards the sky, and thus the developing parachute canopy, to avoid this sensation. This should not be a problem for a parachutist with some experience. So much for the theory. I was the third of 5 in the cage to jump. We were all a bit nervous having not jumped for 4 months. Parachuting is exciting when experienced often, but the butterflies can start after a period away from it. The first to jump disappeared in silence after the command 'go'. The next to jump managed somehow to stand on the foot of the dispatcher before jumping out. The dispatcher then called me forward to jump, and warned me to stay clear of his feet which I did. Unfortunately in doing so, I veered over to the opposite side of the cage exit where there are two trailing static lines, (the webbing that is attached to the balloon/aircraft, which is in turn attached to the parachute to enable deployment), and trip up and go hurtling out of the cage. Of course my Static Line was hooked up before the cage commenced the ascent, but for a second or so, I forgot that this was the case as I travelled down to earth from 800 feet. This put me off any similar experience of Free Fall parachuting in the future. An hour later I made another parachute jump, this time employing the 'look up' technique and all was fine.

My next two jumps were possibly, indeed as far as UK forces were concerned, the last from a Hastings aircraft which were about to be replaced by C130 Hercules operating out of RAF Lyneham. The first of the two, was a routine day jump at Salisbury Plain onto an alternative DZ at Fox Covert, but my final jump from a Hastings was a memorable farewell to parachuting from this aircraft. The Squadron took part in a night descent which involved a departure at sundown from Colerne, and then a farewell flight over the Bristol Channel before the final night drop at the Fox Covert DZ. This last drop was also memorable for me as it turned out to be the biggest stick I was ever to jump in, which was of 30 paratroopers in Sim 15s, one more than the usual maximum of Sim 14s from a Hastings. I am aware that following the introduction of the C130, much larger sticks are not only possible, but are also the norm. I also note that parachute pay has increased from seven and sixpence a day!

In between the parachuting activity with 2 Squadron, I enjoyed two periods of accumulated leave which arose after I had re-engaged up to 22 years. Unlike normal annual leave, which was deemed a privilege, re-engagement leave could not be denied. In respect of normal annual leave, most airmen always managed to achieve the full quota, or alternatively carry forward any leave which cannot be taken for operational reasons. Even after the additional parachute pay, and previous overseas allowance, I was still not very well off, and so I spent some of my extra periods of leave working as a labourer, employed by the son of a nurse who worked alongside me in SSQ. The nurse put in the usual 'good word' for me with her son, who sub contracted work from building sites, plus the authorities responsible for minor road and path repairs. I was told by the contractors mother, that her son had reacted to her request to employ me with a some surprise, as I did not fit the 1960s stereotype of a medical orderly! In the end he has happy to employ me on various schemes in the summer, and also for some work the following winter. Looking back, it seems sad that I thought it necessary to spend some of my leave working, but at the time I did not mind, and in fact I enjoyed the experience.

Before leaving for Aden in October, I completed two more jumps which were unusual. An experimental unit at RAF Boscome Down asked for volunteers to jump using a modified parachute assembly. The modification was simply some added material attached to the edges of the canopy, called a 'skirt'. This modification was designed to prevent rigging lines crossing over the canopy during deployment, which greatly reduced the effectiveness of the parachute, and required the operation of the reserve parachute to compensate. If the reserve parachute was brought into use, then this could result in serious problems for the parachutist. We were reassured that the modified parachute had been extensively tested, and our contribution was just so that the required number of test jumps could be made before the parachute would become standard issue. Thus reassured, a group of mainly tradesmen from 2 Squadron, boarded an Argosy at Boscombe Down, along with other parachutists who were set to do trials with free fall equipment. We were all given some white cloth covering for our boots, for the filming of the jump. I started to feel a little apprehensive at this stage, particularly when the aircraft door opened and I saw a small aircraft flying alongside for the filming. It seemed to be too close for a start! Of course all was well, and I made another successful test jump at Boscombe 12 days later from a Beverley. Having bade farewell to the Hastings, this was now the final jump from a Beverley. Soon the C130 Hercules would take over from both of these ancient aircraft, but meanwhile, the squadron would be going to Aden a week later, to take part in the withdrawal of the British forces, prior to the handover of power, but exactly to whom was still being fought for on the streets of the Colony.

On the 11th of October 1967, most of the squadron departed from Gatwick on a civilian VC10, which flew non stop into RAF Khormaksar. This was an unexpected luxury after the last time when we traveled to Aden via Cyprus and Bahrain. We were even allowed to drink on the flight, at least until the Squadron Warrant Officer, Warrant Officer Norrie Chapman, became concerned after a small fire broke out on a seat being utilised as a card table, and therefore advised the cabin staff, that he would not be responsible for what might happen next if the bar was to remain open. It was then closed! We soon arrived safely at RAF Khormaksar for what we thought would be for 3 months, but subsequently became just 47 days when we departed for good this time on 27 November. The heightened state of emergency was made immediately apparent with a briefing, before we even left the Air Movements, (Passenger Section), by a RAF Regiment Officer who was carrying a SMG! We then proceeded to some temporary accommodation on the camp, and shortly after to the NAAFI for a few beers, as it was now the evening local time. The next morning, we marched at the double to the camp cinema for yet more briefings. The double time, (in effect jogging), was seen and noted by the Senior Medical Officer, Wing Commander Riseley-Pritchard, who gave me a note to pass on the squadron's Commanding Officer, a Squadron Leader O'Dwyer Russell, to the effect that running in the Aden climate was best left until after acclimatisation! I expect that this was known, and the idea was simply to create a good impression of the squadron. Whilst we wore the same tropical uniform as the other RAF personnel on the base, we also wore our own unique squadron light blue stable belt, plus of course we had para wings on our sleeve. We were certainly different!

After the briefings, I reported in to the SSQ. I was surprised to discover that two of the staff who were there when I last left in April 1965, were still there, otherwise there had been a lot of changes. The withdrawal was well and truly under way, and the staff was already greatly reduced. The administration side was now the responsibility of a Corporal Gordon Wannell, who was also the aeromedical evacuation NCO, and was the last RAF medic to leave Aden with the SMO on the final day. In preparation for the withdrawal all the station personnel medical documents and associated records had been despatched back to the UK. There was a system in force whereby airmen who required anything more than very basic medical attention, and those unlikely to be fit for duty much before the final withdrawal date, were returned home on the next available aircraft. After the closure of the RAF Hospitals at Steamer Point and Khormaksar Beach, SSQ, had now taken on the role of a small hospital, but wherever possible treatment would be limited, and patients would normally be evacuated to United Kingdom as soon as possible for long term treatment. Alternatively there was full medical facilities on HMS Eagle, an aircraft carrier moored in the harbour. This facility was so seldom used, that when a film crew wanted to film an evacuation of a patient to the carrier by helicopter, a 'fake' casualty had to be employed. The daily routine of SSQ continued with the morning sick parades, but very few patients were reporting sick. All the families had been flown back to the UK a few months ago, so after the morning sick parades, there was no other routine work. There was no routine medical examinations or inoculations and vaccinations being carried out, so there remained only the in patients to be attended to by the remaining medical officers, soon to be just Wing Commander Riseley-Pritchard other than Royal Naval Medical Officers from HMS Eagle.

The shortage of patients not only caused some film-makers a problem, but also almost caused another problem when a concert party came to give a performance at SSQ for all the patients. The background to this was that in the summer of 1967, *The Sun* had run a campaign to get more shows for the troops in Aden. There is an organization called the Combined Services Entertainment, (C.S.E.), who normally arrange concerts for British Troops serving abroad, but for some reason, Aden was seemingly not getting any touring concerts at this time. I think that there was a problem in getting artistes to go out to Aden at this troubled time. The campaign was very successful and three shows then visited the colony and gave several concerts. Tony Hancock was one of the first to volunteer, followed by Mike and Bernie Winters. The last of the CSE shows featured the very popular 1950s singer Ruby Murray, (number 1 in 1955 with 'Softly Softly'). In addition to shows at the remaining few barracks in Aden, a show had been scheduled for the patients in hospital, which was now SSQ. The problem was that there was not that many patients left on the day of the concert. However there were a few left in the ward who were duly wheeled onto the patio where the concert took place, and with everybody on the SSQ staff and other invited guests to swell the number of 'patients'. Ruby Murray and the others in the CSE party were able to give a shortened version of their show, apparently, to many 'patients'. For this final stay at Khormaksar I did not stay in the SSQ staff's accommodation, but instead joined the rest of the squadron who were living in empty married quarters. This was an excellent arrangement. We lived in comfortable accommodation, and this also gave the impression to outsiders that the camp had a lot more people still stationed there than there actually was. This idea extended to the barrack blocks, where just one or two airmen would be still living in a building meant for 30 -50. Whilst we lived in married quarters we were fed in the messes, but whenever we could, we scrounged tinned rations and cooked our own food in the houses. As ever, we made the very best of things.

Other than the CSE shows, there was an ever decreasing amount of entertainment at RAF Khormaksar and in Aden generally. The cinema had closed, all servicewomen had returned to UK with the imminent closure of the Steamer Point base, and there was very little sporting activity save for occasional *ad hoc* football matches. This was mainly because of the reduced manpower in Aden, but also because those remaining were generally working much longer hours. The NAAFI clubs remained open until very near the last days of of the British presence, but of course there were no more dances, and just the usual bar and food outlets. A favourite snack at the time was a fried egg roll, which meant that the roll itself was fried. This tasted delicious, but this may well have been because normal bread was not that tasty for some reason. One small but popular pastime, was when the UK newspapers arrived, and whilst these were up to a week old, they were made available to read for free in the clubs. On the popular music front, the BFBS had closed down when the staff were amongst those the many nonessential personnel that could therefore be repatriated to the UK ahead of key workers. This left just the BBC World Service, which broadcast very few popular music programmes. Therefore the tune heard most often was the World Service signature tune of 'Lily Bolero'. Whenever I hear it now, I am transported back nearly 40 years to those days when I would tune in mainly to the news, and often find out things that were happening in Aden of which I knew nothing! The one thing I and everybody else on the Squadron wanted to know, was when we would be leaving, but this was strictly on a 'need to know' basis only. There was one really good night's entertainment near the end when the band of the Royal Marines gave a concert in the NAAFI at Khormaksar. This was a really excellent show. The band's versatility and range of the music played, was a very pleasant surprise to me and most others in the audience. One of the songs which as the saying goes, 'brought the house down' was undoubtedly The Animals 1965 hit, 'We've gotta get out of this place'!

On the work front, 2 Squadron generally worked a 24 hours on and 24 hours off pattern, as they continued security patrols on the camp. However, they also supported other military formations by relieving some hard pressed units by taking over check point and other security duties for a spell. In this way the Squadron gained some valuable experience and respect, although their contribution may not always have been officially acknowledged. For myself, I continued to work exclusively at SSQ, which included a sleeping duty at more regular intervals and no day off afterwards. In common with everybody else, I did not mind the extra work, as the days to the end of the tour seemingly passed rapidly by. Just as on the previous detachment, I went to Crater. This was however a totally different experience to 1966. On this occasion I went to recover a soldier of the Argylls and Sutherland Highlanders, who had been wounded. The RAF was at this stage providing a limited ambulance service for what remained of the British troops in Aden. Crater had been recaptured, and subsequently occupied by the Argylls following a withdrawal immediately after massacres on 19 June in which 22 soldiers had been killed in ambushes by local Arab police, and mutinous elements of the South Arabian Army, (SAA). Ever since the Argylls had recaptured Crater, security was very tight, and at every road junction the Argylls were out in force, halting all movement. So armed with my SMG, I sped to the Battalion Headquarters in a small ambulance where the wounded soldier was being treated for his wounds. I was accompanied by an Army medical officer and a driver. However, this was almost a false alarm in that a soldier had indeed sustained a gun shot wound, (GSW), but his wound was somehow caused by the soldier himself during a fire fight, when he had literally shot himself in the foot! There was no question that he had deliberately done so, as he was an experienced senior NCO. Before we returned to Khormaksar with the casualty, we stopped for a cold drink and a chat with the Argylls. As we did so, one of the Argylls invited me to look at the bodies of three terrorists that had been shot dead, and were lying in a alley outside the HQ building. The three lay side by side, covered with an army blanket. The story emerged that the three were spotted driving in a car in Crater along with another man. At the time, four Arabs in a car would arouse suspicion, and the occupants must have known that they would be stopped and searched. Before the Argylls could take any action, the car stopped and three of the occupants got out of the car and commenced what was described as a 'wild west' shoot out, which resulted in their death. The reason for this seemingly suicidal action was that the fourth man in the car was being kidnapped. I read an account recently, where the author claimed that four terrorists had been killed in this incident, but I am certain it was just three as it is something I will not forget, having never seen anything quite like it before, or since for that matter. I did not feel sorry for the deceased, but as with others who die in their youth, (terrorists in Aden were invariably young, sometimes children), I had a sense and no more than that, of regret for a life suddenly cut short. They, and those British soldiers who were massacred back in 1967, would be about my age now if they had lived, which seems sad. As was the case in this and other insurrections, even the victors are sometimes no better off in the end.

The Crater incident was the last time I attended an incident off base, and as the British forces gradually handed over control to the South Arabian Army, (SAA), terrorist activity against the British declined, although there was still some sporadic attacks by those wanting to enhance their status with the imminent ruling party. The handover to the SAA in the outlying districts of Aden, coincided with fierce fighting between the rival NLF and FLOSY factions. This power struggle pre independence, resulted in an overwhelming victory by the NLF, who therefore by force of arms, i.e. by 'eliminating' the opposition, took on the role of 'Government in Waiting' and were therefore recognised by the British, who then entered into talks with NLF representatives in Geneva. The talks concerned the actual handover and final withdrawal date, a pre withdrawal ceasefire, and financial aid to what would become the South Yemen. Soon after my Crater experience, the planned withdrawal seemed to accelerate, as Royal Marine Commandos based off shore on Royal Naval ships started to take over security duties in Aden. As the final day approached, a Royal Navy medical orderly, who I assume was my equivalent, in that he was attached to the Royal Marines, turned up at the Khormaksar SSQ, along with a Royal Naval Medical Officer. Whilst Wing Commander Risely-Pritchard and Corporal Gordon Wannel were still in post, and had the overall responsibility regarding the disposal of any final withdrawal casualties or any acute illnesses, the Navy medic, considered that the Royal Marines, and therefore himself and a Navy Medical Officer had taken over SSQ and that it was therefore no longer a SSQ, but a Royal Naval Sick Bay! By this time nobody at all was 'reporting sick' anyway, and as there was also nobody wounded in action, and no other casualties that I can recall, the Sick Bay was never utilised! Before I bade farewell to SSQ on the penultimate day of RAF Khormaksar, I was in the SSQ office, or whatever the Navy wanted to call it, when a British Army Soldier called in to SSQ with an enquiry about a former patient. The Navy medic's moment of assumed authority had arrived. He asked the soldier to remove his service cap, as he was now in a Navy Sick Bay! It was light hearted and humorous, but for the two remaining RAF medical personnel, this attitude must have rankled at the very least.

The penultimate day of British rule in Aden and the final withdrawal of British troops resulted in a final massive airlift for almost all but the Royal Marine Commandos. They would depart by helicopter to HMS Eagle on the very last day. 2 Squadron would hand over their duties to the Royal Marines and would be ready to depart late on the last full day. One of my abiding memories of RAF Khormaksar, which was one of the all time major RAF bases, is strolling back to the former married quarters after the final meal in the Airmen's Mess, and passing the very large accommodation blocks, all of which were still lit up, but which were now almost deserted. I am fairly certain that the temporary occupation of former married quarters, and distributing the remaining RAF personnel, would have created the impression of a greater rearguard presence than was the actuality. Instead of clogging up the departure lounge at the Air Movements section, 2 Squadron assembled at the Corporals Club. I never used this facility on either tour, and had forgotten that it existed. It was now closed for good so I would never ever use it. We all waited outside the club waiting to be called forward when our flight to Bahrain was ready, and had our final meal in Aden which consisted of roast beef sandwiches, which were very dry and unappetising. After this final reminder of how awful bread could taste, we boarded a Britannia and departed from what a Pathé News commentator described as a 'troubled land' and 'inhospitable shores'. A few hours later all the remaining troops departed, with the Royal Marines from HMS Albion covering the withdrawal until they in turn departed by helicopters to their ship. On arrival at Bahrain, we all had to change from our combat dress to civilian clothes before continuing our journey home via Cyprus. This observance of some international protocol always struck me as nonsense, as we were travelling in a RAF Aircraft clearly marked as such, with all the crew dressed in RAF Uniform! It was then on to RAF Akrotiri in Cyprus, where the resident RAF Regiment Squadron treated us to some cases of beer, which was a nice gesture. We were exceptionally allowed to consume the beer in the Air Movements section. This at least made the final seven-hour leg back to RAF Lyneham feel slightly better. When we finally landed at Lyneham we felt a lot more than slightly better to be back home, with some leave and then Christmas to look forward to.

After a short period of leave, I returned to work in SSQ, but it was not long before I had some time off for boxing. This time it was to represent Transport Command at RAF Uxbridge, and involved just three days off work, but this was very welcome and gave me the chance to see some of 'swinging London' at first hand. On the day of the contests, which were in the evening, a party of boxers went into central London for a look at places such as Carnaby Street, and it was obvious from what we observed than at least in terms of clothing, London was markedly ahead of places such as Bath. As is the case with any group of young men, we enjoyed watching and trying to chat to almost any woman in a mini skirt! Before getting back to Uxbridge, we visited a professional boxing gym, and spent some time chatting to one of the trainers. I will write about the evening's bout in Chapter 11, which will be all about my boxing career.

A few days before we started the Christmas break, the squadron was introduced to the C130, Hercules aircraft. Before the first jump, we had some familiarisation training on a stationary aircraft. There was a different layout of the seating for parachuting, which would enable a much larger number of parachutists to exit the aircraft at the same time, than any other aircraft the Squadron had jumped from. The most significant difference for parachutists was the the Hercules had a higher minimum cruising speed. This meant that the speed of the aircraft when employed dropping parachutist was higher than for example the Hastings and Beverley aircraft. To partly reduce the speed of the parachutists in the aircraft's slipstream, a shield was placed near the door for the drop period. The crucial difference for parachutists was that they should refrain from carrying out the forceful exit previously employed, and instead just trickle out. If a forced type of exit was employed, the parachutist would clear the shield, and then be subject to the full force of the slipstream. This might possibly cause a problem when the parachute was deploying, although the parachute that I had been testing at Boscome Down would or should prevent problems. There was also a chance that a parachutist exiting the aircraft via the full slipstream, might collide with another parachutist in the air. We therefore had to unlearn our normal exit drill and practice the technique of just stepping out of the exit door. On 20 December, the Squadron successfully carried out it's first jump from a Hercules on to the DZ at Weston on the Green.

For the first two months of 1968, the Squadron had no parachute jumps, and I had no boxing contests, so I had a couple of months working in SSQ for a change. In March, the Squadron more than compensated for this lack of jumps with a series of 5 jumps in 8 days, commencing with a return to the Argosy for a big jump at Everleigh on 5 March. We jumped in a Sim 10 formation, and I was the first out on the starboard side for a change. Just 3 days later we went to RAF Hullavington for some more Balloon jumps. I managed to do two jumps without any more scares. It was then a return to the Hercules just 4 days later for a night descent again at Everleigh, and this time I was last in a Sim 14 formation with full equipment. The Hercules could cope with a much larger stick, but even one this size felt cramped when we stood up and prepared for the jump. The next day the Squadron all jumped with the modified parachute which some of the Squadron including myself, had been trialling the previous year at Boscombe Down. Once again we all landed safely at Everleigh. A few days later we flew out to Libya for an annual airborne exercise, which this year would involve the Hercules. This aircraft is notorious for being uncomfortable for passenger use, with the normal seating configuration being webbing seats down the sides of the aircraft. They are extremely noisy, and nowadays passengers use ear defenders, but these were not supplied in the early years of the aircraft's UK operation. There was however the consolation of far less flying time than the Hastings, and a direct flight to RAF El Adem.

The Libyan base seemed the same as it did the previous year, but this time we did not have to wait long for the first jump, which would be made once again at the desert DZ at Raz-El-Eleba, but this time at night and with equipment. The sticks were small and consisted of Con 6s from the Port exit only. I jumped at number 5. All was well with my exit and descent until I neared the ground, when my rate of descent rapidly increased and I made a very hard landing. What had undoubtedly occurred was that the parachutist who jumped after me, a cook called Gary Sloan, had drifted underneath me at a critical point near the ground and in parachuting terms 'stole my air'. This caused my parachute to slightly deflate and cause an increase in the speed of descent. If this had occurred at an earlier stage, I would have dropped a little and then my parachute would return to normal. As my air was 'stolen' near the ground, I therefore ploughed in before it could re inflate. It is the normal practice for parachutists to always steer away from others in the stick once their parachute has deployed. However drifting below another parachutist at the last minute, and particularly during a night descent is almost impossible to avoid. After landing I was in extreme pain from my back. This would have been partly because of my landing speed, and also that I would have adopted the standard landing position with both legs together and push slightly back under my body to absorb the impact. My legs were therefore uninjured, but the force of landing had damaged my spine. I was attended to on the DZ by a RAF Medical Officer who initially thought that I had severe bruising, as I did not have any apparent nerve damage. When the severe pain did not diminish, I was given some morphia which did not seem to help at first, but eventually eased the pain. I was clearly unable to travel back to El Adem by road that night, so I stayed at the DZ with the Medical Officer, a medical orderly and a driver. After a very restless and painful remainder of the night, I was airlifted out by a small helicopter in the morning. This was a scary and indeed an uncomfortable experience. I was carried on a stretcher, in a contraption outside and at the side of the helicopter. The crewman told me that if I was feeling sick or in any pain, I should signal my discomfort by waving my head from side to side. At this point the back pain had dulled, so the discomfort came about by my being over conscious of any excessive head movement. I constantly felt like moving my head about, but was afraid that any such movement may have been interpreted as a signal to stop, so I therefore felt I had to restrict my movements. With hindsight, I wonder why some other signal such as a hand movement could have been used. I was relieved when I landed back at El Adem after about an hour's flight.

Soon after being admitted to the SSQ, I had yet another scary experience. This was the X-Rays. There was no qualified radiographer on the base, but a nursing attendant stationed there had been trained to a standard whereby he could take some X -Rays. However, the nursing attendant told me that he had taken so many x-rays recently that he was reaching the stage where he would have to stop soon, as his radiation badge was indicating that he was near the maximum level of exposure to radiation allowed. He therefore decided that what he would do, was to set up the x-ray equipment, and then retreat whilst I pressed the button to take the x-ray. He moved all the necessary pieces of the machine into position, then handed me a lead with the start button which I was to press when he gave the signal. He then left the x-ray room and went down an adjacent corridor. It reminded me of something from the radio comedy programme 'The Goon Show' as I listened to his retreating footsteps. I then heard him shout OK, at which point I had to press the button and x-ray myself, and then confirm I had done so. He then returned to the room and after repositioning me, this almost bizarre procedure was repeated. I do not know if this method was employed as I was a medic and therefore ought not to be worried, but the thought of all this radiation that the operator was avoiding did indeed worry me. The x-rays were not of a very good quality – perhaps I was shaking with fear, but showed that I had crushed at least one of my lumbar vertebrae. I had visions of a spell at Stoke Mandeville, but as I no loss of sensation in my lower body, this was most unlikely to be necessary.

After viewing the x -rays, the medical officer at SSQ El Adem, considered that as I was unable to travel back to UK sitting in a Hercules, I might be allowed to travel back on a stretcher along with the rest of the squadron in a few days time. Unfortunately, this was vetoed by those responsible for all medical evacuation world wide, so it was then arranged that I would travel to Cyprus accompanied by a trained aero medical attendant on the flight, and at Cyprus I would connect with a fortnightly aeromed flight back to the UK. However the flight from El Adem was delayed 24 hours due to a *shamaal*, which considerably reduced visibility on the airfield. I therefore arrived in Cyprus hours after the UK aeromed flight had departed for UK, and had to wait two weeks for the next routine UK aeromed flight. In the meantime I was temporally lost! When enquiries were made at the RAF Hospital at Wroughton, (known as the PARAF Hospital as in Princess Alexandra), regarding my condition etc, the hospital had no record of me. Naturally the squadron was insisting that I must be in the hospital somewhere. This was 1968, and I imagine that before I was 'found', numerous signals would have been flying round between Akrotiri, El Adem, Wroughton, and Colerne. None of the established systems of communication could seemingly cope with my unusual pattern of movement. I can well imagine all the recriminations and blame shifting that took place after I had been found.

By the time I had reached the orthopaedic ward at Akrotiri, I could manage to walk a short distance to the toilets. When I explained my progress to the nursing sister on the ward, she was very uneasy about somebody with a fractured spine walking around in her ward. I was therefore confined to bed until I had seen an orthopaedic surgeon the next day. Before I saw the surgeon I had some proper x-rays of my spine, which showed that I had a crush fracture of the first and third lumbar vertebrae. These were quite severe, and incidentally were still showing up on X rays and scans over 30 years later. I was cleared to continue my rehabilitation and was allowed to walk, with the usual proviso not to overdo it. Within days, I was strolling round the grounds of the hospital, and enjoying a pint in NAAFI bar in the grounds which bore the notice ' No Patients'. I made sure I walked as normally as possible, and seemingly nobody thought I looked like was a patient as I always got served! In the second week of my hospitalisation, I travelled by bus to the main RAF station at Akrotiri to meet up with SAC Ken Prout, with whom I once shared a memorable parachute jump from a Hastings. By the time the aeromed flight was due, I was quite mobile, but for my comfort during the flight, I was classified as a stretcher case which was fine. However it was also decided that I would board and disembark the aircraft on a stretcher. I was able to persuade the aeromedical crew to let me sit on a normal passenger seat and walk to the toilet etc. When I finally arrived at the PARAF Hospital Wroughton, I made a Lazarus type entrance leaving the stretcher behind, and walking into the reception ward in my Para smock! I had to explain that I had made a good recovery, and had been returned to the UK as that was where I was stationed. I was spared any return to a strict bed routine. Shortly after arrival, I met the Hospital Registrar, who in service hospitals was the deputy Commanding Officer. It was Wing Commander Riseley-Pritchard, affectionately known as 'Grisly Dick', who of course knew me very well from Khormaksar just four months earlier. He immediately appreciated my position, and told me that I would see an orthopaedic specialist the next day, and I would then be discharged to sick leave to recuperate further at home. As he promised, I was discharged the next day to sick leave, but before I left the hospital I was officially medically downgraded to UK service only, and officially forbidden to parachute or carry out any strenuous duties such as lifting stretchers, for 6 months. This was to be expected, but was still a bit of a blow, as it would cramp my style a little, and I would also lose my parachute pay after 90 days. As I was driven home from the hospital, I was already reconciling my fate, and considering how best to cope with it.

After two weeks on sick leave, I returned to work, mainly at SSQ, as I was now medically unfit for parachuting. Shortly after my return, two young former RAF apprentices, Steve Woods and Allan Dines arrived. They were both part of the very first batch of apprentices in the Medical Branch. They had been very well trained over a 12 month period, and were qualified up to the rank of corporal in the trade of Medical Secretarial, (Med Sec), and to Sergeant and above educationally. After a slow start due to manpower reductions in the Medical Trade Group, Steve went on to have a really good and very interesting career, before retiring in the rank of Flight Sergeant after 28 years service. Sadly Allan Dines was murdered during a private holiday in Belize whilst he was still very young. The two ex apprentices had one thing in common with the RAF Regiment airmen on 2 Squadron, which was that the Flight Sergeant Pitman, who was still in charge of SSQ, did not like them either. He seemed suspicious of their training, and appeared unwilling to accept just how much they knew, which was not the best of starts to their careers.

As always, I soon found a way of escaping from the office. The Junior Medical Officer at SSQ, a Flight Lieutenant Foote, who was a very fit and active individual who played rugby, agreed that I should spend time at the gym to increase my strength and fitness, and in particular my back. These exercises would in theory anyway, be under supervision of a Physical Training Instructor, and therefore they would be carried out in working hours. I hardly needed much encouragement, as I set about getting really fit, and in addition to the sessions in working hours went on runs, and often trained twice a day. As I got fitter, I started to train for boxing once again. I was supposed to be unfit for such strenuous activity, but I was able to join the Support Command boxing squad for a week's training. Although I was officially medically downgraded, I was now clearly fit to carry out the full range of duties, including lifting and carrying stretchers. A visit to a orthopaedic specialist at Wroughton resulted in my being declared fit for all duties and also boxing.

Whilst I had now been upgraded, and had become even fitter than before the parachute accident, I had now completed the normal three year tour on the Squadron. It was sometimes possible for certain trades to extend their tour, but the RAF Records Office department responsible for Medical Branch postings, decided that my time was up. At the time in September 1968, the number one hit record was appropriately 'Those were the days' by Mary Hopkin. The Beatles were still topping the charts with 'Lady Madonna' and also 'Hey Jude'. Cliff Richard, who was still touring and recording in 2006, was just about getting into his stride in 1968, with yet another number one, 'Congratulations'.

At the end of September I left Colerne for RAF Waddington which was a 'V' Bomber' base just outside of Lincoln. This posting turned out to be in error as I was due for an overseas posting. To rectify matters, the posting was made into a detachment, and I was then posted to RAF Akrotiri in February 1969. So for all practical purposes, my tour with 2 Squadron came to an end. It had been a most memorable three years of my career, and to this day I attend reunions at Colerne village, (the camp is now an Army barracks), and also a five year reunion at the RAF Regiment Depot where the Squadron is based.

My four months at Waddington was most memorable almost exclusively for boxing. It was the most successful period of my boxing career ever, and the details are recorded in Chapter 11. When I arrived on the station, I had to visit the Physical Education department, and when I told them that I was a boxer, I was asked if I would like to represent the station at the Strike Command championships the following week at RAF Uxbridge. This was the first of four championships I was allowed time off for. There was also the Lord Wakefields at RAF Saint Athans, an Inter Command Competition at RAF Locking, and then the RAF Championships at RAF Cosford, before which I spent ten days training with the Strike Command team at RAF Wyton. In addition I had to take embarkation leave and some annual leave. I can honestly say that I cannot remember what work I did in SSQ as I was hardly ever there! I was on the duty after hours roster, which entailed staying in the SSQ overnight, and in turn for the entire weekend. There was ample compensation for any weekend duty, which was to go off duty on Thursday morning after working Wednesday night, until Monday morning. As my married quarters remained at RAF Colerne, I went home every weekend, usually hitch hiking unless I used one of my free railway warrants. I therefore did not see anything of the night life in Lincoln, or indeed on the camp. In February 1969, and I expect much to the relief of the staff of SSQ, who must have hoped that my replacement would be slightly more productive, I returned to Colerne to pack up for the posting to Cyprus.

10. Cyprus

What seemed like a straightforward journey to RAF Akrotiri along with my family, by a Britannia aircraft from RAF Lyneham, became very tiresome. After a delay of a few hours, the flight was cancelled. The replacement flight was a VC10 aircraft from RAF Brize Norton, which would soon become the standard method of travel to Cyprus. The off loaded passengers had to transfer by bus to Brize Norton, which added to the overall travelling time, and meant that mine and the other children on the flight would be getting very tired, and now faced an overnight flight. The good news was that the flight time by a VC10 was less than the ancient Britannias, and anyway my two children enjoyed the experience and even got some sleep during the flight. So on a sunny but cool February morning, we all arrived safely at RAF Akrotiri for the start of a three year tour. After the usual arrival formalities, most of the families were transported to hotels in Limassol, where they would stay for a few days until suitable accommodation had been found. I was met by a Corporal Eddy Bourne from the SSQ at RAF Akrotiri, and he subsequently helped me to find privately rented accommodation in Limassol, and generally settle in, which only took a couple of days. I then reported in to SSQ at RAF Akrotiri was about 10 miles from Limassol.

Whilst 1969 to 1972 was a peaceful period in the history of Cyprus, Akrotiri was a huge airbase, which played a key role in the Central Treaty Organisation, (CENTO), at the time of the so called cold War with the Soviet Union. There was a perceived threat of the expansion of the Soviet Union via what was termed, 'the soft underbelly of Europe'. The station was still an important staging post for flights to the Middle and Far East where the British was still maintaining a military presence. Akrotiri was also certainly unique in the number of sub units either on the base or under it's control. The station was home to a Vulcan Bomber Squadron, a Fighter Squadron of Lightning Jet Fighters, a Transport Flight with Argosy aircraft, and a flight of Whirlwind helicopters. There was a large maintenance unit, a hospital, and a signals unit on the Troodos mountain. There was a RAF Regiment Wing with two Squadrons, one of which was often on detachment, and three rescue teams consisting of Mountain Rescue, Air Sea Rescue based in the port of Limassol, and most importantly for me a Parachute team. The station was considered so large and important that it was commanded by an Air Commodore, and during most of my tour, this was Air Commodore Stacey.

The SSQ was therefore a busy place, with a large RAF staff, and also some local civilians, plus some dependants of service personnel. There was three RAF Medical officers, and mainly male administrative and nursing staff. The local civilians were responsible for all the cleaning, cooking of the patients meals, and two worked in the office and provided some good continuity. There was several wards which catered mainly for the minor illnesses of the single airmen living on camp in communal accommodation. The nursing was carried out mainly be the male nursing attendants, under the supervision of a male State Registered Nurse. There was no WRAF living on the camp at that time. A civilian nurse was also employed to deal with the families who lived on the base and who were registered with the RAF Medical Officers at SSQ. There was a clinic in Limassol staffed by personnel from RAF Episkopi, for families living off base. The working arrangements were reasonable, particularly in the summer when the normal working day was from 7 a.m. to 1.30 p.m, on Monday through to Saturdays. The after hours duties were covered by teams of three corporals and three airmen who would work a 24 hour shift followed by 48 hours off duty. The after duty hours cover, changed half way through my tour, whereby all the RAF staff other than the two senior NCOs did their share of duties. I personally thought that system whereby just some of the staff, carried out all the duties, for which they had compensatory time off, was better than the disruption caused when the entire staff were working irregular hours, even if only something like once a week. However compared to some previous units, the duties were not onerous. My first job was to join the after duty team, and during the morning office hours, to occupy myself with recording admissions to SSQ and the hospital for statistical purposes. I therefore wasted no time in making enquiries about joining the Parachute Rescue team as soon as possible!

Shortly after I started work at SSQ, I had to spend two weeks at RAF Troodos, which was a signals unit at the top of the 6,000 foot mountain of the same name. At the time, the staff at SSQ took it turns to man a small medical centre at this unit. Later that same year, it was decided that a SAC would be permanently stationed there, and the first airman to occupy the post on this basis, was SAC Steve Woods who I knew from RAF Colerne. It was clearly unfair that I should have to spend time away from my family in

Limassol so soon after arrival, but according to the deputy SNCO in charge at the time, a Sergeant Jim Pearson, there was supposed to have been no other option. However when Flight Sergeant Fred Foster who was the SNCO in charge, returned from leave, other options were explored with Sergeant Pearson, but by this time I had done my stint. It was one of those occasions where I had to obey an order that I considered unjust, but happily this was not a regular occurrence in the RAF, or at least not in my experience of the Medical Branch.

After my experiences at Lusaka where few airmen ever darkened the door of the sick quarters, and at Nocton Hall where I passed away the time in the afternoon walking the Registrar's dog, I was partly prepared for two weeks of doing very little actual work at RAF Troodos. There was a doctors surgery, but only once a week when the Medical Officer from Akrotiri made a visit to the unit, and which also incorporated a clinic for the families of airmen on the base who lived in the village of Platres a few miles away down the mountain. At other times urgent cases would be transported down the mountain to Akrotiri. Any accident victims would be given first aid, and taken to the hospital at Akrotiri by ambulance escorted by the resident nursing attendant. There was a male SRN based in Platres, mainly to look after the service families, but who also attended Troodos every morning to assist with any advice of treatment that may have been needed. Except for attending the small medical room on the Troodos base in the morning, I had nothing to do for the rest of day, other than to be on call for emergencies. Due to the altitude, the first few days on the mountain were slightly tiring as I acclimatised. At the time I was not training for boxing, so I took very little exercise other than an occasional walk. March was not the best time of the year to be at Troodos. The winter snow had melted, but it was still cold and there seemed little to do with all my spare time. Because I was on call for emergencies, I stayed away from the small NAAFI club bar, and the only other entertainment was a small cinema. On a Saturday afternoon just before my two week stint ended, I was called out to an accident on one of the steep and narrow mountain roads. A RAF airmen in a Land Rover, had seemingly misjudged a bend, and had skidded of the road. Fearing for his life if he stayed with the vehicle, he threw himself out of it, as the vehicle began what may have been a fatal descent down the mountainside. Two off duty nursing officers were at the scene when I arrived. The driver had been knocked unconscious, but was supposed to be otherwise OK. I put him on a stretcher and went with him to the Casualty Department at the RAF Akrotiri Hospital. The casualty was drifting in and out of consciousness throughout the journey, and I later learned that he had a broken leg. Whilst in theory I perhaps ought to have examined him myself before departing from the scene of the accident, it was accepted this would not have seemed necessary. Two days later I was back at Akrotiri, and did not have do any further stints at Troodos.

Shortly after my return from Troodos, life in general improved a great deal Thanks to a significant pay increase due to overseas allowances, and also to cars being available duty free to servicemen in Cyprus, I was able to buy a new car on hire purchase over two years. The car was a VW Beetle and this enabled my family to get around much easier, and also to be able to visit many of the Island's beaches, now that the weather was becoming increasingly hot. In the summer time, the normal working day ended at 1.30 p.m., and the nearby beach at Ladies Mile near RAF Akrotiri, was a favourite afternoon excursion, as this spot was much cooler than Limassol. After a few months in the rented house, we moved to official service accommodation, called a 'hiring'. This was a pleasant three-bedroom bungalow, still in Limassol. The hiring was fully furnished and cost less to rent than the previous house. There was a good social life with many meals out with friends at SSQ and also neighbours, who were also service dependants. Limassol had plenty of discos and bars with live music, and several service cinemas including an open air cinema in Limassol in addition to those on the bases. There was also a Services Families Club, but this was not so popular other than for teenagers who had their own discos and entertainment there. The most popular meal out was a kebab. This meal consisted of several courses of assorted barbecued meats, accompanied by salad and chapatti bread, and spread out over a couple of hours. The cost of the kebab included local wine, and was very inexpensive. There would be music to dance to in between courses, sometimes live but usually a disco.

The music at the disco was much the same as 1968, in that British groups dominated the charts, and the Beatles and the Rolling Stones both had number one hits. It was the final year of The Beatles as a group and they signed off with their final number ones, 'Get Back' and 'The Ballad of John and Yoko'. The latter hit denied Elvis another number one hit as his 'In The Ghetto' could get no higher than second. The Rolling Stones took 'Honky Tonk Women' to the top spot, and this was to be one of their all time biggest hits which was always included in their concerts right up to 2006! As in 1968, there was also some unusual novelty type big number ones such as 'Lily the Pink' by The Scaffold, Desmond Decker's 'The Israelites', and Zager and Evan's 'In The Year 2525'. One of that years unforgettable number one hits was 'Je T'Aime' by Jane Birkin and Serge Gainsburg. This consisted of Jane and Serge seemingly making love to music, with sexy sounding French dialogue and lots of suggestive sighing etc. It was a big favourite in discos for years. Another slightly unusual record, 'Sugar Sugar' by The Archies, which was a huge transatlantic double number one hit, also kept Elvis from the number one spot with his 'Suspicious Minds'. The Archies were unusual as they were a manufactured band similar to The Monkees, but were all cartoon characters.

After things had started to improve for me socially, my service life also improved when I joined the Near East Air Force (NEAF) Parachute Rescue Team. I had to first obtain medical clearance, and then undergo some ground training, under the watchful eye of the Parachute Jump Instructor (PJI), based at Akrotiri for the team. The skill required to execute parachute type landings and rolls is a little like riding a bike, and I was soon able to be considered fit to jump again, 15 months after my last jump and back injury in Libya. So on the 20th June 1969, I boarded a Argosy feeling very apprehensive about my comeback jump. It turned out to be very easy. I jumped second in a con stick of just 3 parachutists, and without any extra equipment, and made a good landing. I had made the team, and would start to earn parachute pay, and best of all had I now had the means of escape from the office, for one or two mornings a week. There would also be CENTO exercises in Turkey and Iran, another exercise in the Persian Gulf and two trips to Kenya. Both service life along with my personal and social life had now improved considerably in the four months since arriving in Cyprus.

Before my tour in Cyprus ended in February 1972, I had completed 67 more jumps, which brought my total to exactly 100. I did not jump again after this tour, mainly because the only opportunity to do so, at least to be paid for jumping, would have been to go back to 2 Squadron. Whilst I may have enjoyed rejoining the squadron, there was also a fair chance that I may not. I was however certain that I would not want to spend time away from my family, particularly now that at the end of the Cyprus tour, they were aged 6 and 8. I would have to rely now on sport to get me out of the office now and then, or at least for a good few years, when I took the opportunity to be a Flight Nursing Attendant (FNA). I will not write about all the remaining 66 jumps, other than mainly those undertaken on exercise, or any jumps that were in some way or other different from the normal. The vast majority of my remaining drops were onto Ladies Mile DZ at Akrotiri, and usually on a Friday morning, for no particular reason other than that was the day set aside for parachuting by the Transport Squadron planners. There would be a session of ground training each week, which became compulsory before a jump.

After four of the standard Friday morning drops onto Ladies Mile, all from an Argosy, I had the first of two water jumps into Akrotiri Bay. This required mastering a technique whereby just before touching the sea, the parachute harness is released so that it does not encumber you in the water. If the parachute is abandoned too soon, then a fatal injury might occur. All the parachutists wore the standard inflatable life jacket called a Mae West, which had to be inflated on impact with the sea, and not before. Along with the rest of the team, I made a safe landing, and the only danger seemed to come from the RAF Air Sea Rescue launch that was rounding up the parachutists, which occasionally got too close for my liking. The very next day, I had the first of two jumps from a helicopter. This was from a Whirlwind onto Ladies Mile. The exit technique in the aircraft was for the parachutist to sit on the floor, and then shuffle forward to sit on the sill of the open door, then push off on the word 'go'. As with a balloon jump, there would be a sickly feeling, but this would be mainly eliminated by looking up after exit, which I did. My first year on the team concluded with three more jumps from an Argosy onto Ladies Mile.

In 1970, I made 33 jumps with the team, starting out with nine in the first two months, one of which was another from a Whirlwind Helicopter. All the jumps were made at a DZ at Evdimu, near Episkopi. This was partly due to the flocks of flamingos, who were breeding near the Ladies Mile DZ. In 1971 and 1972 we also did not use this DZ in January and February. The Evdimu DZ was a ploughed field, so there were no hard landings for a couple of months. When parachuting started again at Ladies Mile, I had two reminders that there was an element of danger involved. On one occasion we were cleared to jump in what was at least borderline weather due to strong gusts of wind. After 58 jumps, and I was reasonably experienced by this time, I hit the ground at some speed due to strong winds and injured my shoulder, although no bones were broken. Later there was a fatal accident when a member of the RAF Falcons Free Fall Parachute Display Team was blown off away from the DZ, and drowned in the nearby sea. Before this accident, life jackets were never worn, even though the approach to the DZ was over the sea, and the DZ itself not far from the sea. Following the accident, we were all required to wear a life jacket for parachuting at Ladies Mile.

Whilst the team were very well trained in the parachute role, they had seldom been in action. Before I joined the team in 1969, there had been at least one 'hearts and minds' operation. The circumstances were that a woman on a small Greek Island, was having complications with childbirth and required urgent medical attention. The island was not accessible by boat, due to very rough seas. The RAF then stepped in and a RAF doctor with other medical staff, parachuted in and saved the life of the mother and her child. In my time on the team which covered almost 3 years, there was only one incident when the medical team might have been utilised. This was when a small ship had gone missing, and a search was being carried out. Myself and one of the two Medical Officers on the team, a Flight Lieutenant Stothers, joined a search aircraft complete with all the equipment required for a parachute descent into the sea, plus medical equipment to treat casualties until rescued by another vessel or by helicopter. Presumably the search was outside the range of helicopter or an air sea rescue vessel. The ship was not located and we returned to Akrotiri, without our moment of glory! There was never any proper system for a call out of the team in after duty hours, so it was presumably considered very unlikely that the team would ever be called out at relatively short notice, if at all. With the presence on the team of RAF Regiment gunners, and other non-medical personnel, the team clearly had another role to play, which may remain classified information to this day. Parachute training continued throughout the summer of 1970, and I completed another 8 jumps at Ladies mile, which included a Sim 25 from an Argosy, which was the largest number I ever jumped with, and I noted in my Log Book, that this was a demonstration jump for CENTO officers. This was no doubt a rehearsal for a forthcoming CENTO exercise in Turkey.

In September 1971 I joined the NEAF Para Rescue team on the annual CENTO exercise, which this year took place in Turkey. The host country for this annual exercise, rotated between Turkey, Iran and Cyprus when it was the UK's turn. These three countries were joined by the United States Air Force which was operating out of military bases in Turkey. The exercise lasted one week, and each of the four CENTO member countries provided aircraft. The UK supplied two Argosy Aircraft plus the Para Rescue Team. The teams were all based at the Andana Air Force base, which was a shared facility with the United Sates Air Force. Whilst the accommodation was reasonable for a week's stay, the food in the Turkish Air Force Mess, whilst supplied free of charge by the Turkish hosts, was not palatable to us. After the first meal which was very unappetising, partly because we were unsure what it was we were eating, the Medical Officer with the team, A Flight Lieutenant Nansen who was normally based at the RAF Hospital Akrotiri, was easily persuaded to sign the necessary official RAF forms which would enable the team, to be compensated in advance by the payment of lots of American dollars, which could then be spent eating at the American Air Force messes. We therefore had a week eating inexpensive and appetising American food. It was just like a holiday, with just two parachute jumps thrown in!

The first of the two jumps, was at a DZ near Tarsa, in which we dropped in sticks of sim fours carrying our medical equipment. On landing we simply walked off the DZ and were then driven back to Andana. The next day, we dropped at a DZ near the Andana base, again in Sim fours, but this time we were required to treat mock casualties. These were local Turkish forces, so to make it easy, if not too easy, each casualty wore a bib which described his injuries in English! The team performed brilliantly of course, and then returned to the base to continue the week's break! We were made very welcome in the American Forces social clubs, and enjoyed at least two nights at dances. On the first occasion the club was packed, and a live rock group was playing. The following night, there was another dance but the club was only half full. The group was just as good if not better than the previous night, so one of the Para team asked an American airman sat at the bar why this was. He simply replied, 'Tonight is soul night'! We then realised what he really meant, which was that this was the night when mainly black Americans, or whatever they were called in the 1970s military, had their night with their music! In addition to the music, I enjoyed playing the fruit machines which had an apparently higher percentage of payout, and huge jackpots. I subsequently managed to win several jackpots and was a lot better off when the team returned to Cyprus. I was also weighed down with a large amount of goods, such as toys and records bought from the American equivalent of the British NAAFI, the PX. This was the best military exercise I had ever experienced before or since, even though the next two with the team, were also very enjoyable!

Back at the SSQ, a Flight Sergeant Lloyd had replaced Fred Foster at the end of the previous year. He had different ideas regarding the management of staff, which was of course to be expected. One of his previous posts had been at the RAF Records Office at RAF Innsworth, in which he acquired a very good knowledge of the standards in the trade group, and therefore knew what could or should be expected of the Nursing Attendants, and other Medical Administrative trades. He invariably adopted a quiet but firm and fair approach to his management position, and was a very effective manager. The duty roster was now shared amongst all the staff, other than the two Senior NCOs, one of whom was the SRN in charge of the wards and the treatment room. I was put in joint charge of the Medical Stores with another Corporal, and whilst this was hard work at times, such as the monthly stocktaking of drugs, and annual stocktaking of equipment, I did have a fair degree of autonomy, and could plan my workload accordingly. I could for example take a trip to the Medical Equipment Deport which was based near the RAF Hospital, when I wanted a break or change of scene.

On the home and social side, things were much the same as the first year. In the summer there was trips to the nearby Ladies Mile beach of an afternoon, and trips to other beaches at the weekend or periods of annual leave. The most scenic parts of the island were in the North, and whilst they could be reached after a couple of hours by car, once most had been visited a couple of times, the longish drive in the hot weather was not something to undertake regularly. Trips to the capital Nicosia, where also infrequent, mainly for the same reason. I can only recall two visits to Nicosia. One was to see a special exhibition after the first moon landing, as the event was not shown live on Cyprus TV, and the only other occasion was to go to as horse race meeting.

The number one hit records of 1970, were evenly split between the UK and the USA with seven for each country. Elvis was still at the top, but his sole number one hit of 1970, 'The Wonder of You' was to be his last whilst he was still alive. His 'Way Down' which topped the charts in 1977 was after his untimely death. Unusual records remained a feature with Hank Marvin singing his way to the top with 'Wandering Star', and the Norman Greenbaum's 'Spirit In The Sky. It was a Football World Cup year, and the England team had a number one hit singing 'Back Home', which was of course much more successful that their team performance when they lost to West Germany in the quarter finals after leading 2-0.

At the end of 1969, I tried to get some boxing training started on camp. There was a facility for boxing with the usual bags and a ring, but no team or trainer. There was also very little boxing going on in Cyprus either service or civilian. However there was a limited amount of interest, and whilst the training petered out in the summer months, it started again in the autumn of 1970, this time with a proper trainer, Neil Hempstead. The two main members of the team were SAC Ian Pinks, and SAC Lloyd Oliver. Both had been successful RAF boxers before they were posted to Cyprus. The focus of our training became the forthcoming RAF Championships at RAF Wattisham in January 1971. We considered that a week or more off work and a free trip back to the UK would be possible, which was something of an incentive of course.

After all the excitement of the CENTO exercise, it was back to training jumps at Ladies Mile. I brought my total of jumps up to 76 after a further 7 jumps. The first 5 were from an Argosy, and then the C130 Hercules took over, and other than a helicopter jump, the remainder of my jumps would all be from Hercules. It was the end of an era of jumping from old aircraft such as Hastings and Beverley. After a jump on 18 December there was a 4 month gap before the next jump, either for operational reasons or those flamingos again!

At SSQ, I was not required to work over Christmas, as the single airmen who lived on the camp volunteered to provide cover. After the Christmas break, those including myself who did not work over the holiday, did extra duties so that the volunteers could be compensated. On New Years Eve, I therefore did an after hours duty with Corporal Eddy Bourne. Eddie and myself had made a New Year resolution to stop smoking. This was something that I had not attempted for about 10 years, and reflected my aim to do well at the RAF Boxing Championships. At 10 minutes to midnight, we lit up what we had decided was our final cigarette, before we ushered in the New Year. About 30 minutes into the new year, I responded to an emergency call to a road traffic accident a few miles away from the camp on the road to Limassol. On the way there, I broke my resolution. When the ambulance driver lit up as usual on the way to the scene, I joined him! I did however otherwise keep to my resolution for a week, but only as far as smoking cigarettes was concerned, as I then started to smoke small cigars. The inevitable return to smoking followed, initially with a resolve to just cut down.

In early January, I travelled to UK with the RAF Akrotiri boxing squad of just two boxers, Ian Pinks and myself, and the trainer, Neil Hempstead. On arrival at RAF Brize Norton, I stayed with Ian at his parents home on the Brize Norton base for a couple of days, before meeting up with Neil at RAF Wattisham the day before the start of the Championship. Whilst serving in the RAF in Cyprus was certainly not arduous or unpleasant, we both really enjoyed being back in England, even in cold, frosty and foggy weather. We particularly enjoyed the taste of food such as bread, which was a problem for Ian as he always had a good appetite, and could not afford to put on weight before the start of the boxing when he had to make the light middleweight weight limit at the weigh-in before the contests commenced. On the Saturday before the start of the competition, we travelled first to RAF Wyton to meet up with some of Ian's friends and other boxers, and then on the Sunday afternoon, we travelled to a fog bound RAF Wattisham. The journey was particularly memorable as the taxi driver taking us from the railway station, overshot a turning to the camp, saying as he did so in a broad local accent, which was reminiscent of Alan Smethers, (the Singing Postman of the 1960s), that he often missed this turning in the fog. He then reversed the taxi, notwithstanding the fog, to get back onto the Wattisham road. The next chapter will relate the further excitement of the boxing!

After a gap of 4 months, parachuting on Ladies Mile started once again on 23 April, when I had what the first of what would be my last ever 24 jumps to reach the magic total of 100. The next jump was slightly unusual as it took place at night, which was one of only three night descents the team undertook during my tour. Four jumps later I had another hard landing in high winds, and injured by shoulder. This was on yet another demonstration jump for visiting CENTO officers, so no doubt the conditions which were at best borderline! The remainder of my jumps were carried out safely.

After 3 months back at SSQ following my trip to UK for the RAF Championships, it was time to go on another 'jolly' as sporting trips were often described. This time it was trip to Bahrain with a combined RAF and Army team of boxers from Cyprus. The arrival in Cyprus of the Royal Green Jackets a few months earlier, resulted in a revival of boxing in the service community. There was still insufficient RAF participation for a inter-services tournament in Cyprus, but a tournament with a combined services team at

Bahrain was arranged. The RAF members in the team were Ian Pinks and myself, who were joined by SAC Llloyd (Ollie) Oliver. We spent about a week away from Cyprus and apart from one single training session in a gym soon after we arrived, and just one bout each, we had a most enjoyable week's holiday. It was also very interesting for me to see the changes to the RAF camp at Muharraq that had taken place since I left 10 years earlier. As often it seems to be the case, when the British are due to quit a base, there were lots of new buildings such as barrack blocks and also a hospital. The British forces were due to leave Bahrain in a few months time by mutual agreement with the Bahrain government, although they would be destined to operate out of Muharraq, as agreed with the Bahranis, for future operations in the area. The newly built hospital was already running down, and had only a very small staff remaining. When I went there to have a look round, I was greatly amused to see the hospital telephone system had seemingly remained unchanged, and as a result the same person answered all the phones quoting the name of the almost extinct departments such as, Out Patients, Admissions Office etc., which he knew was ludicrous, but it also amused him! After an enjoyable week, I returned back to Cyprus for the summer months, after which there would be three more trips with the Para team, and another back to UK for boxing, all in my final 4 months at Akrotiri.

Meanwhile my very good social life continued, and now included friendship and social occasions with fellow boxers Ian Pinks and Ollie Oliver and their wives. Ollie was a singer and guitarist in a rock group called 'The New Edition' who played at local venues, and I became one of his fan club members! In the summer months, I had a two week camping holiday with my family. This was split between Troodos and Aya Napa (which was then a very small peaceful place), and both spots were pleasantly cooler than Limassol. The Troodos climate was cooler due to the altitude of 6,000 feet, and at Aya Napa, there was invariably a pleasant sea breeze. When the summer hours routine commenced at RAF Akrotiri, I finished work at 1.30 p.m. on most days, other then when it was my turn to do after hours duty. After finishing work, I would get into my VW Beetle, and with the windows wide open because of the heat, head off home to Limassol as fast I could. As soon as I had left the camp area, off would come my uniform shirt and cap for the 10 mile drive, and I would always turn up the car radio to listen to the latest pop music on BFBS radio. If I were to choose one tune which would remind me of those days, and was typical of the eclectic mix in the pop charts for 1971, it would have to be the Waldo de los Rios's version of 'Mozart 40' which reached as high as number 5 in the top 20 pop chart.

The comparatively hectic schedule of activity with the Para Team commenced with a very brief exercise at Sharjah at the end of September. This involved the team parachuting into the desert at the Sharjah, and nothing very strenuous afterwards. After landing the team were met by the RAF Sharjah Desert Rescue Team, who had erected tents for the team to spend the night. They had also brought food and some beer on ice! It was dark by the time we had settled in, and that was the end of the first day of the exercise. After a pleasant evening meal, some beers and a good sleep, we set off early in the morning on a compass bearing, towards a rendezvous point a few miles away, where we were met again by the Desert Rescue Team and transported back to RAF Sharjah. After a trip into Dubai for some duty free shopping, we spent a night on the camp before returning to Akrotiri the next day. I hope that the staff at SSQ thought that I had been engaged on something slightly more strenuous!

Shortly after the desert exercise, the team were engaged on a somewhat unusual operation, which was connected to a private visit to Kenya by Prince Charles, and by Princess Anne in her role as the newly appointed President of the Save The Children Fund, and who was also accompanied by the Valerie Singleton and a production team of the children's television programme 'Blue Peter'. For reasons which I still do not know, the Royal Flight which was a VC10 aircraft was accompanied by two C130 Hercules, both of which contained members of the NEAF Para Rescue Team. Due to the slower speed of the Hercules, one of the two aircraft flew ahead of the VC10. This level of backup for presumably any untoward incident, was in my experience unprecedented, and begged the question of why such a visit was being undertaken if this level of backup was deemed necessary. Whatever the reason, the team enjoyed two weekend trips to Nairobi with stays at decent hotels and a good allowance for our meals. Presumably the cost of accommodating the team in Nairobi for two weeks, was either too expensive or the Hercules were required for other tasks, so the team returned to Cyprus after the inbound trip, and returned two weeks later for the return leg. Our stay in Nairobi was very brief, but for some of the team including myself, it was spent at the famous Stanley Hotel which seemed to have changed very little since colonial days.

In complete contrast to the luxury of the Stanley Hotel, the next assignment for the Para team was the annual CENTO exercise. This was held at Bandar Abbas in Iran and involved the team being accommodated in some basic temporary accommodation at a civilian airport. The food was slightly more international than that offered by the Turkish forces the previous year, but was not to our liking. However there was a good restaurant in the vicinity where we could at least eat a good main meal. As we were advised not to drink local tap water, we received a generous allowance to purchase drinks in sealed containers, and as the local tinned beer was inexpensive, we made the very best of things! Due to adverse operating conditions, in the week that we were involved in the exercise, the team made only one jump, and that was without any equipment. I assume that the team were a mere adjunct to the exercise which involved aircraft from Iran, Turkey, USA and UK. It was on the whole, a very boring week spent mainly hanging around the airport.

After returning from Iran, I had my final 5 parachute jumps, which were all out of a Hercules onto the Ladies Mile DZ. All the jumps took place over a 3 week period. I had in mind, my 100 jump target before the end of the year, when there would probably be an annual break, and also when it would be the end of my tour with the Para Team. Because I had been parachuting regularly, I was really enjoying the experience, particularly when for four of the last five jumps, I was jumping at number one. I liked the excitement of standing by the door with one eye on the ground below, and another on the red/green light, waiting for the green and 'go' command from the dispatcher. Whilst the parachutes in use at the time could be partly controlled by assessing the direction and speed of any drift, it was not easy to land and remain standing, which was known as doing a 'stand up'. The practice of trying for a 'stand up' was discouraged, and parachutists were told that they should carry out a parachute type roll immediately on landing. However this instruction was often ignored when there was little wind, and many of the more experienced members of the team would achieve 'stand ups' whenever possible. On my final jump, the team jumped in a Sim 15 formation, and for some reason I had to jump at number 3 starboard, rather than my favourite number 1 port. I was determined to end my tour with a 'stand up' on my 100th jump, and I was pleased when I managed this quite easily. I had laid on a crate of beer for the team to celebrate my 100th and final jump, and before returning to work at SSQ, I had a drink on the DZ, and also a chat with the Station

Commander Air Commodore Stacey, who had also parachuted in on the same drop.

My 100 jumps and time with the team was commemorated later at the annual team Christmas Party, when I was presented with an inscribed tankard. I still have the tankard which has a significant slight dent on the base, when the tankard slipped off the top of my head when it was full of beer and I was fooling round a little at the party! As was the case during the previous two Christmas periods, there was also a SSQ Christmas party to attend, and many other social occasions with a large circle of friends, many of which, 35 years on, I am still in touch with.

With less than 2 months to the end of my posting at Cyprus in February 1972,, I had yet another trip back to the UK for the RAF Boxing Championships in January. This time I was on my own, but I greatly enjoyed meeting many of the boxers and officials who I knew very well by then. The championships were held at RAF Brize Norton this year, so I had no additional travel in the UK after landing at a snow covered Brize Norton, the day before the start of the competition. After the end of the championship, I spent another enjoyable six day holiday whilst waiting for a flight back to Cyprus. I am sure that the staff at SSQ hoped that my replacement would spend a lot more time there than I ever did!

A few weeks after arriving back at Akrotiri, I was packing up ready to leave for my next posting. This was to RAF Halton, and specifically the hospital, which was entitled The Princess Mary's RAF Hospital Halton. The location suited me as I had asked for posting to the south of England. This was not because I particularly wanted to live down south, but mainly because there was many stations in Lincolnshire, Norfolk plus others in the North that I did not particularly fancy for one reason or another. Somehow or other, I had managed to accumulate some annual leave, and that coupled with two weeks disembarkation leave, meant that it would be several weeks before I started work at the hospital. During this long leave, I moved into a RAF rented house on a very pleasant private estate in Aylesbury for what was to become a stay of over four years, and the longest ever stay at one unit for all my 25 years in the RAF.

11. My Boxing Career

My boxing career was once described as illustrious. However this was the word used by a RAF Medical Officer on a referral note, which he hoped might persuade a plastic surgeon to consider spending time changing the shape of my nose! The referral was made after I finally hung up my gloves, if that is what boxers are supposed to do when they retire, after a period covering 13 years, but which included several years of inactivity. In total I had 26 bouts if I count every single time I entered the ring, but I much prefer to ignore the first half dozen which were unrecorded on my Boxing Medical record, and were all at what was the wrong weight limit for me, due to my inexperience and lack of expert advice. I might therefore to be able to claim a more even split between wins and losses, with 10 wins and 10 defeats. Furthermore, there is also an additional 'win' recorded in my now dog eared record book, that on closer inspection is actually a 'walk over'. This term describes a situation when an opponent in an official tournament fails to be available for some reason, so the other boxer is declared the winner. This is only after the other contestant has entered the boxing ring in his boxing kit, and has then walked over to the opposite corner to touch the corner post and then walked back to his own corner, usually to polite applause! In my account of my career, I have strived to record as accurate an account as possible, based mainly on my memory of events, but backed up by official records such as my Boxing Medical Record Card. I note that the Record Card which did not exist when I commenced my boxing career in 1960, but was issued to me in 1966 is headed ' Imperial Services Boxing Association' and that an official has deleted 'Imperial' and substituted ' Combined', which I consider to be an interesting piece of historical evidence.

The first of my initial six bouts, which I think could be disregarded in respect of my overall tally took place at RAF Steamer Point in late 1960. My weight at the time was around 9 stone, and I entered the Middle East Command Championships in the lightweight division, which was for boxers who 'weighed in' before the bout under 9 stone 7 pounds. I would probably have been able to 'weigh in' under 9 stone and thereby compete as a Featherweight, that is under 9 stone, but I did not appreciate the difference at the time. 47 years on, I can still recall the excitement of not only the actual bout, but also the build up to it such as entering the ring and the announcements. Of course the boxers were simply introduced by an Master of Ceremonies who would just say 'In the red corner, Corporal Thompson, representing RAF Bahrain and in the blue corner...' and nothing like the ring announcers for present day professional boxing. The introductions would of course be accompanied by partisan cheering, and on this occasion mainly for me as an RAF boxer boxing an Army sergeant. I started off well in the first round, but I was feeling the pace and already breathing heavily. At the end of the second round, I became even more tired as I was being out boxed, and in the third round, the referee stopped the contest in favour of my opponent, 'to save further punishment' as is the official phrase when a contest becomes too one-sided. However everybody thought I had done well against a more experienced opponent, and I suffered no after effects and was undaunted.

The next year when I was stationed at RAF Henlow I joined what was a large station team, which was training for a novices boxing tournament, called the Lord Wakefield Championships. This was an annual event which took place in early November at different RAF Stations, and was open to boxers who had not previously won a novice championship and who could fairly be described as a novice. With National Service still in operation, the overall standard even at this level was high, and there was a large entry for the tournament which this year took place at RAF Bridgnorth. Those who were due to compete for the station were allowed time off work for the week before to train for the tournament, plus a week off for the actual tournament, providing the team had performed well, when the Station Commander would invariably grant a long weekend for the team.

I was selected to box for the station, again at lightweight. However, this time I made a good start and won my first round bout on points fairly comfortably on the first day. I was not scheduled to box in the next round until the next day, so I basked in the glory of still being in the tournament, when many had already been eliminated. In the next round, I made a nervous start wondering how much harder it might be up against somebody who had also won their first round bout. I finally got going in the third and last round, but it was not enough for the judges, who quite rightly awarded the decision to my opponent. It was my experience that there could be some perverse decisions in amateur and indeed professional boxing, so providing you went the distance, there was always hope.

On the strength of my win, I was invited to go to RAF Melksham for a trial with the Technical Training Command team. This involved a couple of days off work again altogether, but I was not selected after some sparring with other hopefuls. In early 1962 I had three more bouts at civilian shows, but all against RAF Boxers. The first two of these bouts were against more experienced boxers when I was outclassed, but I managed to go the distance and gain some experience. One of the bouts was with SAC Chris McMahon who went on to win the RAF championships. In my final bout of the season, I lost again in a much closer bout against a boxer who tended to indulge in some wild swinging punches. Whilst I evaded most of them, some blows did land, often on my nose as I dodged them. As a result, I sustained a deviated nasal septum, which required a surgical operation to improve my appearance and breathing. I subsequently had an operation that summer at PMRAF Hospital Halton. This involved the removal of a part of the nasal septum. I made a good recovery and was passed fit to box again in the autumn of the same year.

In the autumn, I had started to live out in Bedford after getting married, and my training was limited to sessions at lunchtime and runs at night. I entered the Lord Wakefield competition again, but this time there was no time off work to train, partly because there was not so many boxers taking part from RAF Henlow. This was doubly unfortunate as the tournament was taking place there. As National Service was almost at an end, the Lord Wakefield was to becoming dominated by young airmen from the ranks of the apprentices and boy entrants at large training camps such as Halton, Locking and Cosford. Whilst I was still only 23 years of age, I started to feel old, and when I was clearly out boxed by one of these youngsters, I felt ancient! With hindsight, the problem was that I was not training properly, but at the time, I thought it best not to continue boxing. It had been an interesting but largely unsuccessful venture to date.

My interest in boxing was revived after I joined 2 Field Squadron at Colerne. All but one of the stations boxers were members of the squadron, and I got to know them all, and I was also friendly with Mick Nolan who was a corporal cook on the squadron, and a good standard middleweight. We often trained together, and as he was also a RAF champion at race walking, I would accompany him on his training walks, by jogging alongside him. The big difference in our respective weights made sparring difficult, but Mick was willing to take it easy with me, so that at least I could get some benefit from a session in the ring. I had now moved down to featherweight, a weight which I could reach without any undue fasting etc. I therefore made my debut as a featherweight and made a comeback after a four year absence in October 1966 at the Transport Command Championships at RAF Lyneham. I went straight to the final which was against a Junior Tech Jeff King, who was probably one reason for the absence of any other featherweights! He was a useful boxer with a good punch, but below average size for a featherweight, and smaller than me. In the final I had to take the fight to him and not allow him to get into his stride. When he came in, I would get into a clinch and hang on until the referee parted us. These tactics were fine, but were too tiring for my level of fitness, and I was breathing very heavily at the end of the first round. As I tired in the second round, Jeff was starting to unload some good punches, and soon after a mandatory count of 8, the bout was stopped. Whilst I went through the motions of expressing disappointment at the referees decision, I was glad it was all over!

Two weeks later, I tried for the third time to win the Lord Wakefield Championship. As most of the other boxers on the squadron were too experienced for what was officially a novice tournament, there was only two boxers entered from Colerne. The other boxer was a SAC clerk sec, who was the same weight as me. As we could not both enter the competition at the same weight, and neither of us was willing to go up a weight to lightweight, I decided to go down to bantamweight, as I could not persuade him to lose the weight. As soon as I got to RAF Cosford, I had a weigh-in, and then started to sweat off a few pounds by wearing a 'sweat suit' whilst skipping and shadow boxing in a 'drying room'. This was a room in the barrack block which was primarily intended for drying wet clothes of the occupants. It was a little like a Turkish Bath, but it was very effective for rapid weight loss. Before most major tournaments of this type, there would often be some boxers in either a 'drying room' or in the station ' boiler room'. All the trainers knew where the best places to lose weight were. Nobody seemed unduly concerned at the effects of what was mainly extreme dehydration. Whilst I was in the 'drying room' at Cosford, I first met SAC Lloyd (Ollie) Oliver. He was also on a mission to reduce his weight down to bantamweight, and he was bigger than me. The reason Ollie was losing weight, was that he thought that he would have a better chance of winning the championship at bantam-weight than at featherweight, because there was a featherweight boxer taking part who looked to be the hot favourite to win that division.

The next morning I managed to weigh in at bantamweight and so did Ollie. This we both achieved by not taking in any liquid until after the weigh in. I cannot imagine what we actually weighed after rehydrating as much as possible and eating breakfast. It must have been debatable if I would ever manage to weigh in again at this weight again, should I have proceeded past the first round in the competition. As it happened I did not need to bother trying again, and have never ever got my weight down to below 8 stone 7 since, even when I was running over a 100 miles a week. In the ring I met a young Craft apprentice called Playle, who was smaller than myself, not surprisingly. If he was at all concerned at meeting an older and bigger boxer, he did not show it. Fortunately for me, he was not a big puncher, and his tactics were to attack at speed and then move swiftly out of reach. He completely out-boxed me and I lost on points. Before I left the ring, his trainer congratulated me on a sporting contest. He must have been worried about his boxer. Later in the day, I met up with Ollie – in the NAAFI club bar of course! I asked him how he had got on, and he related that he had suffered the same fate as myself against another fast young boxer. Ollie explained that the young so and so was far too fast, and he hardly could hardly manage to lay a glove on him. I think that we both felt better after swapping stories over a pint or two. We had certainly both learned our lesson and Ollie went on to win the competition as a featherweight the following year, whilst I succeeded two years later, after having to miss that year whilst serving in Aden.

Regardless of yet another defeat at the Wakefield's, I was invited to join the Transport Command Boxing team for a week's training and then the annual inter command boxing competition at RAF Halton. The training took place at RAF Lyneham, and there I met up with Jeff King again, and got to know many of the boxers, particularly some of those based at Lyneham, which then had a good team. The training was normally split into three sessions a day, commencing with a run early in the morning, and then a session in the gym before lunch. After a long lunch break, there would usually be a sparring session in the gym. The evenings would be free, and were usually spent in the NAAFI club which was a very lively place, with a weekly dance every Thursday. The Lyneham based boxers seemed to know many of the WRAFs stationed on the base, and they therefore seemed happy to spend a lot of their time in the NAAFI. I cannot recall them making any trips to nearby Swindon. Whilst the partaking of a couple of pints to relax at night, did not present much of a problem for fit young men, it could cause unwanted weight gains. This was a particular problem for a boxer called Sammy Harvey, who was also a featherweight, and otherwise an SAC based at Lyneham who worked on an aircraft servicing flight. Sammy was a very likeable Irishman who liked to drink Guinness, which meant that to stay below the featherweight limit, he had to lose weight by the traditional method of exercising in boiler rooms – unknown to the trainer, or so he thought anyway. On one memorable occasion, he asked me to join him on one of his weight loss exercise sessions, to time him and keep him company. When we walked from our accommodation, to the boiler room, we passed some vending machines. Sammy then ate a meat pastie and drank a coffee, explaining as he consumed these that he did not like exercising on an empty stomach! I knew what he meant, but it was so funny, I have never forgotten it.

At the start of week two, the team moved to RAF Halton for the competition. At that time, there was eight home commands, and the boxing championships were initially spilt into two groups of four commands, with the winner of each group competing later in a grand final. Transport Command had a fairly big squad, but would always have a problem against Technical Training Command which had a good pool of young boxers to pick from, because the Apprentice and Boy Entrant units were in that command. The four Command teams would have matches against the other three teams in their half of the draw. This was to lead to some shrewd tactical moves, particularly in the featherweight division. Jeff King was probably the best featherweight, but the Transport Command trainer decided to rest him against the best boxer in Technical Training, a young apprentice who had just won the Wakefields. The strategy being that Jeff King would then be fresh to take on the comparatively weaker opponents in the remaining matches, and be almost certain to take maximum points, whereas if he boxed the young apprentice in the first bout, he could possibly lose, or not be so strong for the other two bouts. Sammy Harvey was preferred to me, to take on the young boxer. He subsequently lost after a very hard contest with a very tenacious and tough boxer. Afterwards he joked about the way his opponent had entered the ring. Instead of the usual boxing dressing gown with the name of the RAF Station emblazoned on the back, he just had a scruffy raincoat over his shoulders, which he probably used to look tough! Sammy was honest enough to admit being concerned at the sight of this young man's entrance. I returned to Colerne without having a bout this time, but after a most enjoyable two weeks off work.

I continued to be a member of the Transport Command team, and attended two more competitions with their boxers. As I was stationed at Colerne, in January of the following year, I joined in with the RAF Lyneham boxers at a civilian tournament at Bristol, which took place at the Hartcliffe Boxing Club. I was the very last on the bill, and boxed a young local boxer, whom I managed to outpoint for a very welcome win. I got some teasing about taking so long, and thereby having reduced the team's drinking time at the nearby pub. There was also a good deal of amusement at my prize for winning, which was a chip pan! The next outing with the Transport Command team also resulted in an amusing ending. This was a trip to RAF Leconfield in Yorkshire, for an inter command contest in February 1967. Unfortunately the opposing team could not provide a featherweight boxer, so a bout was arranged between Sammy Harvey and myself. We were good friends by this time, but we did not really mind the match. We could just regard it as more or less sparring which we had done before in the gym. We had a good contest which we both thought we had won, but Sammy got the judges vote. I was slightly disappointed that my winning streak had ended so soon, but that was all. As Sammy and myself had estimated that the boxing match might not end before the closing time at the NAAFI Club bar, we had brought with us in our kit bag, a four pint can of beer which was very popular at the time, indeed there was also a seven pint version on sale! We sat down right at the back of the hall, as inconspicuous as possible to watch the remainder of the nights boxing. We started to drink the beer from the large can, and were unaware that we had been spotted by some of the crowd, who obviously thought it was amusing to see the two former and recent rivals in the boxing ring, behaving in this way.

At the time of the Wakefield Tournament in November 1967, I was serving with 2 Squadron in Aden, but on return I once again joined the Transport Command Team for a tournament at RAF Uxbridge. This trip was more memorable for a visit to London to see places such as Carnaby Street at the height of the so called ' Swinging 60's, as I mentioned in Chapter 9. I ended up boxing somebody from my own team, and also managed to lose on points again, after what I thought was an unfair decision. However this was to be the end of my losing streak, and when I joined Strike Command at RAF Waddington later in 1968, my luck would change at last.

Around the very start of October, I arrived at RAF Waddington on posting, although this was later changed to a attachment, when I was subsequently posted to RAF Akrotiri less than 5 months later. When I was going through the normal arrival procedure, I called in at the Station Physical Education Flight to see what sports etc. was available on the station. When the officer in charge learned that I was a boxer, he asked me if I would like to represent the station at the Strike Command Championships. These were being held at RAF Stanmore Park the very next week, and as the station had no boxers entered, it would be good if I entered. As I had had barely time to say hello at SSQ, I did not expect that the staff would like the idea of losing me so soon, but they agreed, and so after a weekend at home, I travelled to RAF Stanmore Park on the Sunday afternoon for the championships, which were to take place over the next three days. I went straight into the semi finals, and had a comfortable win against a SAC Jenkins, with the referee stopping the bout in my favour in the third round. I was therefore in the final on the Wednesday night, and was overjoyed. In the final, and before a large crowd, I also managed to defeat a SAC Mills with another stoppage in the third round. I was therefore now the Strike Command Champion. I was extremely pleased, partly as my luck had changed, but also because I knew that I would almost certainly be allowed to take time off work to box in the Lord Wakefield's the next month.

As I expected, I was allowed to take time off to compete in the Lord Wakefield Championships which were held at RAF St Athan over three days in early November. I weighed in at featherweight and had my first bout on the first day. This was against a LAC Moran, and I had a comfortable win, particularly as my opponent had to take a couple of standing counts. The next morning of the championships I watched a bout between a SAC 'Geordie' Mercer from Lyneham who I knew very well, and an apprentice who looked good. I knew that I would box the winner of this bout in the semi final later that day. The young apprentice seemed to me to have been a clear winner, and at the end of the bout, Geordie saw me watching and said ' he is all yours Mick!'. However when the referee called the boxers into the centre of the ring for the decision, Geordie was declared the winner on a majority decision. I admit that I was relieved that I would be boxing against Geordie, and later in the day, I had a clear points win against him, and so made it into the final the next day. The finals took place the next day, and consisted of 20 bouts, which comprised of 10 finals for junior stations and 10 for senior ones. The seniority was based on the size, that is the number of personnel serving on the station. As I was representing RAF Waddington, which was a large station, I was in the senior division.

My final was one of six that took place in the morning session, as opposed to the majority of finals which were staged in the evening. This meant that the audience for my final would be mainly other boxers, which was a slight disappointment to me. In the final I boxed yet another apprentice, but this time I was by no means overwhelmed. My opponent was a Leading Craft Apprentice Preston who did not seem to have the answer to my straight lefts, which had become my best punch. In the end I was the unanimous points winner and nobody disagreed with the decision. I was now the champ! I received my winners medal at the evening's final before a big audience from a high ranking officer which was great. When I returned to Waddington everybody was very pleased with my success, which reflected on the station even though I was the only representative. As I was now the Command and Wakefield champion, I knew that I would be selected to represent Strike Command, and that this would mean around two weeks off work to train and compete with the team in the Command finals.

About two weeks later, I joined the Strike Command team for training at RAF Wyton under the popular trainer, Les Bolton. As usual this was a very enjoyable period of two weeks, which consisted of two or three sessions of training during the day, and evenings in the NAAFI Club. The championships were held at RAF Locking over three days the following week. By this time, the championships involved two groups of three commands, so the Strike Command team would be competing initially against two other command teams, one of which was the newly formed Support Command. I was selected to be the Strike Command boxer at featherweight for both matches. For the first of the two contests, my opponent could not appear for some reason so I was awarded the bout by what was termed a 'walkover'. I simply entered the ring and walked over to the opposite corner post, touched and walked back to the usual applause! After this I faced Geordie Mercer who I had defeated in the Lord Wakefield Championship the previous month. This was once again an occasion where I was boxing somebody I was friendly with, but this was OK with both of us. I was confident of winning, so much so that during the bout, I mentally counting the times I had landed a punch. However, I either failed to subtract the punches that landed on me, or miscounted altogether as Geordie was awarded the bout on a split decision.

For Geordie, it was some small recompense for the bad decision he had the previous month. I was only slightly disappointed that my winning streak had ended in this way. My thoughts were now on the forthcoming open RAF Championships at RAF Cosford in January, and of course the time off to train for this.

Sure enough just after the start of 1969, I joined the Strike Command team at RAF Wyton for a week's training before the RAF Open Championships at RAF Cosford. The training for this championship was a great deal more serious than I had experienced before for the Lord Wakefields and the Inter Command Championships, which were mainly for novices. In the case of the Wakefield competition, a win meant that the boxer concerned could not take participate in the competition in future, so these championships were the future for me if I continued my boxing career. Winners of the RAF Open Championships would progress to the Inter Services Championships, and if successful to the finals of the all England Championships. Success at this level could result in an international vest, and subsequently top class competitions such as the Olympic Games. In the 1969 Championships, the winner of the Heavyweight Division, Neville Mead, went on to become the professional Heavyweight Champion of Great Britain. There was therefore a lot at stake, at least for those boxers. For once I was not one of the oldest in the squad which had several very experienced boxers, who had been and were RAF Champions. One major difference in the competition was that the bouts consisted of three rounds of three minutes and not two minutes as in the novice events. During the week's training the team visited Joe Bugner's training Headquarters, and some of the team had a light hearted spar with Joe. After a good week's training, the team travelled to RAF Cosford for the Championships which would be my first taste of boxing at a higher level. In the featherweight division there was only 4 boxers entered that year, so I made the semi- final! That was as far as I got that year, as I was stopped in two rounds by a SAC Norrie Davidson, who was fairly new on the RAF boxing scene, and who went on to almost cause an upset in the final against an ex Royal Navy boxer, LAC Gibbons.

Shortly after the RAF Championships, I boxed in a civilian show at Ely. I found out afterwards when I read the results in the *Boxing News* that I had represented East Anglia in a match against my native Yorkshire! I was out-pointed and outclassed by a boxer from Hull called Taylor, which meant that after my recent winning streak, I had now suffered three losses, although two of these were at a higher level than I was used to. However this bout was not recorded in my official record book, so I can perhaps ignore it as far as the sequence goes! My prize for the contest was a breadboard and bread knife. After the prize giving and a quick drink, I hitchhiked back to Colerne, carrying my prize under my arm as it would not fit into a small holdall I took for my boxing kit of boots etc. Just like a previous prize of a chip pan, it was somewhat strange to say the least! That was to be my last bout for two years, as shortly afterwards I was posted to RAF Akrotiri, where there was very little boxing activity.

In 1970, after personally reviving interest, and the arrival at RAF Akrotiri of two former Lord Wakefield winners, SAC Ian Pinks and SAC Ollie Oliver, a small group of boxers started to train together on the camp under a new coach, SAC Neil Hempstead. In the autumn of 1970, Ian Pinks and myself decided to enter the RAF Open Championships which were to be held at RAF Wattisham. We were granted time off work, but not an official flight back. We could and did apply for what was termed an 'indulgence' flight whereby we could utilise any vacant seats on a scheduled flight. For the return leg, we were reasonably certain of a seat, as Ian Pink's father was a RAF officer in the RAF Brize Norton Air Movements section!

So after an enjoyable five days back in England, Ian and myself were weighing in for the Championships at RAF Wattisham. Whilst the there was a good size entry in the Ian Pinks's light middleweight division, there was only one other boxer in the featherweights, the reigning RAF and Combined Services Champion, Corporal Phil Moyes, who was one of three brothers who had entered the championships. There was no doubt that Phil Moyse was the reason for the lack of featherweights that year. Any concern I had about this were outweighed by the thought that I would at least be a finalist, and providing I went the distance, I would have a chance of winning, however remote. For the first two days at Wattisham, I had nothing to do except watch the preliminary bouts including Ian Pinks's quarter and semi final contests. Ian had two clear points wins, and was looking like the next champion, so we were both in the finals, much to the delight of ourselves but also our young trainer Neil Hempstead.

The final bouts were scheduled to take place in weight order starting at Flyweight and ending with the Heavyweight final. There was no Light Flyweight or Super Heavyweight at that time. My bout was very similar to my previous RAF Open contest. I had only one chance and that was to be as aggressive as possible and hope for a lucky punch. I also had to keep in close to tie things up if necessary. I had no hope of out-boxing Phil who was a very talented boxer. However the effort of carrying out these tactics was to prove too much for me yet again. I had my moments in the first round, but ended the round breathing very heavily. When Phil pressed his attack in the second round, I had no answer to it, and the referee stopped the bout to 'save further punishment' as the well-known boxing phrase goes. An amusing incident occurred in the changing room after the bout. Phil's brother Billy who had retained his bantamweight title by stopping SAC Stan Foxe in the first round, tried to cheer me up by telling me that I should not be disappointed at not beating his brother Phil, as even he could not beat him! The Moyse brothers failed to make it a family treble when their younger brother Johnny lost to the superbly fit, SAC Tony Meakin on points.

Three months after returning to Cyprus, I joined Ian Pinks and Ollie Oliver on a trip to Bahrain as part of a combined Services Cyprus squad. A tournament against a Combined Services team at Bahrain had been arranged by the boxing trainer with the Royal Green Jackets Regiment based in Cyprus. All the bouts were to be between boxers of equal ability as far as possible. In addition to the individual boxers record cards, some of the team, including Ian Pinks had to get into a boxing ring for a brief sparring session, shortly after disembarking from a long flight in a C130 Hercules! After the matchmaking, we had a few days to train and see something of the island, which was very enjoyable. I was matched with a SAC Grey who was a member of 2 Field Squadron, some of whom were on a detachment at RAF Muharraq. I knew my opponent slightly as he was on the squadron when I left in 1968, but I did not know of his boxing ability. I worked out that as he had not boxed in the RAF Championships that I was aware of, he would not be a Phil Moyse!

The boxing tournament took place in what was the open air cinema, before a good crowd which included a Prince from the ruling Royal Family. I tried my best to 'psych out' my opponent with a fierce warm up of skipping and shadow boxing, which also helped to calm my nerves after three defeats since the Lord Wakefields. After an even first round, I stepped up my attack and achieved a knock down in the second round. SAC Grey was holding his stomach and seemed to be wanting the referee to rule that I had struck a low blow. He got up before the count of 10, and I tried in vain to achieve another knock down. In the final round, which was curiously a minute longer, I continued to dominate the fight and was surprised that the decision was split, although still in my favour. When the announcement of the result was being made by the M C, as soon as the word 'majority' was said, Ollie shouted out 'rubbish', as I had surely won decisively.

In January of 1972, I entered the RAF Open Championships for the third time, which it transpired was also the last time. I was still at Akrotiri but was able to get a flight back to RAF Brize Norton where the championships were being held that year. This time I was the only boxer from Akrotiri and I travelled on my own without a trainer this time. On this occasion I arrived the day before the start, so the day after my arrival I was in the ring for a semi-final bout with non other than Phil Moyse! On this occasion I lasted a round longer, but was stopped in the third round. Phil went to win the title once again. The following moth I was posted back to the UK and to RAF Halton, and I spent the remainder of the boxing season settling in to a new married quarter and also a new job at the hospital.

At the commencement of the new season in the autumn of 1972, I started training again under a Sergeant PTI called Jackie Baker. Jack was an excellent coach, and was responsible for guiding the former British Heavyweight Champion, Neville Meade, through to the final of the national amateur championship, which he won before turning professional (with another trainer much to Jack's disappointment). Jack was the RAF Team coach at that time, and whilst I was not strictly a RAF team boxer, I tagged along with him to shows which featured members of the RAF team, and on a couple of occasions boxed as a team member with a RAF vest etc. The first of the two bouts as a RAF team boxer was very memorable. It took place at a working men's club in Leicester. As was often the case, some boxers either failed to show up for one reason or another, so there was some last minute match making. I entered the ring with a Terry Hyslop who was clearly heavier than me. The *Boxing News's* account of the bout described him as a welterweight. I doubt that he was that heavy, probably a light welterweight. The weigh in was one of the first using kilograms, which was the likely cause of an obvious error – which strangely the referee either did not spot, or stayed silent about it. Jack told me not to worry, and just see what Hyslop was like. He may have been useless. However, if he was not, and he hit me hard, I should go down and stay there for the full count. Very early in the bout, it was obvious that Hyslop was useful so I therefore 'took a dive' in boxing parlance. I came away more or less unhurt and with a nice clock as a prize.

After two consecutive losses, I was back on the winning trail with my very next bout, which was on my 33rd birthday at RAF Conningsby. I had not been scheduled to box, but travelled as a sort of reserve. One of the boxers on the show had been severely delayed on the journey to Coningsby so I took his place. I had by now developed a much stronger punch in the right hand to go with a very good left lead. This combination was too good for a SAC Cooper, and the referee stopped the bout in my favour in the second round. When the boxer whose place I had taken turned up after the show had ended, I was enjoying a celebrating my win and birthday at the bar, with my prize which was a radio!

Three weeks later, I was once again back in action with the RAF team. This time it was at a big Dinner and Boxing show in Sheffield. In addition to the RAF team, the Army team were also boxing on the same show. On this occasion my opponent did not show, so Jack Baker tried to match me up with another opponent. I could not avoid listening to a conversation Jack had with the Army Team's trainer, who knew me from Cyprus, when he was in charge of the Combined Services team I went to Bahrain with. The Army trainer told Jack that he only had a bantamweight who was not matched up. Jackie said that he did not have a bantamweight, but there was a featherweight, (7 pounds heavier) who he would like to match. When he told the Army trainer it was me, he agreed to the match. I was worried. Just how good was this bantamweight, whom his trainer was willing to let him box a featherweight I wondered. Oh well I would soon find out. For some reason the audience seemed to be favouring the RAF boxers, so as I entered the ring there was a lot of shouts, of 'come on the RAF' etc. When the MC introduced the boxers, I got by far the biggest cheer. What effect all this had on myself and my opponent I do not know, but one of my very first punches staggered Lance Corporal Donaldson so much that he was given a standing count of 8. I could scarcely believe it. When the bout was allowed to continue I charged in and after landing some more good blows, the referee stopped the bout, much to the delight of the very pro RAF crowd. As this was Sheffield, my prize was of course cutlery!

After a first round win against an Army opponent, I should have considered retiring at what was a comparatively old age for amateur boxing. I would be most unlikely to better this experience, and it would have been a fitting end as my first opponent was also an Army boxer. However, I had no thoughts of retiring at that time, and when the Inter Command Championships was staged at RAF Halton, I was in action again against a SAC Paterson. This was a very hard contest in which we both had knock-downs. I was able to land some hard punches once again, but was not fit enough to withstand the response by a determined younger boxer. There was not much in it, but I lost on points. My final bout came a few weeks later in January 1973, and this was also a Inter Command fixture against a SAC Vaughan. I was not initially selected to represent Support Command at first for this fixture, but the first choice boxer, a young apprentice, was dropped from the team after a problem arose regarding his attitude to training. I was to set an example regarding personal fitness, and was expected to win against a boxer who was experienced, but had not won any significant boxing championships. Soon after the start of the bout, I was breathing heavily, and when Vaughan scored a good body punch, I went down for the count and a much needed breather. However, I somehow misjudged the count and was counted out as I was getting to my feet. I was very disappointed with my performance, but I blamed my demise on my age and not the fact that I was not achieving the required level of fitness because I smoked and did not train hard enough. With hindsight, I could have achieved a lot more if I was fitter and trained as hard as I did when I started to take up running five years later. In the meantime, whilst I did some coaching for a few years, my boxing career in the ring ended after this bout.

12. PMRAF Hospital Halton

Soon after arriving back in England from Cyprus in February 1972, I took over a very nice furnished three bedroom house which belonged to the RAF, and was located on a large private housing estate called Bedgrove, just a mile from Aylesbury town centre. My wife and children moved in a couple of days later, just after all our personal effects had arrived from Cyprus. I expected to stay at RAF Halton for a few years, and remain in the same house, and as it turned out, that was what happened, and I subsequently stayed at Halton and in the house for over four years. This was a very welcome period of stability, and one which all the family enjoyed. After a few week's leave which consisted of the usual disembarkation leave, and annual leave which I somehow managed to accumulate in between sporting and parachuting diversions, I reported for duty at the hospital. The official title of the unit was Princess Mary's RAF Hospital Halton sounded the same as the RAF Hospital in Cyprus, which it was. To distinguish between the two, which of course was scarcely necessary, the Cyprus version was *The,* my italics, Princess Mary's Hospital! The hospital was mainly administered by RAF Halton, formerly a Training Command station, but because that unit was still concerned with training of apprentices and adult aircraft tradesmen, it belonged to Support Command, whilst the Hospital was a Strike Command Unit, with it's own Commanding Officer of Group Captain rank.

Whilst the workload of the hospital must have decreased after the end of National Service, and the subsequent reduction in the strength of the RAF, it was the major RAF Hospital which included several specialist units. There was a Oncology Unit which was named the Cade Unit after a former distinguished RAF surgeon, a Plastic Surgery Unit which included a Burns Unit, and The Institute Of Pathology and Tropical Medicine which had a role to play in the investigations following fatal aircraft accidents, and in addition provided laboratory services for the hospital and nearby RAF stations. There was also a Renal Dialysis Unit which had a capability to be transported to overseas units if required. In 1972 there was around 10 wards in daily use. Except for the specialist units, the main wards were of the Florence Nightingale type, but only as regards the general configuration of the beds. There was an average of 150 in patients, who were mainly RAF personnel and dependant wives and children, who resided in the hospital's catchment area. In addition local civilians, mainly those with former RAF service were treated at the hospital. Whilst there was an increased number of male nurses, including SRNs, all the wards had a senior Nursing Officer belonging to the PMRAFNS in charge, plus other Nursing Officers as deputies. They were in turn managed by a Matron and her Deputy. I gained the impression that the Nursing Sisters in general were generally not the tyrants of the 1950s, but some of the more senior ones who were in charge, were seemingly slow to change. Matrons rounds still took place twice a day, with the Senior Matron doing the rounds in the morning, and a Duty Matron, usually a senior nursing officer doing a further round in the evening, but both with less formality than previously, but of course the same high standards prevailed.

The Medical Administration team was headed by the Hospital Registrar, a Medical Officer of Wing Commander rank, but the management of the various departments in respect of administration was the responsibility of a Warrant Officer with a Flight Sergeant Deputy, both of whom were in the trade of Medical Administrator. They had the title of Chief Clerk and deputy, but this was later amended to Medical Records Officer. There was in addition two Sergeants in the same trade, one of whom was in charge of the Out Patients Department and the other dealt with Medical Boards. The Deputy Chief Clerk also dealt with arrangements for the reception of Aero-medical Evacuation patients arriving at RAF Northolt, from Northern Ireland where 'The Troubles' were in full swing.

Of all the various posts for Corporal Med Secs in the hospital, it was acknowledged that the least popular was working in the Reception, formerly called the Ward Masters Office. Whilst many of the tasks undertaken were important to the smooth running of the hospital, and required a high degree of responsibility, particularly during 'after duty' hours, the work was mainly boring and repetitive, and involved working shifts, unlike the remainder of the office staff who worked a 8 to 5 day with a decent lunch break. A further source of some discontent, was a requirement to wear a white coat whilst on duty, of the type usually worn by Doctors on their ward rounds. Whilst I could understand the reason for this, it remained a matter of some irritation to me. Because of the unpopularity of the Reception posts, the Chief Clerk operated a policy of 'last in and last out'. Whilst this was seemingly fair, it took no account of the experience of the corporals who had just been posted in, and might mean a period of two or more years for some whilst others may only have had to stay for a shorter time depending on the movement of the other office staff. As always, it was always possible to make the best of things, as I had been doing for most of the past seven years. However as my boxing career was coming to an end, and there would be no further escaping the office for parachuting, I might have to spend a lot more time in the office than I was used to! Over the next four years, I would however manage some diversions for sport and three training courses.

In 1972, there was an extensive re-building project at the hospital in progress, which would provide a new out patients wing. During this period which lasted for around two more years, the hospital reception was based in a large Portacabin at the front of the hospital. Meanwhile the main car park was at the rear, so most visitors entered the building by the rear door. This meant that if they followed the various signs to departments and the wards, few would need to visit the reception, which contrary to it's name was mainly for in patients booking in and out. Other functions were to deal with general enquiries from visitors and by telephone, run a paging services using a 'bleep' system of portable electronic pagers, keep an up to date list of all key personnel on duty and their whereabouts if outside the hospital area, and convey deceased to the hospital mortuary. During after Duty hours, the reception staff would carry out a check of the bed state, and produce daily and weekly internal statistics, plus lists of new admissions for the a 'laundry list' of people such as the Matron and the Hospital Padre. They would also be responsible for notifying cases where patients were classified a 'Seriously ill (S.I List), or 'Very Seriously ill' (VSIL List) or death, to all those who were required to know. Where at all possible, the next of kin would be informed by the Medical Officer or the Nursing Staff. Whilst from time to time, other tasks would be allocated to the Reception staff, these were the standard tasks.

When fully staffed, there would be five corporals and five SACs who covered the 24 hours in shifts. There was a day shift of 8 to 4 without a formal break, a 4 to 8 afternoon shift that was followed by an 8 to 8 on a Saturday and Sunday, and night shift from 8 to 8. The night shift ended on the Monday morning and after this 84 hour week, there was a week off work. This pattern required only 4 corporals and SACs, leaving the 5th to cover leave etc. For a few months, it was the case that if no leave was being taken, one of the staff had an additional week off. This was stopped perhaps not surprisingly, but the shift pattern remained fair. Whilst I disliked shift work, I did not mind this too much. What I did not like was the general pattern of the work, which was extremely repetitive and was mainly a case of following set procedures. The workload varied from being extremely hectic to extremely dull. During the morning shift, when routine patients were being booked in for admission, and numerous 'essential' forms had to be completed by hand before they could proceed to the ward, it was sometimes difficult to keep pace. For emergency admissions the paperwork was of course completed when possible later on the ward. In the evenings there was little work other than the bed state, lists and preparation of documents as far as possible for the next day's admissions. There was very little difference in the work of the corporals to that of the SACs, other than the corporal was 'in charge'! Other than this distinction, it was the corporals responsibility to complete the bed state, and also to take any deceased to the mortuary. It was the role of the SAC to do whatever running around was necessary such as admitting emergencies on the ward. At the time of starting this job, I had almost 15 years service, 12 of which were as a NCO. This was not at all unusual with the constant reduction in the size of the RAF, and in particular the Medical Branch. Two other corporals in reception had similar experience. Whilst there may not have been an ideal solution to this apparent waste of experience, at the hospital level, it might have been better if the Record Office had not posted very experienced NCOs to posts where their experience would be superfluous. So for a whole year, without any breaks other than for annual leave, I stayed in the same job, and in the same office (or Portacabin to be exact), doing more or less the same things every day. However it made a change, and in the meantime, I had plenty of things to occupy myself with outside of work.

Just as in my previous 15 years of RAF service, pop music played a big part in my life, and the tunes of the period are often evocative, and bring back memories of the events of the period, when various hits were first heard, as of course many still get played on mainstream radio. My immediate memory of 1972 hit records, without the need to check first, is Don McLean and his two hits, particularly 'American Pie' which stayed in the charts for 16 weeks (I did check this), but was prevented from reaching number one T Rex's number one, 'Telegram Sam'. Don McLean did make number later in the year with 'Vincent', which is rarely heard these days, whilst T Rex had another number one with the better remembered 'Metal Guru'. This was the start of the so called 'Glam Rock' period which was at it's peak in 1973 with groups such as Slade and Wizard. There was a continued presence of unusual records making number one, such as a Pipe band playing 'Amazing Grace', and Lieutenant Pidgeon's 'Mouldy Old Dough'. Later in the year, a young Rod Stewart took 'You Wear It Well' to the top, following up on his 1971 number one hit, 'Maggie May'.

Whilst my work was somewhat tedious, life outside was anything but. For a long time, I appreciated being back in England, and all things English after three years in Cyprus. I loved the scenery, the climate, the food, and as I was living only about 40 miles from London, the possibility of experiencing every type of sport and entertainment. After three years with practically no television, it was great to stay in and watch the three terrestrial channels in colour, particularly as this has been acknowledged as a very good period in the history of British broadcasting, with great drama, comedy, documentaries and all the major sports broadcast free of any extra charges. My son started to become interested in football, and it was then possible to attend any first division match in London without pre booking for a comparatively modest sum if you did not mind the crush. For a time we visited most of the big grounds on the traditional Saturday afternoon, before switching allegiance to nearby Luton Town FC. My daughter was interested in ballet for a while, and was able to go to watch the National Ballet in London. She also attended a local ballet class and was a member of a Brownie Pack. Compared with Cyprus there was not so much evening social life other than at Christmas, especially now that I had just one job, but this did not matter at all. In the summer we took a proper holiday in Cornwall for the first time, and greatly enjoyed it, although we never went back there. This period of my RAF service was the opposite of the previous seven years, in that it was the off duty that was the most interesting. Going in to work on a non flying unit, and having to wear a white coat amongst others similarly dressed, hardly seemed like service life, and indeed mine and many other posts at the hospital, could have been filled by civilian employees, and of course some 24 years later when the hospital closed for good, this was more or less the case, when patients were dispersed mainly to civilian hospitals.

After about 9 months of work in the hospital reception, I did actually start to go to work in civilian clothes for two months. This was because I had been 'volunteered' to attend an audiometry training course in London at the Central Medical Establishment, (CME), which was situated in Central London. For the duration of the course I was based at RAF Uxbridge and travelled in to CME on the underground. It was the policy of all three services, that those working at offices and other establishments in Central London wore civilian both for travelling and also whilst working. I was even granted an allowance for the wear and tear on my civvies. Whilst I had not volunteered for this course, it was a welcome diversion, and meant that I would not stay bored for too long. The purpose of the course was to train sufficient Med Sec corporals in the audiometry, to a level where they could carry out specialised tests at hospitals for Ear Nose and Throat, (ENT), specialists. At all the RAF Hospitals there was insufficient need for a full time audiometrician, and it was not considered cost effective for patients to have to travel to just one or two specialist centres. When I had completed the course and passed the requisite examination, I would only have to carry out about 6 tests a week. Like almost all RAF training courses at that time, it was extremely thorough and erred on the side of too much information rather than too little. The anatomy and physiology of the ear was of course a basic requirement, although none of the tests involved contact with the ear other than earphones. However this aspect was covered in some depth, as was the physics of sound. As physics was never my favourite subject, I struggled a little with this part of the course. Finally we were eventually taught how to carry out all the various hearing tests, which was comparatively simple! I managed to pass the examination at the end of the course and returned to Halton.

Prior to the 1970s, the system of testing RAF personnel for hearing disorders using audiometry was not normally carried out after the initial medical examination on entry. A simple hearing test would be conducted at the annual medical examination of all officers and aircrew only. As the incidence of noise induced deafness became apparent amongst not only aircrew but also ground staff, all unit Medical Centres, (the title of sick quarters had changed), were required to test all those tradesmen and women who were exposed to excessive noise at least annually. They did so using a very basic audiometer. Those who failed the test at unit level would be referred to a ENT specialist for assessment. Before they saw the specialist they would be retested by an audiometrician, who would use a more sophisticated audiometer, and where necessary carry out tests for other diseases of the ear. Sometimes, and with certain individuals the testing procedure would be somewhat tortuous. The requirement for all the tests was the ability to make a decision. This was was almost beyond the capabilities of some, although of course there was often a great deal of anxiety and fear of failing the tests and having to subsequently change careers. Top of the list for this was aircrew. In a basic test, a sound would be delivered to each ear, starting at around 100 decibels, and reducing down to zero or even below (technically possible). When the lower limits were reached the person being tested had to decide if the sound could be heard. To eliminate guesswork, they had to press a button only when the sound was present. It was always explained at the start that no matter how good the hearing was, there would come a point when it would be impossible to hear anything, particularly at the higher frequencies. The audiometer could deliver a 'sound' as low as minus 10 decibels, and whilst some individuals might be able to discern sound delivered at minus 5 decibels, minus 10 was almost impossible. The test would commence using the lower frequencies, which were rarely affected, and then proceed to higher frequencies, where even in the normal and acceptable ranges, would not produce results as good as the lower ranges. Some patients would continually ask me to 'play it again' no matter how much reassurance they were given. For those suspected of having certain diseases of the ear, a balance test was carried out, which often caused those who were indecisive for any reason to have even more problems. For this test, sounds were sent to each in ear in turn at varying frequencies and decibels. The patient had to simply say when the sounds were thought to be of the same loudness. This was nigh on impossible for some, and such a test would take a lot longer than the average time, with repeated requests for another 'go'.

There was however one very good thing about my part time role as an audiometrician, and that was after a couple of months, it was decided that it would be best if I was more generally available during the day, rather than one week in four when I was working a day shift in reception. So just before my summer holiday, I said goodbye to reception and moved to a 8 to 5 job in the Admission and Discharge, (A and D), Office. I kept my white coat to wear when doing tests, as that was how out-patients expected technicians to dress, but I eventually reverted to wearing my normal uniform. I now had a triple bonus of a better job, an end to shift work, and finally an end to wearing a white coat!

In addition to these three joys, I had a two week summer holiday to look forward to. This would be taken during the first two weeks of the school's summer holiday. After a weekend rehearsal camping at Stony Stratford, in which it rained as the tent was erected, I was confident that my family would cope with a camping holiday in Europe, which we did. We camped in Belgium, Holland, Germany and Denmark and other than a couple of rainy days, we enjoyed some good weather. The camping element was simply a means of having a holiday on the continent, rather than for any other reason, but we had a very good time on a limited budget.

As we set off for Dover and the Car Ferry, we probably all sang Cliff Richard's 1963 number one hit, 'Summer Holiday'. I heard somebody say on the radio last summer, that their family continue to sing this every summer holiday to this day! In the summer of 1973, the Glam Rockers such as Sweet, Slade and Wizard were dominating the charts, which remained mainly British. The summer holiday number one was Gary Glitter's 'I'm The Leader Of The Gang', which because of his recent abhorrent crimes has been air brushed from pop history. Two number ones by American artists that still get airplay today were Dawn featuring Tony Orlando's 'Tie A Yellow Ribbon' and female rocker Susie Quattro's 'Can The Can'. The popularity of unusual records was maintained when the Simon Park Orchestra, took 'Eye Level' to number one at the end of the summer.

When I returned to work I settled in to my new job, which in spite of the title of the office, was mainly concerned with the discharge of patients. The admissions other than urgent cases were controlled and administered by the individual departments such as surgical and orthopaedic. I was concerned only with the recording of the admission once the patient concerned had been admitted. When service personnel were discharged, I received their file from the ward and prepared all the necessary documentation prior to what was termed a Discharge Parade. The 'parade' consisted of the discharged patient seeing the hospital Registrar in his role as the deputy CO. The Registrar would formally approve any sick leave recommended by the specialist who had treated the a patient concerned, and if necessary also approve any change necessary in the medical category. This was simply the grading which indicated the patients fitness to work, to proceed abroad, and to fly either as a passenger or as aircrew. Those who were suffering from a severe illness such as cancer would for example be categorised as fit for UK service, and light work only with specific restrictions such as for example 'no heavy lifting'. I also arranged any follow up appointments required. The patient would be asked if they had any complaints and asked to sign to confirm none if that applied. As there was an obvious risk of delaying departure whilst any complaint was investigated, it was extremely rare for anyone to have a complaint! This being the services, leave and re-grading required a fair amount of paperwork, and required a good knowledge of the relevant regulations, as often the specialist may have recommended what was not within his power to recommend. Those who were proceeding on sick leave would be entitled to a free railway and bus warrant if required, and this was also a part of my job. The workload would vary from a few patients being discharged without leave or re-grading being required, to days when there would be almost too many for me to cope with. I managed to develop a quick way of doing almost everything required to get the patient processed, leaving the completion of the numerous forms etc. until later. All things considered, it was about the best job I could have for my rank and trade in the hospital. Whilst it consisted of the same type of work every day, it did present a challenge at times, and I was happy to be in the post. This was just as well as I would spend the next three years in the same job!

Another advantage to working a normal 8 to 5, Monday to Friday only week, was that every evening I was free to take a part time evening job. After the summer holiday, I thought it would be a good idea to earn some extra cash, partly to save for a better holiday next year, and partly to spend on the attractions of nearby London, and maintain a good lifestyle, at least at the weekends. During this period, I was fortunate not to be required to do any additional duties at the hospital, and as I had retired from sporting activities for a while, I had time and the energy available to supplement my RAF salary. So for a year right up to the next summer holiday in 1974, I worked from 6 to 9 p.m. at a factory in Aylesbury which made shop fittings. It was light manual unskilled work, which consisted of assembling things such as clothes rails. The work was quite varied, and I worked with a small team of people, who like myself were in full time employment but wanted to earn some extra money. Whilst it was slightly sad that I felt it necessary to do this, the time passed quickly and the money came in very handy. I also really appreciated the weekends!

As it can be imagined, time in general passed by very quickly during this period. There was a slight change to the routine for my extra job and that was from the start of 1974, the Government had decreed that all industry was to be restricted to working a three day week to preserve dwindling coal stocks. This situation had arisen after a nationwide dispute with coal miners, which resulted in a 'work to rule' and thus a need to preserve fuel as stocks dwindled. The three day week continued into March. Many people thought that this measure had been a great success, and welcomed the opportunity to work longer hours for just three days a week, to achieve the same weekly total, and end up with four days off work. However, as soon as the emergency energy saving measures had ceased, the country soon reverted back to a five day week. What looked like being a gloomy end of the year Christmas and New Year period, did not materialise, as in a sort of Dunkirk spirit, everybody was determined to make the very most of things. Slade's big number one hit, 'Merry Christmas Everybody' could be said to have summed up the mood of the time – "And so this is Christmas" for example.

Soon after the beginning of 1974, I was now starting my third year at Halton, and had no desire to change jobs or to be posted elsewhere, unless I was to be promoted. After National Service ended ten years previously, there had been a slow down in promotion to in general and in particular to the rank of Sergeant. This was partly due to the ever-reducing size of the RAF and medical branch as overseas bases closed, and also because there was an above average percentage of corporals in the trade, there was comparatively fewer sergeants. Some medical centres, such as RAF Colerne had a Flight Sergeant in charge, but no sergeant deputy. Before promotion to sergeant could be achieved in the trade of Med Admin, it was necessary to attend a Senior Trade Management Course, and qualify by passing a series of exams. The last course was held in 1972, and only four corporals attended and qualified for promotion. I was selected to what was the next course in 1974, along with 15 other corporals. However, after making enquiries of the RAF Record Office, I discovered that there were several corporals ahead of me in the queue, and it was unlikely that I would be promoted and posted for some considerable time yet.

The course lasted around 6 weeks and was based at RAF Halton, which now housed the Medical Training Unit which provided basic and advanced training for medical admin trades. There was very little management taught on the course, which mainly consisted of learning off by heart, administrative procedures concerning statistics and accounting for medical equipment. Whilst it was a break from work, particularly for those stationed at other units, it was a most tedious course. Many of the students made a point of memorising procedures to the extent that they might obtain a 100% passmark in one of the exams which were phased throughout the course. Whilst I never managed a 100% individual exam score, I passed with an above average for the course score, and then returned back to my job in the A and D office at the hospital.

In the course of my job, I met all the service patients when they were due to be discharged from the hospital. For those with serious conditions, I might therefore see them several times as they kept returning for further treatment, and get to know them. Unfortunately in the case of those who had terminal cancer, I would therefore often see the deterioration in their condition by their appearance. I was also aware of the wide variation in respect of the effects of cancer. Patients who had been given the last rites would sometimes survive for years, whilst others would reach the end of their lives in months. One example of the latter, was a RAF pilot who developed a growth on his hand, which was found to be malignant. The first time that he was discharged after treatment, he objected strongly to being made unfit to continue flying as a pilot, as he was certain that he was quite capable of continuing to fly, and that he would soon be back to normal. Nobody could have been more motivated, but he deteriorated so rapidly that he died within months. There was also cases of unexpected recovery which would occur from time to time, when terminal cancer would go into remission. An example of this seemingly miraculous event was a patient in the hospital with terminal cancer, whose wife was living in Malta, and was due to give birth. He naturally wanted to see his forthcoming child before he died. Unfortunately he was far too ill to be able to fly out to Malta, and his wife's pregnancy was too far advanced to her to be able to fly to England to give birth. This awful set of circumstances, was however resolved when against all the odds, the patient recovered sufficiently to be able to see his child.

Outside of work, I was enjoying life, particularly the weekends. In the summer, there was another camping holiday abroad, this time in Denmark, which all my family enjoyed, particularly as the weather was fine, which is essential for a good holiday with young children. After a year of working in the evenings, I was much more able to afford the holiday and not be totally skint afterwards. However, I did not continue with the second job after the holiday, and wondered how I had coped with such a routine for so long. After the gloom of the three-day week, life in general seemed a lot more cheerful for many people, and I think that this was reflected in the music charts. The charts were still dominated by mainly UK groups and artists, but the 'Disco' period had arrived when the Swedish group Abba had the first of 9 number one hits with 'Waterloo'. Other notable newcomers were The Three Degrees who topped the summer charts with 'When willI see you again'. The novelty number one was provided by Ray Stevens and his amusing hit, 'The Streak'.

After a few weeks back at work, I had to have a diversion. This came about in an unusual way. After retiring from boxing, I thought that it was time to get my nose reshaped. It had become decidedly and most notably flat, mainly due to sparring with large gloves. I rarely suffered any blows in actual bouts. The resident plastic surgeon agreed to do his best, with a warning about silk purses and sows ears! I was therefore admitted for surgery, and had about two weeks off work. The result was an improvement, but the surgeon offered a further operation to improve the shape even more. This would involve a more serious operation involving transplanting bone, so after some consideration, I decided to put up with the revised shape. I had visions of undergoing surgery and having a sore nose afterwards, only to trip up and ruin the surgeon's handiwork!

After returning to work, I had to undertake a most unusual extra duty. After two years of not having to do any station duties such as Orderly Corporal, I could hardly complain, but I did moan a bit about this duty, which was to act as the barman in the Hospital Corporals Club. At the time, Corporal clubs on RAF Stations were being phased out, as they were not used very much, and were seen as something of an anachronism. On some units that had a high proportion of junior airman on training courses, there may have been a desire by some corporals to have a separate facility for an off duty drink, but there was no such requirement at the hospital. However some corporals at the hospital wanted to have a separate club, and it was agreed that it would continue, and that it would be run as a station duty for a week at a time, by all the corporals stationed at the hospital. The bar was only supposed to be open for a few hours at night, but in practice it stayed open until around midnight. However as with many things in the RAF, there was a good side to this, and that was that even with a small number of customers, the barman enjoyed free drinks and even made a few pounds profit after handing over at the end of the week. Eventually the club became a general hospital social club with volunteers running the bar, and my week's duty was the only one I had to undertake in over four years at the hospital.

Other than normal annual leave, which included a good family holiday in the Highlands of Scotland and Edinburgh, I spent most of 1975 at my primary tasks in the hospital. However in l September, I was invited to attend a boxing coaches course, which was held at RAF Halton and lasted about two weeks. It was being run alongside a training camp for the RAF Boxing Squad, and also a course for boxing officials. The course leader was the new RAF coach, Dennis Wreaford, a Sergeant PTI and former RAF boxer. It was a very interesting and enjoyable course, and at the end I passed the requisite examination to become an official Amateur Boxing Association Coach. A few weeks later I had a few days off work to attend a Inter Command boxing championship with Corporal Billy Moyse, one of the three Moyse brothers, and who had also semi -retired and was now a coach. He was also a PTI at Halton and was attending the tournament at RAF Locking to look after several young boxers from RAF Halton, who were mainly aircraft apprentices. I was attending as his deputy and a boxing second to gain some experience. What I also gained was a very enjoyable week from work, meeting up with old friends from the boxing world. It was during this week, that I started to become known as 'Rocky', which was due mostly to my previous association with the RAF Regiment rather than my boxing prowess, but of course I did not mind what interpretation was put on the nickname! Soon after returning from RAF Locking, Billy decided to let me take over as the coach for RAF Halton. For the remainder of the amateur boxing season, which is similar to the football season with the English and National finals taking place in April, I took over the coaching and arranging bouts for about a dozen young apprentices. These bouts took place at local venues, and once at Oxford University, but were always in the evening, so other than occasionally finishing work earlier, there was no time off work.

Meanwhile in the charts it was roughly the same as the previous year, with mainly British groups and singers. There was two notable groups making their first appearance at the top. In the early part of the year, The Bay City Rollers had their first of two number one hits with 'Bye Bye Baby' and then in July, 'Give A Little Love'. They were responsible for the craze called 'Roller Mania' which resulted in their young fans copying their clothing which included pieces of tartan. A much more significant number one was Queen's 'Bohemian Rhapsody' the first of six number one hits which extended through to 2000, and helped to make the group second only to The Beatles in terms of chart success. There was no shortage of novelty records in 1975. The first was the star of the TV series 'Kojak', Telly Savalas singing or speaking 'If', then Windsor Davis and Don Estelle, stars of a popular TV comedy series, with 'Whispering Grass'. Later came a duo called Typically Tropical' with 'Barbados' which was a 'one hit wonder' that is no other record in the charts ever. At the end of the year, Billy Connolly made number one with 'D.I.V.O.R.C.E.' Some people considered that British pop music was at a very low point with these sort of records, but I, and obviously the majority of the record buying public thought otherwise, and the trend would continue for a few more years through to the Punk period.

At the start of 1976, I learned that I would be posted to RAF Hospital Wegberg, in Germany in June. Of all the postings I could have had, this was the best, and as things stood at that time, it would be my final posting before the end of my service. For reasons similar to my having to undertake audiometry training, I was now required to attend an Electro Cardiograph (ECG) Technician course. The course was held at RAF Wroughton and lasted 4 weeks. It was similar to the audiometry course, in that there was a lot of theory before getting round to actually operating the ECG machines. The course was not particularly interesting and involved some study in the evening on occasions, but overall it was yet another break from work, which was something I had achieved for the past 12 years, and would continue to do so for the next six years. Life in the RAF was never dull for long!

13. RAF Hospital Wegberg

Shortly after returning to Halton, I packed my bags before departing for RAF Hospital Wegberg. My family would be staying at Aylesbury until I had been allocated suitable accommodation, which would take around two months. This was the system in force for all airmen posted to stations in Germany at that time. I had just over three years left of my twenty two years left to serve of my engagement. This was then the minimum period of service required to receive a pension. This requirement was subsequently amended so that servicemen with much shorter periods of service would receive a pension, mainly because fewer service personnel would be allowed to engage for such long periods of service, but this was not made retrospective which has left many of those who retired after less than 22 years service before the change, with a feeling of injustice, and a subsequent campaign for the rules to be further amended. Before leaving Halton I made enquiries about a possible future second career as a Probation Officer, and saw the posting to Germany as a period when I would be a lot better off financially, and an opportunity to see a lot more of Germany. My employment in this theatre was not something that I gave much thought to, as I set off for what I thought was to be my last posting.

RAF Hospital Wegberg was closed in the 1990s following the withdrawal of the Royal Air Force from Germany, as part of the 'peace dividends' following the break up of the Soviet Union, and the end of the 'Cold War'. However in 1976, the Royal Air Force had three large air bases in West Germany, at Laarbruch, Bruggen and Wildenwrath, plus a Headquarters at Rheindahlen. RAF Hospital Wegberg, which was close to RAF Rheindahlen, and near the German town of Moenchen Gladbach, catered for the service population including dependants from all these bases. There was around 130 beds in daily use, but there was contingency plans to greatly extend the number of beds should a situation arise where they may have been required in the event of any engagement with the forces of the Soviet Union. I gained the impression that this was something that was either unlikely or else unthinkable! The configuration of the hospital was a series of single storey buildings radiating like spokes from a central hub, with a separate psychiatric ward called Medical Ward Two. All these buildings, plus around 50 married quarters were contained on a largely self contained unit, in a very pleasant rural setting. The hospital catered mainly for all the basic specialities, such as surgical, orthopaedic, gynaecology, maternity, psychiatry, and general medical. There were resident specialists for all these areas of medicine. In addition other specialists such as Ear Nose and Throat and Plastic surgeons would make regular visits to the hospital for consultations and surgery.

The hospital was commanded by a Group Captain Medical Officer, with a deputy who was a Wing Commander Hospital Registrar, and who also acted as the general practitioner for the staff and for the families who lived in the camp married quarters. The nursing element was headed by a Matron who was a Wing Officer, (the PMRAFNS equivalent to a Wing Commander), with the wards being staffed by nursing officers of the PMRAFNS, and a mixture of male and female members of the RAF. In 1976, the hospital was hosting the training of State Enrolled Nurses, who also supplied much of the compliment of ward staff. The medical administration team, which came under the command of The Registrar, was in reality led by a RAF Warrant Officer, with a Flight Sergeant deputy. The Warrant Officer managed all the medical administrative staff in the various offices, such as Out- Patients, Admissions and Discharges, Medical Boards and the Hospital Reception. The majority of the medical administrative, (med admin), staff were corporals and senior aircraftsmen (SACs) and women (SACWs) in the medical secretarial, (Med Sec) trade. There was in addition some locally employed civilians, but they were mainly typists who also acted as personal secretaries to the specialists. Around two thirds of the med sec corporals and SACs were employed on reception duties. This was similar to other RAF hospitals, and meant that most hospitals including Wegberg, employed a policy of 'last in and last out'. This meant that all newcomers started their Germany tour in the reception, and in theory might stay there for half to two thirds of their three year tour. No doubt to save any squabbling about who ought to be be employed on what was a unpopular job, there was no exception to the general rule. So after nineteen years service, including two tours of duty at RAF Hospitals, I was allocated to Reception. This meant that once again I would have to endure shift work and wear a white coat! Initially I did not mind too much, as it was a change of scene, and there were compensations, although these were mainly outside of work.

When I lived on the camp, the social side of life at Wegberg was very good. I arrived just before a long weekend, when all but essential staff were given an extra day off following a successful annual inspection by the senior RAF Officer in Germany, the so-called AOCs Annual Inspection. I therefore could not go through the arrival process, so I started my tour with an unexpected short holiday. This was the start of the long hot summer of 1976, which made life that much more pleasant. Just before I had arrived at Wegberg, a new SEN course had just arrived from the UK, and through one of the reception staff, who knew one of the course members, I socialised with many of them throughout the summer, and also throughout my tour. The hospital NAAFI club could have been best described as lively. Most nights there would be a good crowd in the bar, and twice a week there was a disco, and every month or so there would be some form of entertainment such as a group. One of the attractions of the NAAFI, was that the cost of the drinks was much less than in normal civilian establishments off the camp. So whatever else life in Germany with the RAF had to offer, there was at least cheap booze and cigarettes. Of course this was seemingly not considered to be totally at odds with health. Most servicemen still smoked and many drank at a level that would now be considered excessive. Whilst the NAAFI bar closed at around 11pm, it was possible to extend drinking by travelling by taxi to nearby bars, some of which also offered food such as chicken and chips! However the food at the hospital mess was very good and midnight feasts would have only been necessary to satisfy hunger after a few beers!

The single accommodation on camp was two-bed rooms, but other than on a temporary basis few had to share. Those who did have to share were usually the married airmen, who were waiting for their families to join them. This meant that the majority of airmen were free to entertain their girlfriends in their room, and whilst this was officially forbidden, it was a order that was never strictly enforced.

The day after my arrival, I went into Munchen Gladbach to watch the famous football team play their last match of the season after they had already been crowned league champions. It was a great experience to watch some of the German national team such Berti Voghts and Rainer Bonhof play, and also a pleasant change not to witness the football hooliganism that existed in England around this time. There was rarely any bad behaviour in German stadiums, and only occasional trouble outside. Any that did arise was kept under control by the German police. Whilst all sport was catered for at the nearby RAF Rheindahlen, at the hospital there was only football during the season, and lots of mixed volleyball in the summer. I was content to just watch the football, but often joined in with the volleyball, partly because it was some form of exercise, and also because it was enjoyable just being out in the sun during that record breaking summer.

After a very nice weekend with my new friends and duty free cigarettes, it was time to get fitted for another white coat, and start shift work in the Hospital Reception until further notice. The duties involved were almost the same as at Halton. The shifts were slightly different, but still involved working a 84 hour week of night duty, followed by a week off. One difference in the standard duties was duties involving the mortuary. In addition to the few deaths that occurred in the hospital, as the most serious case would if possible be transferred to the UK, those who died at other units would be transferred to the mortuary at Wegberg. This was because such deaths would almost certainly be sudden, and therefore a post mortem would be required. This would be carried out by a RAF pathologist based at Wegberg. The mortuary was kept in regular use with a variety of fatal car accidents, an occasional aircraft crash, and other assorted fatalities – some following beer and wine festivals! It was the Reception staff's responsibility, and in particular the corporal's job to receive such bodies and place them in the refrigerated compartments of the mortuary. Thankfully, not very often, it was also necessary to accompany the next of kin to view the body. This entailed taking the body from the refrigerated part and transferring it to the adjoining chapel for viewing. This could be harrowing at first, but it soon became almost routine. Occasionally the body would be in a state of decomposition, and this was something that I never got accustomed to. Even the smell of the standard air freshener spray became nauseous by association.

One small difference between the set up at Halton and that of Wegberg, was the proximity of the out-patients to the main reception, whose role was mainly concerned with staff locations and in patients. This meant that in spite of all the signage, which was always being reviewed and improved, a small number of service patients would come to the Reception desk, proffer their out patient appointment slip of paper, so that they could be directed in the direction of the out patient reception, which many had walked straight past. Often no words were spoken by the visitor. One day a SAC working in reception, who was almost always very polite and courteous, met the umpteenth 'silent' enquiry of the morning. He had greeted the visitor with his usual, 'Good morning, can I help you'? When he received no response, and as usual the appointment slip was poked under his nose, he said 'Thank You', then tore the slip up and proceeded to eat it. The patient fled the scene. It was never discovered which department the visitor was attending, but there was speculation that he had an appointment with the psychiatric department!

Away from the tedium of reception, there was a generally happy atmosphere at Wegberg. Unlike many overseas units, the majority of servicemen and women had volunteered to be posted to Germany, and if they were not so thrilled with their work situation, such as those working in reception, off duty life more than made up for it. One example of general merriment I can recall, was when Elton John and Kiki Dee had their big number one hit with 'Do'nt Go Breaking My Heart' in the charts. If the record was played on the British Forces Broadcasting Service, (BFBS), radio programme, say in the dining room or the NAAFI, the duo would be invariably mimicked. This record was at number one for 6 weeks throughout the summer of 1976, staying in the charts for 16 weeks. This was the height of the 'Disco', and Elton John's success was nothing compared to Abba who had three number ones, 'Mama Mia', 'Fernando' and 'Dancing Queen'. The latter was only at number one for a week, but was in the charts for 15 weeks, and could be regarded as their greatest hit, and is the one that is still played a lot on stations such as RadioTwo, some thirty years later. The charts continued to be dominated by UK artists and groups, and also had some novelty records at number one, with The Wurzels's number one with 'Combine Harvester' being the best example. In addition to the twice-weekly discos at the hospital social club, I joined others from the hospital on trips to local beer festivals. These were traditional German events, which involved country type dances to German 'oompah' bands, and were great fun. This was however the only popular form of German music, as almost all the pop music in their charts was British or American. One exception was the Dutch group Pussycat, who had a number one with 'Mississippi' during this period.

After a couple of mainly happy months on the camp, I took over a large flat in the nearby town of Erkelenz, and my family arrived and settled in. The flat was in a block of flats that had been rented by the RAF to supplement the married quarters at Wegberg. There were other blocks in the area that housed RAF personnel from other nearby stations such as Wildenrath and Rheindahlen. As flats go, they were very nice, and the surrounds were kept clean and tidy. Noise was not excessive, which was probably a combination of local German bye laws and service discipline. As most service families were unused to living in flats, they were not very popular, and for many, including my family, they were seen as just temporary accommodation until a service quarter on the base would be available. Most of the social life remained on the camps, and food shopping locally was limited to bare essentials, as the NAAFI shops on the bases sold all the usual British food-stuffs, and were slightly cheaper than local supermarkets. Education and healthcare also remained on bases, which gave the flats a dormitory feel. As a result of this, socialising with the local population was limited at best. My son joined a local German football team, and of course we both enjoyed going to watch Borussia MG play at home. I knew some families who had never been on public transport, partly because they could not speak any German. I was able to speak some German and always enjoyed such things, and even tended to despise those who never explored the local culture.

One of the perks of a posting to Germany was being able to purchase a duty free car, and of course to earn enough in overseas allowances to pay for it. Whilst the NAAFI was involved in hire purchase transactions for cars, the point of sale was local dealers. When I visited a Ford dealer to discus the purchase of a new Ford Capri, the exchanges between myself and the sales-man was memorable. Before visiting the dealership, I learned what I considered was sufficient German words for motoring matters, and at the dealers I was able to speak sufficiently in German to say what I wanted to buy etc. All was going well, and I was proud of myself that I could manage the language, when the salesman said unforgettably, something like 'now that we have to speak about money, it is better that in English we speak, so there will no misunderstanding be'. I readily agreed! When details of the extra charges were made known, I queried why I had to pay a fee to import the car when this model was actually made in Germany, just a few miles down the road. I was told it was because I wanted a right hand drive car. But surely all Capris are made in the same factory whether they are right or left hand drive, I said. The dealer then told me that the reason was that all the right hand drive cars were shipped to England. Of course I then asked why it was that somebody could not divert those that were to be purchased in Germany, but I knew what the answer would be of course! It was also interesting that Ford would charge the price at the time of delivery and not at the time of sale. Price rises occurred at regular intervals of course, as this was the 1970s! The good news was that I eventually got a well built and trouble free car, which may not have been as likely with some British makes at that turbulent period in the motoring industry.

After I had worked in the Hospital Reception for a few months, my shift coincided with an out patients clinic when a visiting consultant physician required an E.C.G. for one of his patients. I had not carried out an E.C.G. since the course ended in June. At that time the procedure and equipment for a proper clinical examination, were far from straightforward, particularly for somebody who was not performing the tests very often. For example it was possible to attach some of the leads to the body incorrectly. There was of course no 'idiot guide' label on the leads such as 'right ankle'. There was also a knack to attaching leads to the chests of women, which involved gel and suction! As my luck would have it, my first patient since the course was a woman. I managed to do the E.C.G. but was called in later to see the consultant who said that he thought there was a possibility that I had wrongly positioned the leads – he must have known that this was a probability unless his patient's heart was performing in a very strange way, so he was just being very polite about my error. I managed to do another test, which was successful, no doubt to not only my relief but also that of the consultant and not least the patient! My error must have made it obvious that asking members of Reception staff to occasionally stop what they were doing, and go to outpatients to carry out E.C.G.s was not a good idea, and other arrangements came into being soon after.

I spent Christmas day of 1976 working at the hospital until after 8 p.m., presumably because this was also something else where a 'last in' policy applied. I know that I did not volunteer to work. Often there is no shortage of volunteers to work on Christmas Day at Hospitals, as there is a jolly atmosphere, few patients, and it is at least one day in the year when your work is appreciated. Other than when I was stationed in Belize and had returned from leave in Texas on Christmas Eve, did I ever work on Christmas Day, so once in 25 Christmas's was not cause to complain, but I was not very happy about it. To make things worse, the RAF transport which was taking me and others back to Erkelenz broke down, so it was late when I finally got back home much to my family's annoyance – to put it mildly!

Son after the start of 1977, my social life improved when my new car was finally delivered via the circuitous route. It was then possible to be a lot more mobile after relying on RAF and public transport for over 6 months. As I remained on shift work, I could now make the most of off-duty time with trips to places such as Aachen and Dutch border towns such as Roermond and Venlo. A few months later, my wife finally managed to get a part time job as a nursing auxiliary at Wegberg after a year on a waiting list, and I progressed to the top of the waiting list for a married quarter on camp. As my wife felt that she could not take a holiday so soon after starting work, I took our children on the usual end of school year holiday, which was down to Fussen on the German-Austrian border. We had a really good time camping, exploring castles and visiting places such as Munich. On return I found out that I had been offered promotion at long last, but if I accepted it would mean that I was to be posted to RAF St Athan, which was near Cardiff. It was a case of good news and bad news. If I accepted there would be disruption to the children's education, (they were then aged 11 and 13), and an actual loss of income, as the basic pay increase would be much less than overseas allowances. I was also about to take over a married quarter on the camp the following week. In addition, I had had only two more years left to serve at that time, so there would be no long-term advantage to being promoted. I just had to decline the offer. However, when I returned to working in the reception, whilst I knew that I had made the only sensible decision, I started to wish I was a sergeant in Wales and not still a corporal in Germany, particularly as I remained in a job I disliked so much.

As usual I managed to find a means of escape from the office, albeit only for a week later in the year. This was via boxing. I considered that whilst I was too old to box, I was a qualified Amateur Boxing Association Coach, and perhaps I might be able to get somebody interested who worked at the hospital. I made enquiries and three of the staff expressed an interest. One was a member of the Reception staff, SAC Jimmy Ross, one was a cook, SAC Grant Russell, and there was also an SAC called Bob who worked for in the Hospital Admin Office. My first task was to get permission to use the physiotherapy department of the hospital as a gymnasium to train. There was some misgiving about this to say the least, but eventually the officer in charge of the Physiotherapy Department agreed that I could use the gymnasium. Then I had to obtain some basic equipment such as gloves for sparring, gloves and pads for training, plus a heavy bag. To start with these items were borrowed from the Physical Education Department at RAF Rheindahlen where they were gathering dust, and then later I obtained some new gloves. Of the three hospital staff boxers, only Bob had boxed before, but Jimmy and Grant looked to be more than capable of competing in a novice tournament such as The Lord Wakefield's. This year the tournament would be held at RAF Hereford in early November. We must have impressed everyone with our enthusiasm to enter the competition, and I also drew attention to the fact that we would be the first team ever to enter that represented Wegberg, and probably the only team to represent any RAF Hospital. Rugby was the main sport played by medics, partly because of the link with the sort of school RAF Medical Officers would usually have attended! Other than Jimmy Ross, I only ever met one RAF boxer who was a medic, and he subsequently joined the Physical Education Branch!

We were granted permission to enter the tournament, but not to fly back to UK on an official flight. However, a special committee which had funds for sporting projects granted funds towards the cost of travel by my car. By this time, Bob had changed his mind about going, as he claimed to have an injured shoulder. That left just Jimmy and Grant left to represent Wegberg. However, when Grant had a compulsory boxing medical examination, he was not given clearance due to a head injury, which he had sustained prior to his entry into the RAF. There was a possibility that clearance might be given, but this was dependent on obtaining some medical records from the hospital where he had been treated in Scotland. Grant decided that he would still join Jimmy and myself on the trip. Whether his boss in the Hospital Catering was fully aware of what had happened I do not know, but all three of us made the trip anyway.

Grant did not obtain medical clearance, so this just left Jimmy Ross. Jimmy had trained well, and was young and strong. However he would have been a lot fitter if he had not smoked, as of course would many sportsmen, including boxers did in the 1970s. This was also his very first bout. As luck would have it, Jimmy came up against a determined and very fit young boxer, and so lost his semi final on points. He was disappointed to lose, but all three of us made the best of our short stay at Hereford, and indeed the whole trip. As I was faced with a three-hour car journey after the car ferry on the return trip, I could only sit and watch Jimmy and Grant enjoy themselves on the boat as they joined a group of Dutch girls in the bar. However when we arrived back at Wegberg very late at night, the bar was still open as somebody was undertaking a marathon walk throughout the night for charity, so of course the bar had to remain open for the supporters! I am fairly sure that Jimmy Ross, who I have kept in touch with to this day, bought me a pint, but if not he owes me one!

In the 1977, Disco probably reached a peak with Abba's ' Knowing Me Knowing You' and 'Name Of The Game' reaching the top spot, but the most well known disco song of all time, Donna Summer's 'I Feel Love' was number one for a month during the summer. The novelty selection was Wings with 'Mull Of Kintyre' complete with a Scottish Pipe band! One of the most significant events in the music world occurred in August when Elvis Presley died. His 'Way Down' shot to the top spot, and an amazing eight other previous hits charted. The other was the rise of the Punk movement. The Sex Pistols had three top ten hits, and just failed to reach number one with their somewhat irreverent version of 'God Save The Queen', which peaked at number two, in what the Queen's Silver Jubilee year.

The year ended on a happy note, with a family holiday to Fussen, where I had stayed with my children in the school holidays earlier in the year. Our winter holiday included another visit to the famous Neushwanstein Castle, trips to Munich and Oberammargau, (the town which stages a massive Passion Play every 10 years, and also the 1936 Olympic Winter Sports winter sports venue of Garmish Partenkirken. We all walked to the top of the highest ski jump in international competitions, to experience what the Ski Jumpers faced. I have since then remained in awe of them! Our holiday winter holiday ended early on Christmas Day, when after exchanging presents, we drove back home to Wegberg. Near the end of the journey, we became concerned about our car's fuel capacity, as even major motorway petrol stations had closed for the night!

At the start of 1978, I decided to get fit by running and stopping smoking. I measured a 1.5 mile course on roads outside of the grounds of the hospital, and timed myself running round it. I was pleased to note that I could manage to run inside the time allowed for the Army Basic Fitness Test. I continued to run initially on the same course every day, and then gradually extended the distance by running to nearby Rheindahlen which was 2 miles away, resting then running back to Wegberg. Soon after, I progressed to running 6 miles. This consisted of running 10 laps of an internal road in the hospital grounds. I then approached Mike James, a Flight Lieutenant who was in charge of the Hospital Pathology Department, and also the contact for cross country running. He arranged for me to run in a cross-country race, as part of the Joint Headquarters team for which Wegberg competed for in the RAF Germany Cross Country League. I struggled in the race, partly because I had not stopped smoking, and had only cut down. Also I was of course not used to racing over what was a distance I could just manage to run at my own pace. However I avoided coming last, and enjoyed the experience, and have continued cross-country racing to the present day, some 31 years later.

On the work front, I finally moved out of reception, slightly ahead of my turn. After almost two years in this job, it was thought that I had served my sentence. I moved to the Admission and Discharge Office,(A and D), which was a job I had done before at Halton, and was therefore something I quickly got used to. It also meant that I was finished with shift work, and of course The White Coat! Now that I was working regular hours, I was able to go running every lunchtime with several other runners from the hospital every lunchtime. The main group was consisted of Mike James, plus Graham Holloway, a Squadron Leader Orthopeadic Surgeon and Ken Barber, a corporal Dental Technician. I began to improve although I was still smoking a little. Ken Barber wanted to run a marathon, and was contemplating running his first ever marathon at Monschau at the end of July. I decided that I would join him, and started to increase my running to twice a day on weekdays, and to do long runs of up to 20 miles at a weekend. At the same time, my son Carl became interested in running, and we both joined a nearby local Athletic Club, OSC Waldniel. Carl was concentrating on track racing, whilst I started doing road races for the club. Ken Barber also joined OSC, and we often competed for this German Club at local road races. As we were both new to road racing, we competed in races called *Volkslaufs,* which were specifically for novices or athletes coming back after injury. As Ken improved, he looked likely to win one of these events, and one day he did win a half marathon. This was a race held in the large grounds of a Naturist Colony, although those involved in the race wore clothes. Ken won a trophy in the form of a very large cup similar to those presented for Football Cup Finals!

By the end of July, I was confident that I could cope with a marathon, and had entered the Monschau Marthon along with Ken Barber. We were joined by another runner from OSC Waldniel called Manfred Offermans to complete an official team. Monschau is a small town in the Ardeennes on the German/Belgian border. It was not the ideal place to run a first ever marathon, as it was a hilly course, and it was held on a hot day in July. I do not think that we ever really considered these things. On the day, we lined up at the start in very hot weather, but full of hope, with the main object of finishing the race. Notwithstanding the adverse conditions, all three of us completed the race, and finished as the third team. Ken and Manfred finished in just over three hours, whilst I got round in under 3 and a half hours. I was overjoyed, and soon after, I stopped smoking and started to train harder. I was hooked on marathons now.

Back at work, I felt a lot happier now that I was employed on a more fulfilling job, and was working regular hours. I also felt a lot better physically and mentally now that I was once again taking part in sport, and particularly the lunchtime runs. As I approached my final year of service, I started to consider if it might be preferable to re-engage and extend my service to at least the age of 47. As it was possible to give notice if my situation and prospects were to change, I applied to extend my service, and my application was approved. Whilst I had extended my engagement, the date of my return to the UK remained the same, which meant that I would be posted in April 1979, which was the date which would have given me my final six months of service in the UK. I was told that this date could not be changed, which was a reminder that the RAF could be, or at least seemed to be, inflexible in some administrative matters.

In the music charts, the Disco culture received a final boost with the release of the film 'Saturday Night Fever' which featured several big hits for the Bee Gees, including two big number ones, 'Night Fever' and 'Tragedy' (in 1979). They also had hits with 'Staying Alive' and 'Too Much Heaven'. As several earlier Bee Gee hits were included in the movie such as 'How Deep Is Your Love' film, it was a case of Bee Gees hits feeding the movie, and the movie feeding the hits! Another big musical film 'Grease', led to two massive hits for Olivia Newton-John, and John Travolta, and these two spending a total of 16 weeks at number one. 'Your The One That I Want' was number one for nine weeks, and 'Summer Night's stayed top for 7 weeks. In a period that was still dominated by British artists, the novelty element was provided by 'Matchstalk Men And Matchstalk Cats and Dogs' by Brian and Michael, which was a song about the twentieth century painter J S Lowry. At the end of the year, Boomtown Rats with Bob Geldhof, had the very first New Wave number one with 'Rat Trap'.

In the school holidays, there was a final camping holiday in Germany to be enjoyed. I spent a week recovering from the Monschau Marathon, whilst camping at a small northern German seaside resort with just the children, and then the whole family joined up and explored central Germany, and also

Luxembourg. Whilst visiting Luxembourg, I spotted the Radio Luxembourg building in the capital. I was curious what the radio reception would be like at such a close proximity, so I tuned in a portable radio to 208, and then discovered that it was about the same as in England, and just as it was back in 1950s when it was the only source of the Hit Parade as it was then called, to be broadcast in the UK. Another memorable event occurred whilst camping in the vicinity of a United States Air Force Base at Bitburg. I spotted a Starfighter aircraft in the sky which was on fire, and was heading for a crash. Starfighters were nicknamed, 'Flying Coffins' due to a high rate of crashes, although most of these accidents were attributed to pilot error. Whilst I was carrying a camera at the time, it never occurred to me to photograph the scene, and I just stared at the aircraft as it plunged to the ground – after the pilot had ejected I later found out. I would never make a living as a photojournalist. I did take photos of the crash site, along with many others of course!

During this summer holiday, I managed to stop smoking altogether, at least for a few months before succumbing to cravings and having the off cigarette now and then. This led to a big improvement in my running ability. My road race times improved, and when I recommenced cross-country racing in the autumn, I had greatly improved my finishing position. RAF Hospital Wegberg now had it's own cross country team in the RAF Germany league, and perhaps I might have been at least partly responsible for this, although Mike James was the prime mover, and he continued to encourage and coach me. At the end of October I ran in the Essen Marathon, and after an almost unbelievable run, got under the magic three hour mark. The course was a four lap out and back type course, which was alongside a large lake in Essen. I started off at the same pace of a recent half marathon best time, but somehow it was a day when everything went well, and I hung on to run just 10 seconds under three hours. This was one of my best ever races in the whole of my running career, on a misty October morning in Essen. Ken Barber who went to the race to support me, and Mike James who was coaching me, were delighted. In 1978, which was a few years before the marathon 'boom' of the early 1980s, a sub three-hour marathon was a great deal more of a significant athletic achievement.

In the early months of 1979, I was informed that I was to be posted back to RAF Halton, and once again to the hospital. It would have been my first choice of posting before I applied to re-engage, as I intended to settle in the area. Now that I had around 8 more years to serve, Halton was still a good posting, but I had some reservations about going back to working at the hospital whilst still a corporal. Soon after being informed of my posting, I went back to Aylesbury to get a first hand idea of house prices and mortgage possibilities. After interviews with a Building Society and a major agent, it seemed that I may have just 'missed the boat', as house prices in the Aylesbury area had now become beyond my means. I returned to Wegberg disappointed, but relieved that at least there was now no urgency to buy a property.

After going the whole of 1978 without any diversions from my normal working routine, Mike James organised a trip back to UK for an inaugural RAF Hospitals Cross Country Championship, which were to be held at RAF Hospital Nocton Hall. With the time spent travelling, which included an overnight stop at RAF Hendon, we had a very nice 5 day break. We did not manage to win the championships, and had to settle for runners up behind the host team, who of course had some good athletes as they had instigated the event. In February I ran another marathon, this time around the nearby town of Wegberg. On this occasion I was just outside the magic three hours, but the weather was far from ideal for fast times with wind and driving rain, so I was not too disappointed.

A few weeks before I left Wegberg, I offered to work on the day shift in Reception, so that my replacement in the A and D office, would have time to learn the job whilst I was still around working next door. It seemed like a good idea, and it was agreed that for my last few weeks I would work in Reception, whilst teaching my replacement who did not have any previous experience of this job. Unfortunately whilst this was a good plan as far as my replacement was concerned, it turned into a disaster for me. During the period I was working in Reception we had the annual inspection by the AOC. I was aware that it was more than likely that there would be a Fire Drill in the course of the inspection, and that I would be involved in carrying out set procedures. These included operating a Fire Alarm in the Reception Office. On the day, there was a practice Fire Drill, and to my horror I could not find the alarm switch as it had been moved to a different part of the office since I last worked there. The switch was eventually found, and nothing much was said about the matter at the time. I ought to have checked the position of the alarm when I started work in the office, and certainly should have ensured I was familiar with all aspects of Fire Drill before the inspection, but unfortunately the movement of the alarm switch never occurred to me. Shortly after this oversight, a signal was received offering me promotion, and a new posting to RAF Wattisham. However the Commanding Officer did not give his approval, and so I reverted to my original posting to Halton. This was seen as very harsh, and almost unprecedented by my immediate Warrant Officer boss, but there was nothing that he could do about it. I was therefore pleased to be leaving Wegberg, and hoped that it would not be too long before I was once again offered promotion once again.

14. Back To PMRAF Hospital Halton

A week after returning to the UK, I took over a married quarter on the camp, and started to settle in during the remainder of my disembarkation leave. The married quarter was a nice three bed house in a pleasant setting on the edge of the Halton Hills, which were a part of the Chilterns. However notwithstanding that I was not now due for demob, I wanted to get settled in my own house as soon as possible. Whilst property in nearby Wendover and Aylesbury was now beyond my means, I found a new development in Buckingham, which was just about affordable, and paid a deposit. I was then able to persuade the Building Society to let me have a mortgage. The house was expected to be ready for occupation in September, which it was.

When I reported to the hospital after my leave, I was disappointed but not totally surprised to find that the same system of rotation applied to the Reception, and that I would be returning to shift work and white coats yet again. The shifts were roughly the same as before, but somehow I did not mind so much. I had my running and new house to look forward to, and hopefully I would soon get promoted again, and there was not likely to be any problems with any future postings once I was settled in my new house. The new Out Patients wing had now been completed, and the working conditions were a lot better. I just had to stick it out for a while, and make sure I knew where the Fire Alarm was!

Outside of work, running became my main form of recreation, and Carl and myself both joined The Vale of Aylesbury Athletic Club, and both started to represent our new club in a variety of races, and attend training nights twice a week in Aylesbury. In addition I represented RAF Halton in the RAF Marathon Championships at RAF Swinderby, but failed again to get under three hours once again. The reason why I was not improving was because I had started smoking again. I decided to try hypnotism to help me stop, and this was to prove very successful. After my final session, I returned home and was curious about whether the hypnotism would really work. I therefore had a cigarette, and thought that it seemed the same as before, and therefore the hypnotism had not worked. However, shortly after smoking that cigarette, I went to work on the night shift. It was towards the end of the shift that I realised that I had not smoked at all during the night, so it seemed to have worked. It had, and I stayed stopped, at least for over three years, when temptation overcame hypnotism and willpower.

With the strikes of the so called 'winter of discontent' continuing up to February of 1979, the music of the start of the year at least, could not have struck a happier note, when the Village People hit the top with 'Y.M.C.A.'. This very funny 'tongue in cheek' record, along with the follow up, 'In The Navy' have survived to the present day. They were one of only two representatives from outside the UK, the other being Art Garfunklel with 'Bright Eyes', which was from the 1978 movie, 'Watership Down' which was about rabbits. It was the nearest to a novelty record for this year, and spent the longest time at the top spot. The happy mood continued throughout the year with a Ska revival, which resulted in a couple of hits each for new groups Madness and The Specials. The big summer hit was 'I Do'nt Like Mondays' by the Boom Time Rats. Whilst the inspiration for the title came from the words of somebody who shot people at random in the USA – it was his reason for the murders, the mood of the song was that of another fun record. The year saw the rise in popularity of electronic music with Gary Numan taking 'Are Friends Electric' under the group name of Tubeway Army, and then 'Cars' under his own name. The year ended with Pink Flloyd's reappearance in the charts with the massive hit 'Another Brick In the Wall' which was as well known for the accompanying video of course.

In September there was a change of fortune for me in that a new Warrant Officer, Eric Smart, took over as the Hospital Medical records Officer, (MRO). I had not worked with him before but he knew about my recent career as he had worked at the RAF Records Office. He told me that whilst he accepted that it might be fair to everybody if the 'last in and last out' system was operated in respect of Hospital Reception staff, he not only had the right to make an exception, but would do in respect of myself. He considered it ludicrous that my RAF Medical Branch experience, and particularly of working at three different hospitals was wasted if I stayed working in Reception. He also advised me that all being well, I could expect to be promoted fairly soon, probably the following year when a vacancy arose. I thought it was a pity that the MRO at Wegberg did not share his ideas regarding rotation of staff in Reception! I therefore started a new job controlling medical records. It was not that interesting, but it gave me some scope to improve the current system, and to use my experience in tracking down 'missing files' plus a fair amount of autonomy in my daily working routine. It also meant an end, once again, to white coats and shift work! The change of hours, fitted in very nicely with my move to a new house in Buckingham, where I could now commute daily along with my wife who had secured a civil service post on main camp at Halton. There was an after hours duty, which was that of a Duty NCO for the Hospital, who was responsible for minor matters such as closing the Social Club Bar! As all the hospital NCOs were on the rota, this duty did not arise very often. With this exception, I was once again employed in a post that might well have been civilian one, but I was not complaining.

Now that I had stopped smoking, I started to improve my overall fitness, and planned to run my fifth marathon at Harlow in October with other members of the Vale of Aylesbury AC. Before then, some of us decided to run in a marathon at Milton Keynes in September, but mainly as a training run in lieu of a standard 20 miler. I must confess that I did not really want to drop out of the race at 20 miles, and on the day I felt too good to not continue, so I ended up running the whole marathon in 2 hours 50 minutes, which was a really big breakthrough. What was even better was that my time was good enough for me to run in next year's Amateur Athletics Association, (AAA) Marathon Championships. This was also to be the 1980 Olympic Trial race. I was not bothered that I might be the last finisher in such a trial and was overjoyed to have qualified. When I subsequently ran the Harlow Marathon, I did not run anything like as well, but at least ran inside the three-hour mark.

My ambition to improve my marathon time, led me to travel to Barnsley in South Yorkshire at the beginning of December, for what was then a classic marathon. It also had a reputation as being a tough event. It was something of an out and back course with the first half being predominantly downhill, which meant that if too much effort was expended during the first half, which is common, then the final miles would be extremely hard going. I thought that possibly such a course might suit me, and that I could gain such an advantage on the downhill that overall I would still run a fast time. I traveled to Barnsley the day before, and stayed at the home of one of the runners from the promoting club, Barnsley Athletic Club. At this time I considered that I had reached a standard where I could ask for assistance with accommodation, and whilst this was hardly the case, I did manage to receive hospitality from the promoting clubs! The night before the marathon I went to as local pub with my host, and some other runners who would be running the marathon the next day. They seemed very laid back about it all, and enjoyed a few pints presumably as they always did on a Saturday night. One of the runners smoked, and nobody seemed to be bothered about sitting in a pub which was not exactly smoke free and healthy. I gathered that they were serious athletes, and were expecting to run well the next morning. Before the end of the evening, the runner I was staying with drove me round the course. As we approached a hill near the end, he told me in an unforgettable matter-of-fact way, that this was where somebody had collapsed and died in the race the previous year! I was not put off by this revelation, and had a good attempt at a fast time the next morning, but the course denied my ambition. However I was happy to get under the 3 hour mark on such a hard course.

The start of 1980 was marked by the good news that my promotion had finally been approved, and I was to be posted in March to RAF Wattisham in Suffolk. As my family was now settled in Buckingham with my children at local schools, they would stay put, whilst I would live in the Sergeants Mess from Monday to Friday. As the regulations stood at the time, my accommodation and food would be free, which was an added bonus on top of my pay rise. In addition, I would be entitled to claim some additional travel expenses which would cover some weekends commuting, and in any event the distance involved was only around a 100 miles. Shortly after I had been told about my promotion, an officer at the Hospital who was looking for a news story for the RAF News, asked me about how my running was going. At the time it was going very well, and I was running up to three times a day, covering 140 miles a week. At the start of 1980, I had the idea of aiming to complete 1,000 miles by the end of the 50th day of the year. Fortunately for this mad ambition, the final days before the target date, I was on annual leave and was able to achieve my target after dropping slightly behind. I mentioned this to the Hospital Press Officer, and added that I was training hard for the Olympic Trial Marathon in May. The result of these revelations was the publication of my story in a subsequent edition of the RAF News. The story, which about my move to Wattisham, my high mileage and marathon running ambitions, was accompanied by a photo of a very thin Mick, complete with a military moustache, which I shaved off soon afterwards! I have kept all my old passports, and the one that covered a period whilst I was a member of the Parachute Rescue Team is Cyprus, has a similar photo of me with a moustache. The contents of the passport include some strange looking visas for Iran, Turkey and The Trucial Oman Sates, whilst my occupation is listed a Government Official. Whilst the passport, which was issued by the British Embassy in Nicosia, was nothing out of the ordinary whilst I was on the Para Team, when I travelled around afterwards, it was invariably scrutinised more carefully than average at airports. I was glad when it expired and I could just keep it as a souvenir!

15. RAF Wattisham

My final days at Halton included a visit to the station tailor, to arrange the necessary, and indeed long overdue, sewing on of my sergeant stripes. I thought that they suited me a lot better than the corporal ones! The Hospital Medical Records Officer, Eric Smart was pleased that I had gained promotion, and assured me that I would enjoy life both in my new job in charge of the RAF Wattisham Station Medical Centre, and also living in the Sergeants Mess. He proved to be right on both counts.

On a midweek morning, I drove to RAF Wattisham feeling slightly apprehensive, but happy overall. I arrived at lunchtime, and as I did not wish to enter the Sergeants Mess for the first time on my own, I went to the station gym, got changed and went for a run. After the run, I went to the Medical Centre and met the outgoing sergeant who introduced me to the Senior Medical Officer, (SMO), and the rest of the staff. He then took me over to the Sergeants Mess to introduce me and get me sorted out with accommodation. After visiting the Station Headquarters for my arrival procedure, I was then introduced to key contacts such as the Barrack Warden who controlled things such as the issue of furniture and bedding for the Medical Centre! Back at the Medical Centre I met up with Steve Woods for the third time at the same station. He was by now an experienced corporal, and would be my deputy, and invaluable at the 'hands on' management of some of the more junior members of staff. Later after settling into my own room at the Sergeants Mess, I had a very nice evening meal, cooked and then served in the exclusive catering and dining facilities of the Mess. In the evening I went out to a local pub with the SMO for a couple of pints and a chat about work, and also so he would get to know me better. This was very nice, and notably a huge contrast to my initial reception at previous units.

RAF Wattisham was one of the many RAF Stations that still remained active in East Anglia in the 1980s. It was, just like all the others, a long way away from any large cities, and several miles from any but small towns, and was therefore deemed to be 'out in the sticks'. In Wattisham's case the nearest small towns were Needham Market and Stowmarket, with the much larger town of Ipswich about 12 miles away. The main role of the station was to house two fighter squadrons of Phantom aircraft, as part of the air defence of the UK. After the front line squadrons based in Germany, this was the next line of defence in the 'Cold War', and any aggression by Soviet Union forces. The preparation for any possible future conflict was constant, and was intensified with regular exercises which involved the entire base for up to 72 hours, called Tacevals, short for Tactical Evaluation Exercise, or Minevals which were as the name suggests, a smaller version. In addition RAF Wattisham was the parent unit of RAF Bawdsey which contained Bloodhound guided missiles, and also a small radar unit. This small unit had a SAC medic from the Wattisham Medical Centre, and the services of a local general practitioner. The RAF Wattisham Medical Centre was staffed by two medical officers, the SMO and a Flight Lieutenant junior. Then there was myself and my deputy, Steve Woods, and six SACs, plus a civilian nurse and a cleaner. In addition we had the services of a civilian typist, and also a permanent ambulance driver who remained at the Medical Centre when flying was in progress, plus other drivers as required. They were all under my control whilst employed at the Medical Centre, but were otherwise managed by their own section managers. After the comparatively calm world of Reception and Medical Records etc. at Hospitals, this return to the what was the real RAF, justified my earlier feeling of apprehension. Shortly after I had taken over, there was a Minieval exercise on camp. This started with a call out of all personnel in the small hours of the morning. I went in the Medical Centre, where some of the staff had already reported in. The SMO was on annual leave but his junior was in attendance. Both the Junior Medical Officer and myself were both somewhat hesitant as to what was the best thing to do first, as neither of us had any previous experience of these exercises. After some thought, the medical officer made a decision. Eager faces waited for his words of wisdom as we stood around in the Decontamination Area of the Medical Centre where casualties, real or pretend, would be received and treated. He suggested that we dismantle the Table Tennis table in the centre of the room! That done, there was then a pause, but fortunately Steve Woods had arrived by this time, and was more than able to come up with more practical suggestions!

Whilst I was previously able to successfully negotiate time away from work for sporting activities, as a SNCO, this became even easier. My boss would always trust my judgement as regards the necessity of my absence in respect of a particular sporting event. It was always more of a question of whether Steve Woods was available to cover for me, as there was no realistic alternative. My first sports trip whilst at Wattisham was the RAF Marathon Championship race at RAF Swinderby at the end of April. Whilst this race required only a short absence from duty, the race was to take place on the final day of a major Taceval exercise. I was however allowed to leave the exercise on the day before the end, so that I could travel to RAF Swinderby for an overnight stay in the Swinderby Sergeants Mess. RAF Wattisham had two good marathon runners in Mick Hurd and Dave Todd, and we stood a good chance of winning the station championship. The race took place on a two lap course on quiet flat roads in the vicinity of the camp, and included the Inter Services Championship. The weather on the day of the race was unseasonably hot, and when I finished in a disappointing 2 hours 54 minutes, I was soon reassured that I had run well as all the finishing times were well down due to the heat. Mick Hurd won the race, and was closely followed by Dave Todd, whilst I was the third scorer. Wattisham were both the first RAF team, and the first team overall in the Inter Service Championships, whilst I won the first of three first RAF veteran trophies.

Not long after the Swinderby race, I was asked if I was interested in taking part in the Nijmegen Marches in July. This is an annual event which takes place around the town of Nijmegen in Holland, and consists of non competitive marches on four consecutive days. The distance of the marches varies between 30 and 50 kilometres each day, and is dependant on whether a back pack is carried. I was considered to be fit enough to be able to cope with this event, and I had only to complete just one trial walk around Wattisham in order to book my place on the trip. Our six man team travelled to Holland on the Friday before the start of the marches on the following Tuesday morning. After arriving in Holland, I travelled to Wegberg to meet up with Ken Barber. I had a great weekend and got some good training runs in, which included a long run on trails with other runners from RAF Germany, before travelling back to Nijmegen on the Sunday night. The following day was spent mainly sheltering from incessant rain in our tents, and then moving the tents after some flooding. Thankfully, the weather improved a lot by the start of the marches the next day. My team had opted to walk about 40 kilometres each day, which was not too daunting, although their desire to start very early in the morning was not something that appealed to me. The reason for the early start was simply to finish early in the afternoon, so that there would be lots of time left to visit Nijmegen and join other marchers in favourite bars.

On the first day I coped very well with the distance marched, and enjoyed the camaraderie amongst the groups of marchers. The majority of the marchers were military personnel from NATO countries, which included lots of United States forces teams, who are renowned for their chanting as they march. When I got back to the camp, I went out for a 12 mile run which consisted of running back down the course for 6 miles and then running back. Apart from wanting to maintain my normal running mileage, I figured that by the time I returned, the rest of the team would have departed for the bright lights, and I would not be tempted to join them. This pattern of running after the march continued at the end of days two and three, but I was feeling the overall effect of the long days spent on my feet, and reduced the distance spent running. At the end of the last day, my feet were somewhat sore, so I skipped the run and had a few beers at the camp with other marchers instead. The event ended with a march past of the marchers on the Saturday morning. This was an optional extra that I had no hesitation in declining!

As I settled in my job, I thought about how I could improve on the training of the junior staff, and make their work more interesting. I had of course some experience of boring jobs! One of the first innovations came after receiving some criticism from an Air traffic Controller, following a practice emergency alert on the airfield. It seemed that the medic and ambulance driver had encountered a problem with a map reference, which was given out when the alert was sounded, and which indicated the point where the ambulance was supposed to proceed to. The normal procedure was to dash to the airfield and simply watch where the fire engines were heading. However this system failed to work on this occasion for some reason. I ascertained that there was not a problem reading the map of the airfield, and that it was a case of not having enough practice at finding a particular location. As alerts were infrequent, some of the medics might not have had hardly any previous experience of the procedure. I therefore arranged for regular alerts which could involve only the ambulance crew. After several practice alerts, Air Traffic Control was happy that something had been done about the problem, and the staff had enjoyed the practice, which was a lot more exciting than routine paperwork. I suspect that it was still a matter of following the fire crews to the reference point, but at least there was an alternative strategy in place now.

Because the SMO spent time at a hospital in Ipswich as a part of training for a professional qualification, I asked him to explore the possibility of the Medical Centre staff, spending a week at a time working in the hospital's busy casualty department. The idea was that they would gain so much more experience of dealing with a variety of casualties, than they would have in a year or more of duty medics on the station. This was agreed and all but one of the staff enjoyed the experience. The scheme lasted long enough for them all to have two separate weeks, after which it was considered that they had probably received sufficient benefit to end the practice, particularly as there was now some reluctance to continue working at the hospital by at least one of the staff.

The normal training for the staff as regards medical administration was carried out by Steve Woods, who successfully guided most of the staff through the necessary examinations required for promotion. There was of course some exceptions, who were happy not to bother trying for promotion. This was a time when promotion even to corporal, could be slow, and some airmen were on comparatively short engagements. There was rarely any problems with discipline, and with only the odd exception, the staff could be trusted to work without undue supervision. One of the exceptions was an SAC who was the staff member who worked at RAF Bawdsey. On one occasion, I warned him that we would be getting a visit by staff from Command Headquarters, as a part of the formal annual AOCs inspection. The inspection team carried out very rigorousness checks on local accounting for medical equipment, particularly drugs, the handling of medical documents, and what efforts were being made to ensure schedules for regular medical examinations, inoculation's etc. were being kept. They would also expect the medical centre to be scrupulously clean. I was assured that everything necessary would be done before I paid a preparatory visit myself. When I did visit, very little of the necessary work had been carried out, and to make matters worse, one of the rooms in the small medical centre was in a mess. I therefore placed the medic concerned on a charge. This was considered a somewhat extreme action which should be avoided if possible. I soon found out why. The charge was to be dealt with, not by the SMO as I expected it would, but by another officer in the Station Headquarters. I had to fully justify what orders were given, and what they consisted of. In general we were dealing with a failure to carry out routine duties, not all of which would be specified in the form of an order. I was made to feel that I was on trial, but in the end the charge was proven, and some minor punishment imposed. As somebody else had to go and sort out the mess, I considered that I was justified in my approach to the problem. There was only one other occasion during my time at Wattisham when a formal charge was thought necessary, but this was for something more straight forward, although not too serious, and it was dealt with appropriately.

In the summer of 1980, I went on what would turn out to be the final family holiday, with my wife and daughter. An argument which arose en-route to our holiday destination in South Wales, was never properly resolved, and subsequently led initially to what is legally described as an estrangement, and a year later to divorce, after 19 years of marriage. It is unnecessary to recall any of the details, other than whilst it is possible that the midweek separation could have led to problems, this was not the major cause. There were others living in the Sergeants Mess, who readily blamed their marriage problems on living apart for most of the week, but very often there was of course many other reasons involved, and judging by the ages of those concerned, the so called 'middle age itch' may well have been a major factor! For the remainder of the year, I continued to come home to Buckingham at the weekends, mainly to see the children, and also with the hope that our marital problems might somehow be resolved.

In spite of my domestic problems, I remained focussed on both my job and also on my running. My job was going well, and I was still enjoying my management role at the Medical Centre. After the Swinderby Marathon, I took part in four more marathons before the end of the year, which made this my most prolific year ever for the event. All of these races were very memorable starting with the Olympic Trial race at Milton Keynes. I finished this race in 2 hours 51, which was my second best ever time, but I was only 177th of 195 finishers. I would therefore not be selected for the Olympics in Moscow! I observed afterwards the nearest I got to the winner Ian Thompson, was in the race programme! It was a great experience mixing with the best marathon runners in the UK at that time. After this year, the annual UK marathon championships have been included in the London Marathon, and they are no longer run as a separate race.

At the end of May, I joined a group of RAF runners from RAF Halton who were going on a Twin Town visit to Liffre in France, to represent nearby Wendover. This was a very enjoyable long Bank Holiday weekend, spent staying at the homes of the very hospitable hosts, and which included participation in a marathon on the Sunday afternoon. On the Saturday evening, one of the host families invited some of the marathon runners to a sumptuous evening meal at their house. The preparation of a huge four course meal was severely delayed, and in the meantime, the host offered various aperitifs which consisted of some strong spirit concoction, which became increasingly inviting as the evening progressed. When the meal was finally served, there was of course lots of wine flowing, and as a result we all consumed a fair bit, just to be social of course! This was not the best preparation for a marathon the next day, but whether the host was just being very sociable or else mischievous I do not know. As luck would have it the next day was very hot. When I went for a jog in the morning, I had a slight hangover and was regretting the night before. By the afternoon, my powers of recovery had kicked in, and I managed to run 2 hours 55 minutes. How much faster I might have run I could only speculate, but two of the team, former Olympic Pentathlete Don Cobley along with John Foden, who avoided the excesses of the pre race dinner, both had very good races. Before we left Liffre, we enjoyed a gala post race meal followed by a dance to end a memorable visit.

My appetite for marathon running was undiminished so at the end of August, I travelled to Glasgow for the World Veteran Marathon Championship. As the minimum age for men was 40, this was my first attempt at a world championship, and in theory my best chance in the Over 40 division and overall. There are five yearly age divisions in such championships. For me it was possibly a marathon too many as I struggled on what I thought was a fairly tough course, but others from my running club at Aylesbury all had very good runs.

My final marathon in 1980 was in Holland, and this was a much better experience all round. The RAF champion Mike Hurd from Wattisham used his network of contacts with race organisers, to arrange an all expenses paid trip not only for himself, but also three other runners, one of whom was myself. Mike negotiated travelling expenses to take us in his car to Zwolle, where we would enjoy a 2 night stay in a decent hotel with all our meals included. In the race programme, we were listed as an England team, and in general at that time, if you were not a native in Holland then the next best thing to be was British, as the Dutch had long memories of the Second World War, and had retained great affection for the British, particularly the RAF and the Airborne forces. Mike Gratton who subsequently won the London Marathon in 1983, was the other England representative. On the day of the race, the weather was very hot and humid, but I had a good race finishing in 50th and the third England finisher ahead of two of the other invited runners, in 2 hours 53 minutes which was my third best finish at this time. Mike Gratton finished in third, and Mike Hurd was 9th, after both of them had been affected by the hot weather. After the race and the usual food and drinks at the post race reception, we returned to the hotel for a nice meal and some drinks on the race organiser. This was to be my only experience of elite athletics, and I regretted not having started marathon running until I was 37 years old.

In addition to my five marathons, I also had some track races, albeit only on a grass tack at Wattisham. These took place at the Station Sports Day, when I entered the 1500 and 5000 metre races. I came second in the 1500 but managed to win the 5000 race. This was the first time I had won any race, and whilst it was a race restricted to RAF Wattisham personnel, it was a great experience. Even though I established a lead after the first lap, it seemed like a very tough race, probably as I was unused to both track racing and also being in the lead in a race. In addition to the 5000 winners trophy, I also won a trophy for being the best Over 40 athlete after I had taken part in a variety of other disciplines over the course of the previous week. These had involved scoring points based on set standards for events such as throwing the javelin and the high jump.

1980 was the final year that I regularly tuned in to Alan Freeman's 'Pick of the Pops' which was then broadcast in the early evening slot, having moved from the previous Sunday afternoon when it started in the 1960s. I would always tune in as I drove back to Wattisham, which would greatly cheer me up and make the journey time pass quickly. As was the case in 1979, there was a great variety of music, and plenty of what would now be considered to be Karaoke type songs to sing along with as the miles sped by. The Detroit Spinners and their number one hit 'Working My Way Back To You' was a good example of this. In term of number one's, newcomer Blondie had the most with three top spots with 'Atomic', 'Call Me' and 'The Tide Is High', whilst the The Police with 'Do'nt Stand So Close To Me' spent the longest time at number one, which was four weeks. Disco music was still not quite finished and Abba had their final number one with 'Super Trooper', and Odyssey took 'Use It Up and Wear It Out' to the top spot. The Ska revival continued with another number one for The Specials, 'The Specials Live', an EP, and the New Wave group Jam managed two top spots with 'Going Underground' and 'Start'. As seemingly always, there was a novelty hit, this time with the Saint Winifred's School Choir and 'There's No One Quite Like Grandma', which was never going to be a huge Karoke song!

At the end of the year, the untimely death of John Lennon led to a revival of his previous hit, 'Just Like Starting Over'. This was followed by two more number ones the next month, 'Imagine' and 'Woman'. This reflected a great sadness amongst a wide section of the general public, particularly those of the so called 'Beatles' generation. An example of the effect of John's death was the effect that it had on a football match at Ipswich which I attended along with Steve Woods, on the Saturday after John's death. Ipswich were at that time one of the top teams in the old First Division, which is now known as The Premiership. They went on to finish second in the league, and also win the EUFA cup that season. Liverpool who finished fifth in the league were very much in contention for the title when they met at Portman Road. There was naturally a very a large crowd at the game – I cannot say a sell-out crowd, as somehow in those days with the terraces, it was a matter of squeezing in, rather than not getting in. The P.A. system played mainly John Lennon's hits, and this seemed to have a noticeable effect on the crowd, as there was none of the usual aggressive chanting prior to kick off. It would not have seemed proper to denigrate Liverpool at this sad time, and therefore there was none of the usual jibes back about yokels and 'carrot crunchers'. As if on cue, the game ended in a draw, and probably helped to retain the neutral atmosphere on this day.

On the work front, the year ended for me with a course at Brize Norton. This was the Air Ambulance Attendant Course, some twenty years after I had performed these duties whilst at Bahrain! The reason I was now undergoing formal training for the task, was that I was due to be posted to Belize in either January or July the following year for a six month posting. This would entail me working at the Army Hospital on the main base in Belize, which was just outside Belize City. I would be the RAF representative who would liaise with all concerned regarding any internal medical evacuation by helicopter, or external flights to either the USA or to the UK. It was partly an administrative post and partly hands on. The course consisted of a two week phase learning standard aircraft emergency procedures both in the classroom, in a swimming pool, and on standard aircraft, including Puma Helicopters. There was also lots of administrative procedure and regulations to be absorbed. The second half of the course involved two aero medical flights. The first one was to RAF Wildenrath in Germany where patients from RAF Germany and also the NATO base at Decimomannu in Sardinia, which had a British contingent, were returned to hospitals in UK on the special aero medical flights. For those on the team who were not required for the Sardinia leg, there was a pleasant overnight stay in a hotel near Wildenrath. I took advantage of the trip to visit Ken Barber at Wegberg, and go out for a run with him. Ken was now on his second consecutive tour. This was because he was in the relatively small, specialised trade of Dental Technician, and seemingly few in the trade were interested in a posting to Wegberg. I had a good run around Wegberg, before returning to the hotel for a meal and a few drinks. The allowances for even this short trip were sufficient for cover not only accommodation, food and drink, but also for me to buy a pair of training shoes!

The final part of the course involved a stay of about five days at RAF Akrotiri, where, along with others on the course, I sat a final examination. After I passed I had my new aeromedical 'wings' badge sewn on my uniform by the station tailor. The badge was a small pair of wings with a red cross in the centre. I wore mine underneath my parachute wings, as that seemed the right place, as I did not know anyone else who had both sets of wings to guide me. I was pleased with the way my uniform was now looking, with Collar Dogs, Medal Ribbons and two sets of 'wings' on my sleeve, plus of course the sergeant stripes. Before returning to the UK on an aero medical flight that started at Hong Kong, I had an opportunity to visit the street where I had lived in Limmasol about ten years earlier. The owners of the house still lived next door and were pleased to see me again. I did not spoil their joy by telling them that my marriage was over. There was also a day out for the course at Paphos, which included a nice lunch at the restaurant where an ancient pelican hovered about waiting for tit bits from the diners. I returned back at Wattisham just in time for the pre Christmas celebrations in the mess. Shortly after, I returned home to Buckingham for what was to be a final and subdued final family Christmas, before returning back to Wattisham in the new year.

At the start of the year, I sold the family car to settle some joint debts, and partly because of this and the virtual end of my marriage, I started to spend most weekends at Wattisham in the Sergeants Mess. There was only a fraction of residents remaining at the weekend as most of the married men went home for the weekend. This left just a few who were required to work at the weekend, often just a station duty such as Orderly Sergeant. In addition there was a few confirmed bachelors, and some like myself who were recently divorced or separated. One of the latter with whom I became friends, was a Sergeant Trevor Evans, who worked in the General Duties Flight of the station. Trevor belonged to a club for the Divorced and Separated in Ipswich, and used to go to a dance on Saturday nights, and other social activities. He suggested I joined him for the Saturday night dances which I did. These dances took place in various venues such as school halls, and were invariably discos, with the members bringing their own drinks and refreshment. I started to go along, and enjoyed the dances particularly when I got to know a few of the members. Trevor had started seeing somebody he had met there, and I tended to tag along with him, particularly as he had transport. When Trevor was posted to Belize, I started to go to the dances on my own, on a RAF cycle, which I hid somewhere when I arrived at the venue for the dance. This led to some amusing incidents. The first was when a woman asked me for a lift home. I explained that I only come on a bike. She said that did not matter, as it was unlikely that the police would bother to stop me if she was not wearing a crash helmet. When I told her that it was a push and not a motor bike, she could not believe it at first, so I had to retrieve the bike from its hiding place to show her. On another occasion, as I cycled back to camp, I was stopped by the local police, who wanted to know where I was going etc. When I showed my service I.D. Card, they apologised and said that they were looking for a local burglar – on a bike?! At this time, I was training quite hard for the Swinderby Marathon again, and had travelled over to Leighton Buzzard in Bedfordshire by public transport to a ten mile road race. In addition to running the ten miles, I had also run a couple of miles warming up, and then after the race, I ran a few miles to the railway station as there was no bus due for a while. As soon as I arrived back at Wattisham, I got on my bike and cycled to the Saturday night dance as usual, stopping off at an Off Licence for a couple of cans of beer. I sat in the dance hall near a couple of women who I knew only slightly. They were talking about a gym they had started going to, when one of them told me that some exercise would do me a lot of good. I did not bother to correct her, and was pleased that I was obviously so fit, that I looked ill!

In April I had to get permission to leave a major Taceval exercise a day early once again, so that I could travel to Swinderby for the marathon once again. Whilst the conditions were not perfect with some gusty winds around the Lincolnshire lanes, I achieved a breakthrough and finished in a personal best time of 2 hours 45 minutes, which was a time that I only managed to beat twice in my lifetime. I was the first veteran again, and once again helped Wattisham to retain the inter station trophy, this time as the second team scorer as Mike Hurd did not compete this year. Later in the year, I also repeated my success at the annual Station Sports Day by winning the 5000 metres and once again coming second in the 1500 metres. Before I left Wattisham for Belize, I wanted to run in a big marathon, and decided to enter the Copenhagen Marathon in June. When I sent off my entry form, I enclosed a letter asking if any assistance with accommodation was possible. I received a reply from the race organiser Erik Nielsen to say that I could stay at his home, which was a very nice gesture, particularly as I was not an elite athlete.

After going for over four years without having to attend a training course, along came another earlier in the year. This was a management course mainly for newly promoted senior NCOs with management responsibilities, although many of those attending had been promoted some considerable time, and others in some technical trades had limited management responsibilities. However I suppose it was a case of making a start, as previously management courses were limited mainly to individual trade groups, and did not have much of a personnel management content. The course was held at RAF Newton near Nottingham and lasted for two weeks. Other than ongoing tests throughout the course, there was no final examination at the end, so the students could relax a little. It turned out to be an excellent course, and was stimulating and thought provoking. Part of the philosophy was that being a part of a strictly structured society, could result in a lack of original thought, with the need to conform and obey orders. To illustrate the point, an exercise early in the course, consisted of splitting the course into small groups, whereupon one member of the group had to go to a room with a stable type door, and describe a structure at the far side of the room to the group. The only rule was that entry into the room was forbidden. Nobody turned on the light in the room, although the view was somewhat dim without it. Everybody assumed that although there was no rule forbidding the turning on of the light, it was seemingly part of the exercise to do without. There was plenty of these sort of group exercises, which sometimes led to heated debates when results were debated at the end of the exercise. No doubt this was expected and part of the course, but sometimes it almost got out of hand, particularly if somebody particularly disagreed with one of the basic themes of the course. From my own experience, I always considered that most members of the RAF were very innovative and resourceful. Even the most junior airman, would discover a legal way of saving time on any job that was allotted, so allowing time to relax, or in the RAF jargon to 'skive'. Higher up the management tree, it seemed not only to me, but to others I have discussed this with, that no matter how skilfully any section had previously been managed, the new occupant would invariably find ways to make further improvements. This concept, together with the regular turn round in staff, must have added to the overall efficiency of the service.

As I neared the end of my posting at Wattisham, I decided to book a couple of weeks leave, and spend a holiday in Denmark before and after the marathon weekend, which would be spent with the Nielsen's in Copenhagen. My leave would end just before I left for my new posting to Belize. I also arranged to run in a big 25 kilometre race in Bruges, Belgium the Sunday after the marathon, before heading back to Wattisham. I travelled to Denmark on a ferry from Harwich to Esbjerg, which had a large party of mainly young women from Lapland on board. They had all been to see Pink Floyd at Earls Court, presumably as the band's World Tours did not extend to Lapland! One of the group was taking advantage of a warm sunny afternoon before the ship sailed, to indulge in a spot of topless sunbathing on the top deck. This looked like being an interesting overnight passage to Denmark! There was a disco in the evening which was of course dominated by the Lapland Branch of the Pink Floyd Fan Club, who persuaded the Ship's Disc Jockey to play 'The Wall' at regular intervals. As the young Laps, seemingly liked a drink or three, it was certainly an enjoyable night. Around lunchtime the next day, I disembarked at Esbjerg without any telephone numbers or addresses of the Laps, to start a two week stay in Denmark. It was twenty years after my very first visit, and I was in effect single again.

Except for my stay with Erik in Copenhagen, I would be camping out, having borrowed all the equipment from Wattisham, which was set aside for 'adventure' training. I considered that my two major international races, qualified as an adventure, well at least I was excited about it. The first three nights were spent camping at Esbjerg, which at that time was a small town, and considering that it was a seaport, it was very quiet. If there was any jolly bars with lots of young Danes drinking Carlsberg, I never saw them. This was fine for me, as whilst I wanted to wind down my training in preparation for the marathon on the Saturday afternoon, but I also wanted to relax and get plenty of sleep. On one of the evenings I went to a local football match, but on the others I went for a walk after cooking an evening meal on a camping stove. Then when feeling suitably tired after all the fresh sea air all day, I retired early, after tuning in to the World service on my radio. During the day, I went for some easy runs around the seafront and visited cafes for some fast food. I particularly liked the local Polser boiled sausages, and this was after all, a time to load up with carbohydrates! As well as a lack of any night life, there was also very few shops to spend time shopping or window shopping, so this was an inexpensive short but restful start to my holiday.

On the fourth day, I set off for Copenhagen on the train, arriving just after lunch, spent a little time walking round the city centre enjoying the sights, before travelling to Erik's house in the northern suburbs. I was welcomed into the home and enjoyed the Nielsen's's hospitality for the next three days. This included some delicious vegetarian food cooked by Erik's wife's Ingelise. On the day before the marathon I spent time exploring Copenhagen on what was a fine summer day. I also spent time playing games in the garden with the the Nielsen's youngest daughter, and making a fuss of the family cat called Pusa.

The marathon started in the city centre and consisted of a 10 kilometre loop, before heading to the north of the city and the finish 32 kilometres later at a sports stadium, via a long and mainly flat stretch of road near the seafront. The majority of the runners were from Denmark, and there was also some from Sweden, Norway and West Germany. I was one of only two runners from the UK, the other being the subsequent race winner, Malcolm East, who was living in the U.S.A, at the time. He was one of the invited elite athletes which included the second placed runner John Dimick from the USA, and two East German athletes who finished 4th and 6th. At the time I was a member of the Vale of Aylesbury AC, but I was listed in the Race Program as RAF. As Denmark is one of those countries like Holland that was occupied during World War Two, the RAF who waged war for the entire duration, retains an affection by Danes, so I got some extra cheers and shouts of encouragement during the race. The race went very well, and the only problem was with my stopwatch, which meant that after the 10 kilometre point, I did not know what my split times were. I was aiming to run under 2 hours 40 minutes, and thought I was running at about that sort of pace, but when I got to around 40 kilometre, I found that I was too far outside to make my target. I felt tired after that and had to concentrate on finishing without losing my position. I subsequently crossed the line in 2 hours 46 which was my second best time after the Swinderby race that April, and was placed 50th overall which was some compensation. In the evening I attended the post race reception with Erik, the Race Director, and the elite runners. I tried out my German on the East German athletes, who were making the most of the hospitality which included a strong brand of Carlsberg lager, called 'Elephant'. I do not know if it was the effect of a hard race, the lager, or, as was more likely a combination of both, but the DDR pair and their coach, rested their heads on the table to snooze for a short while, before resuming to enjoy the hospitality. Perhaps they just wanted to escape my German language! There was also some music and some dancing which lasted well into the night, before Ingelise kindly drove Erik and myself back home.

After a lazy Sunday at the Nielsen's's, I said my goodbyes to Ingelise and Erik drove me to the railway station in Copenhagen to catch a train to the south of Jutland, and continue my holiday. I camped near the beach at a small seaside resort which had a mixture of German and Danish holiday makers. The weather was ideal for camping, and I enjoyed just lazing around on the beach for some of the time. My stay included the 'longest' midsummer day, where partly because of the time difference, it was daylight until well after 11 p.m. That night there was a good crowd on the beach to celebrate the occasion with some local games and customs. On another night I splashed out and had a meal at a restaurant which also had a disco, and had another opportunity to try out my German where it was necessary, but mostly it was not, as everybody, especially the Danes spoke English. I knew that the Danes did not expect their visitors to be able to speak their language, so I felt comfortable with just speaking a little German. When the post race stiffness had eased, I went for some cycle rides on a hired cycle, and then started some gentle jogging on the beach. By the end of the week, I felt able to run more or less normally, and started to look forward to the 25 Kilometre race on the coming Sunday. On the Saturday morning I caught a train to Bruges. I was impressed by the punctuality as it arrived at intermediate stations bang on time, and also how comparatively inexpensive it was to travel without pre booking on a one way journey. The journey was also very interesting as a variety of people boarded and left the train, starting with Danes seemingly out for the day, and likewise Germans on Saturday outings, and concluding with Belgians going out for a Saturday night. I arrived on time in Bruges and linked up with runners from Aylesbury AC, who were staying in some student accommodation. After a good nights sleep, I ran somewhat surprisingly well in the 25 kilometre race the following day, finishing in 93 minutes which was a time I only ever bettered the once. There was a dance and lots of wine in the evening, which was very enjoyable at the time, but regretted the next day on a rough channel crossing.

Shortly after arriving back at Wattisham, I was told that my flight to Belize had been cancelled and I would not now be travelling out there for another ten days. Steve Woods who was deputising for me in the Medical Centre was happy for me to continue leave until then, so I enjoyed another unexpected but very enjoyable week's holiday in Suffolk. I spent some time cycling round the nearby Constable Country, and was also able to successfully compete in the Station Sports day as mentioned earlier in this chapter. My enjoyment was enhanced at the weekend, when I went to the Saturday night dance for the last time, and became romantically attached to a woman I had met briefly at past dances. My previous meetings with her at noisy discos, led me to believe that she was a policewoman. This was because she told me that she was a potter, and I thought she said she was a copper! I never really explored aspects of what I thought was her profession, as it seemed a bit of a conversation stopper to me. Having sorted out this misunderstanding, I spent a lot of time with her during my final week at Wattisham. On the final Friday, we went together to the Summer Ball at the Sergeants Mess. This was the first time in my life that I had ever been to such a formal occasion, and I enjoyed it very much. The ball lasted until the early hours and ended with a cooked breakfast. The following evening, we went to see the film 'Chariots of Fire', and she fell asleep watching it! So after a memorable final weekend, I packed my bags and said goodbye to Wattisham, and departed for RAF Brize Norton and an overnight stay before an early morning flight to Belize.

16. RAF Belize

After an unscheduled stop in Canada, due to a technical problem, and a scheduled stop at Washington, I finally arrived in Belize in the early evening. I first met up with Trevor Evans at the airport, as Trevor delivered the usual briefing to new arrivals about security. There was of course no terrorism in Belize and never had been, and the talk was alerting servicemen, (there was no female servicewomen), to the possibility of a bit of mugging down town after dark! I then met the sergeant I was replacing, who showed me round the mess and the army hospital, to which I would be attached to for the next six months.

Belize, which was previously known as British Honduras, was due to be formally granted independence in September of 1981 by the mutual agreement of both UK and Belize. The British presence was mainly to act as a deterrent against any invasion by neighbouring Guatemala who had made sovereignty claims. The RAF element was based just outside Belize City at Airport Camp which adjoined the main Belizean airport, and consisted of four Harrier aircraft and the necessary servicing element. The Army presence was spread around the colony, with just a company of infantry, plus back up of engineers etc., based at Airport Camp. There was a Jungle Training School for 'special forces' in the colony, and also a small detachment of Special Air Service troopers, known as 'F Troop' at Airport Camp.

At Airport camp, there was a small hospital which was staffed by members of the Royal Army Medical Corps, and commanded by a medical officer of Lieutenant Colonel rank. There was also a 'Mash' type unit based there, and this mobile surgical unit would occasionally deploy to isolated villages in Belize and perform minor surgery on the local population. The RAF element which dealt with the health of the RAF personnel, consisted of a Flight Lieutenant Medical Officer, myself and a SAC on a month's detachment from RAF Odiham. In addition to dealing with the health of the airmen, the three of us were concerned with all aspects of aero medical evacuation. This would range from internal flights using mainly Puma helicopters, to arranging emergency flights to the USA or to the UK, either by scheduled aircraft or in extreme urgency by Lear Jet to the USA. Except for when being actively engaged on aero medical matters, there was not much work to fully occupy any of us. I took it turns with the SAC to have every other afternoon off, during the five day week. The living accommodation in the Sergeants Mess was somewhat basic, and consisted of two bedrooms, which were cooled only by ceiling fans going full blast all day and night. The climate was hot but not extremely humid, so acclimatisation did not take long, and then the fans were adequate. The hospital building was air conditioned, and seemed cold in comparison. The mess was run on Army lines which led to some petty rules, such as having to wear long trousers with a shirt with the sleeves rolled down in the public rooms every evening. This was known as 'Planters dress without tie'! There was the usual bar with it's own rules, and a kitchen/dining room attached. The food was reasonable, and by Army standards of the day, very good indeed. The entertainment in the Mess consisted of tape-recorded television, (there was no Belizean National Television Service), occasional film shows and every Saturday night a dance with a live band and a barbecue style buffet. It was seemingly part of the arrangement, that the members of the band would avail themselves of the buffet food, which seemed to lead to an ever-increasing numbers in the band, but they always sounded great. Transport would collect local females and bring them to the mess for the dance. This was similar to the dances at Freckleton some 24 years before.

There was not very much entertainment outside of the camp in Belize City other than some bars, some of which were out of bounds to servicemen. The town itself was not out of bounds, but was deemed a bit risky after dark. There were just a few shops, but this was a poor country and there was very little worth buying. I assume the local rich folk either used mail order extensively, or did their shopping for all but essential items on trips to nearby USA. I would occasionally visit the town to buy American magazines and some music cassettes from a bookshop, and I also ran to the outskirts of the town and back every Sunday for my weekly 'long run'. There was only one occasion when I visited the city at night, and that was for a meal at a posh hotel with Trevor. The food was fine, but the overall cost including taxis to and from the city, was not worth the expense as far as we were both concerned. Other than the guests of the Sergeants Mess every Saturday night, there was not a lot of social activity with the local population. Whilst the natives were generally friendly towards the British servicemen, there was a cultural gap between the generally poor Belizeans and the comparatively wealthy British. There did not seem to be any effort made by the service authorities to forge any links, possibly as the two sides lived in peace, which is not always the case in respect of overseas bases, even in friendly countries.

Not long after my arrival, Prince Charles was married to Diana. There was no television service in Belize at that time, but a tape recording of the wedding was sent out to Airport Camp. Everybody claimed that they were not remotely interested, but when the recording was shown in the Sergeants Mess, the room was packed out! The normal size audience for all other televised programmes would be around half a dozen! There was a local radio station that broadcast in English and Spanish, but it was very amateurish, and other than some record request programmes, it was largely ignored by the servicemen, so it was back to The BBC World Service and 'Lily Bolero'. I listened mainly to tape recorded music for the duration of my tour. To cheer up the entertainment starved servicemen, The Combined Services Entertainment (CSE), sent out variety type shows to Belize. I think there was a couple during my tour, with the basic formula of a good looking female singer, who might have had a hit record in the past, plus a blue comedian and a small music group. I suppose they were fine for what they were, but I could never be bothered to attend.

I continued my running, and went for a run twice a day during the week starting with a run early in the morning on my own, as nobody else would join me. In the evening I joined up with a small group of Army and RAF runners, who were all quite good runners, so this was excellent training for me. I also went swimming in the camp pool, although this was more to keep cool and to sunbathe. There was no regular races to compete in, but around the time of Independence Day, there was a special race put on in the city to celebrate. It was over approximately 6 miles and started and finished at a very run down athletic stadium. I entered a joint service team in the race which we duly finished as the first team. The winner was a local athlete, who finished ahead of the service team's best runner. When the pair were running through the town section of the race, the Army runner noticed that some spectators were laughing at him, and he could not understand why, particularly as he was having a good race. The reason for the laughter turned out to be mainly that he was wearing a sweatband on his head. For some reason this signified homosexuality, and therefore there was in the eyes of some at least, the double humour of him being unable to catch the leader and in turn the remainder of the runners, (who were all men), seemingly trying to catch him! It was probably a good example of the cultural differences!

On the work front, I tended to share any internal aeromed trips with the SAC, and there was not so many during my tour. Some of what were almost routine evacuations from remote army camps in Belize, did result in some excitement for me. On one occasion, I flew in a Gazelle helicopter piloted by an Army Air Corps officer to collect a patient with abdominal pain, who it was considered could be transported as a sitting passenger. In the helicopter, in addition to myself and the pilot was an army Lance Corporal who was being given a lift back to rejoin his unit in the south of the country. The pilot asked him if he had flown in a Gazelle before, and when he said that he had not, he then asked him if he would like to have a go at the controls, to which he readily agreed. It was meant to be simple, and all that had to be done, was to hold the joystick steady and follow the path of a straight road below. All went well to start with, but then the straight road had a small double bend in it, and to my horror, this trainee pilot jerked the controls to follow the road exactly, just as he had been told! I thought for a second that the extent of the banking would be fatal, but the pilot calmly took over the controls, saying 'I have control now corporal', and we carried on to our destination, to my great relief with the pilot in charge again! On another occasion there was no Puma helicopter readily available, so a civilian light aircraft was charted to collect a patient from a far-flung outpost in Belize. As we sped down the runway prior to take off, I started to get slightly concerned as it was taking longer than I thought it would for lift off to take place. At this moment, unbelievably, the seemingly laid-back pilot, reached for can of soft drink and which he placed between his knees to open the can with the ring pull, just as the aircraft eventually took off! I was happier flying in the Puma's which had a good safety record, but they had a habit of developing what were probably minor faults, which were worrying to me, but seemingly not to the crew, who would sometimes joke about such things, for example asking me to look out for oil leaks!

For aeromed flights to the UK, when there was no immediate urgency, there was normally a weekly, but sometimes fortnightly, routine VC 10 aircraft, which would if necessary include aeromed crews. One crew would disembark at Washington, whilst the other would continue to Belize and then escort any patients back to Washington, where the first crew would take over for the flight back to RAF Brize Norton. If the flight coincided with the return of the SAC after a detachment, or the aero medical sergeant at the end of his tour, then they would escort the patients on the Belize to Washington leg. In cases of extreme urgency, patients would be transferred to an American Military hospital by Lear Jet, but for cases where evacuation to the UK was necessary, but was so urgent that they could not wait for the next routine flight, arrangements were made for them to be escorted back on a civilian flight via Miami. Not long after I arrived such a case occurred, when a soldier sustained a fractured jaw after a brawl, that required surgery. He was escorted back to UK with the SAC as escort, because he had his jaw wired and there was the possibility of airsickness en route. This trip was memorable as when the patient arrived at Miami for the UK flight, British Airways denied all knowledge of the booking, and were not prepared to off-load two passengers on a fully booked flight to accommodate the patient and escort. Showing great initiative, the SAC telephoned the British Embassy staff in Washington to ask them to bring some pressure to bear on British Airways. Unfortunately, this was a Sunday afternoon, and as a mere SAC, he was unable to get in contact with anyone who had any authority to deal with the matter, so using his own credit card, he booked on another airline. As I fancied a trip back to the UK for a few days holiday, I was waiting for some similar urgent evacuation requirement, but none was forthcoming.

However, my luck was to change in this respect, and I achieved a flight back to the UK in a most unusual way, shortly after Independence Day. As a part of the the celebrations, a formal ball was held at the capital, at which some music was provided by a military band of the infantry battalion currently serving in Belize. At the ball, a member of the band was seen to be acting somewhat strangely, in that at one part of the evening, he left the bandstand and started to mingle with the guests instead of serenading them! I assume that this was not the only aspect of his behaviour that gave cause to concern, as the Army Medical Officer soon afterwards arranged an appointment with a psychiatrist at the Army's Psychiatric Hospital at Netley in the UK. A flight on the next routine VC10 was arranged, and the bandsman was to be escorted by an Army NCO who was due to be returning to the UK for other reasons. However when the RAF Medical Officer heard about this arrangement, he pointed out that only qualified personnel of the RAF Medical Branch were allowed to escort patients, and as the bandsman was in effect a patient, he would need to be properly classified as such, and escorted by an aeromed attendant. As luck would have it, there was no other patients due to be returned to the UK, so I got my trip back to the UK and 6 days holiday before flying back to Belize on the next weekly flight. During the flight from Belize to Washington it was my responsibility to ensure that the 'patient' I was escorting stayed well clear of all the emergency exits, and was under observation for the duration of the flight, including the toilets. I think I told him in advance about this, so he would go before we set off if possible! It was an uneventful but very boring flight, as the sociable bandsman hardly spoke at all, and I was forced to stay awake to watch over him. I was pleased when the plane arrived in Washington and somebody else took over escort duties for the final leg of the flight back to UK.

After 5 days in Suffolk, I flew back to Belize to continue my tour. It took me a couple of days to reacclimatise to the heat after the comparative cold weather in England, and then I was back in full training. Work was uneventful, but I did manage a brief diversion, which was a trip to the small town of Orange Walk, in the north of the country, with the Army Mobile Surgical Team. The team made visits to small towns in the country, set up their tents and then carried out operations on the local civilians. Apparently a common minor operation was the removal of a sixth toe, which was an affliction that occurred in those of Mayan descent. The growth of an additional small toe was seen by some, to be the mark of the devil. Removal was a very simple surgical procedure, and the army medics referred to the operation as decimalising the natives!

Back at Airport Camp, I was working in the office one day when a RAF serviceman called in and asked me if 'George' was about as he thought he might have an 'Audi'. This was obviously some sort of code which I knew nothing about. I discovered that 'George' was a RAMC Sergeant Laboratory Technician who operated a Venereal Disease (VD) clinic in a small room at the back of the hospital – suitably out of sight, I assume. An 'Audi' is another name for NSU, but in this case the N.S.U. stood for Non Specific Urethritis! This was a common form of VD in Belize at the time, and George would perform a blood test and then provide the necessary treatment, which was normally a course of antibiotics. Occasionally more serious forms of VD would occur, which led to an amusing incident at the hospital during an inspection by a visiting high-ranking Army Officer. At the time, there were several in-patients in the hospital, some of whom were awaiting the next aeromed flight back to the UK. The visiting General was escorted around by the Commanding Officer of the hospital, and when they arrived at the wards the visiting officer spoke to some of the patients. These included a soldier with VD, another SNCO soldier who had an alcoholic problem, and another with infected leg wounds. The wounds had been inflicted by another soldier when the pair were engaged in a bizarre game involving machetes, after taking drugs! I found out later via the RAF Medical Officer, that the CO of the Hospital had been reprimanded by the Camp Commander for not keeping such patients out of sight during the visit!

Outside of work, I continued to train very hard, as I now had a couple of races planned. One of these was a 20 kilometre road race in San Antonio, Texas, and the other was a half marathon at Belize which the Army had arranged Boxing day. Before these races, I took part in a charity run which took place on the roads just outside of Airport Camp. The object was to run as far as possible in one hour. I fancied my chances of achieving the highest mileage, partly because I was used to running early in the morning, and the one runner who would probably have beaten my total did not enter the event. I suppose not everybody took the event as seriously as I did, but I managed to run 10 miles in the hour, which was a whole mile further than the next highest which was achieved by a serious runner. Much to my delight, the results were included in the next edition of base Part One Orders, a copy of which I still have with all my racing souvenirs.

Annual leave at Belize was generally very restricted, in order to reduce the number of troops serving there, but a week outside the country was usually permitted. A favourite destination was Miami, but I was keen to run in a road race in America, so when I discovered a race in San Antonio, I opted to spend a week there.

The week before Christmas I flew to Houston and then took a bus to San Antonio. I was not offered any free accommodation this time, but I was otherwise treated as an elite athlete and given the Race number one, plus I was invited to a Post Race party. In the race I finished in 20th place and was the 3rd Over 40 finisher. I finished just behind a woman who I did not know, and when I spoke to her afterwards, I was unaware that she was a top class middle distance runner, called Carol Urish, who but for the American boycott, would have run the Moscow Olympics. I think I probably said something to the effect that she would do well if she kept on running! She was too nice to put me right. The Post Race party did not take place until the evening of the race, and was a somewhat curious affair. Any hope I had of drinking Budweisers and eating large burgers etc were dashed as there was no alcohol, and the buffet consisted of healthy vegetarian food. I did not discover why this was, as I did not like to ask. I noticed that nobody stayed at the party very long, and neither did I.

In the winter of 1981/82 there was some record low temperatures in Texas, and there was even snow in some parts for the first time. As San Antonio felt cold to me after Belize, I headed down to Corpus Christi on the coast which was a little warmer, aboard a Greyhound bus, which was a nice experience, and felt like I was in a movie. I spent a pleasant few days there at a small hotel, and spent lots of time running and sight seeing. It felt a little like Esbjerg earlier in the year as I was lonely, but it was very restful. I had plenty of fast food, partly because that was what was mainly on offer at the inexpensive food outlets. On Christmas Eve, I flew back to Belize and took over duty from the SAC, who was then free to enjoy the holiday as best he could. For my part, I had a very quiet Christmas Day as I was determined to do well in a half marathon race on Boxing Day. My sobriety partly paid off as I finished 4th overall and first over 40. I was hoping to do better, but all the good runners took part, and presumably they also had a sober Christmas day!

Whilst I was in Belize, I lost touch with the music charts, and tended to just listen to cassettes of artist sand groups that I liked. These included John Lennon, who had some chart success after his death with three number one hits as mentioned in the previous chapter. Before I left UK, Shakin Stevens continued with his version of rock and roll with two more number ones, 'This Ole House' and 'Green Door'. There was no doubt as to what the novelty record for this year was, when Joe Dolce took 'Shaddup Your Face' to number one in the UK. This amusing song was also a massive worldwide hit. The Specials, Police and Queen continued to have number one hits, as did David Bowie who teamed up with Queen to take 'Under Pressure to the top spot. The most notable newcomers were Adam and the Ants, who started what was known as 'new pop' which involved dressing up and melodic music. 'Stand And Deliver' and 'Prince Charming' were two number ones that were also two of the biggest hits of 1981.

As I neared the end of my tour in Belize, I was reminded of the fact that even in peacetime, life in the services carried a risk to life, when two fatal accidents occurred. The first occurred at the Jungle Warfare Training School, when in the course of an exercise using live ammunition, a Special Forces trainee officer sustained a fatal gun shot wound. The other fatality was the army driver of a lorry, which when deploying to a remote location at night, the vehicle overturned into a river causing the driver to be trapped underneath the vehicle. As a result the driver was drowned. At the time of this accident, I was in the vicinity to collect a Gurkha soldier with appendicitis, and after the body was discovered, I deployed to the scene, and when the body had been retrieved from under the vehicle, placed it in a body bag and returned with it to Airport Camp. It was suggested to me that I should not have removed the body before the police had seen it. I did not consider that there was any point in leaving the body in the river any longer, and in any event there was not any police, service or civilian readily available in the middle of the jungle. At least on this occasion, nobody suggested that a Medical Officer should be summoned to declare that life was extinct! I heard no more about the incident.

Also around the end of my tour, an amusing incident occurred in the Sergeant's Mess. One night there was an impromptu party which went on late, and in the opinion of the Garrison Sergeant Major, (GSM), far too late, as it had become very noisy. The GSM was one of several key personnel who had a married quarter on the base, and when he grew tired of the din, telephoned the Mess to ask that the noise was drastically reduced immediately. The telephoned was answered by an RAF sergeant, who had no doubt consumed a few drinks, and was not impressed by the tone of the GSM's observations. The GSM belonged to a Guards Regiment, and was not somebody who was used to anything other than instant compliance with any order or instruction he might see fit to give. The sergeant asked the GSM if he knew who he was speaking to? When the GSM said that he did not, the sergeant suggested that therefore the GSM could eff off! Very shortly afterwards, the GSM arrived at Mess, ordered that the bar was shut, and that everyone should leave immediately and go to bed!

In January of 1982, my tour in Belize came to an end, and I looked forward to getting back to the UK once again. I was posted to RAF Halton, but this time to the Medical Centre on the main camp. It was not my first choice, which at the time would have been a return to RAF Wattisham, but clearly this was not possible, so Halton was a good alternative. Unusually, my flight back to the UK, included acting as an escort to some patients as far as Washington, but none of these required any close supervision. I handed over to other escorts at Dulles Airport, Washington who would be escorting the Belize patients plus some others who were normally based at Washington back to the UK. When we were about an hour from landing at Brize Norton, we learned that the airfield there was snowbound, and amazingly, so were alternative airfields in the south of England, after what I assume was an extremely heavy and unexpected snowfall. Our flight was therefore diverting to Manchester. On arrival, I was given the option of waiting at Manchester until runways in the south were cleared, or proceeding by train. I opted for the train and headed off to Suffolk via London, where I noticed that whilst the roads were clear, the pavements were still covered with a considerable amount of snow, which was possibly the very last time to date that this has occurred. I arrived soon after in Suffolk, which had also been affected by snow, and enjoyed some leave and even the cool weather after six months of the other extreme. However my girlfriend did not share my enthusiasm for the cold, so before I reported to RAF Halton we took a holiday in Majorca!

17. RAF Halton

So just two years after leaving Halton on promotion, I arrived back there, but this time I would be living in the Sergeant's Mess, and working at the Medical Centre, which was known as a Regional Medical Centre, (RMC), as it was staffed and equipped to provide in patient care for other small units in the area which had no facilities for in patients. These were called Station Medical Centres (SMCs). The RMC had several small wards to accommodate mainly single service personnel, who required some nursing care, but not sufficient to merit admission to hospital. Nursing was normally undertaken by State Enrolled Nurses, but after duty hours, the Duty Medic would be responsible for their care. As at all other Medical Centres, the majority of the staff worked in the offices on administrative duties. There was a Flight Sergeant in charge and I was the deputy. For the very first time in all my service, I was working at a Medical Centre that was staffed mainly by members of the Women's Royal Air Force. I had of course worked with members of the WRAF at hospitals, but at all other stations there was no WRAF element, and therefore only RAF staff in the Medical Centres. This turned out to be pleasant change, especially as they all seemed keen to do well and make progress in their careers. There was a reliable corporal WRAF to whom the most junior members of the WRAF and RAF were directly responsible, and whilst I thought that on occasions, she appeared to be over zealous in her supervisory role, I got on well with her, and indeed as I did with all the staff. There was two medical officers at the RMC, who dealt mainly with the Flight Sergeant unless he was on leave and I was in charge, but they were happy to let us both get on with running the RMC whilst they saw to the medical side. For some reason there had not been a permanent Flight Sergeant at the RMC for some time, and the role of the deputy was filled only on a temporary basis by a sergeant from the hospital. This situation had seemingly led to a backlog of administrative work for the new Flight Sergeant, who was something of a perfectionist, and was also hopeful that if he made some significant improvements, he could expect promotion at some stage in the future. He was a married man who lived in the mess during the week, and did not mind doing work in the evening if he thought it necessary ' to get things straight'. He never asked me to work late, and I would invariably leave work bang on 5 p.m. and be in the Mess dining room shortly afterwards.

Life in the Sergeants Mess was very comfortable, and I eventually acquired an extra room so I could spread out my possessions and still leave one room reasonably tidy. The food was usually very good, and there was a bar which had very flexible opening times, although I did not use it very much when I first arrived. I was soon back in training for the Swinderby Marathon in April once again, and whilst I only trained in the evening on two evenings a week, when I went running with the Vale of Aylesbury AC again, I was watching my diet and weight. I did of course run every morning and lunchtime during the week, and was clocking up about a 100 miles a week every week. I seemed to have benefited from my 6 months in Belize, where I trained hard all of the time in the hot climate. At the end of March, I went back to Wegberg to run in the Bruggen 10 mile race, and also to catch up with Ken Barber, who had now separated from his wife, and was also living in the Sergeants Mess. I had a good race and clocked 57 minutes 42 which was my best ever time, and was the third Over 40 in a very good class race. On the Sunday, I went for a really long run of around 22 miles on footpaths around the famous Wegberg Ring, which was a former race track. As far as running was concerned I was on top of my form and the world.

However my social life suffered a setback when on my return to Halton, a letter from my girlfriend awaited me, which was effectively a 'Dear John'. I went to see her a few days later at the start of the Easter break to talk about it, and whilst we would stay friends etc., our brief romance had definitely ended. I returned to Halton for the Easter holiday, and without any set plans, I had plenty of time to think about my future in general, and in particular my career in the RAF. At the time, I was not very well off financially after my divorce, and the subsequent financial implications of maintenance, particularly in respect of my daughter, who was now undertaking further education. I started to reconsider my previous plan to retire after 22 years and start a new career, although I was no longer interested in becoming a Probation Officer. I thought that it might be better to start a new career at 43, because if I stayed in the RAF until I was 55, whilst I would get a much better pension, I would find it harder to find further suitable employment. I also had started to grow tired of moving around, sometimes to places that I did not particularly wish to go to. But at that time, the one big advantage of retiring early, would be that I would be entitled to a gratuity which would solve all my current financial problems. For example, I had not been able to afford to buy a car since returning from Belize, and was using a scooter to get around, and I had to borrow money to finance my last short trip to Germany for the Bruggen race. When I returned to work after the Easter holiday, I gave 6 months notice of my intention to retire on my 43rd birthday after 25 years and six months service – the first six months were discounted for pensionable service for some strange reason!

In the spring of 1982 I continued with my run of success in road running, that turned out to be my best ever. After a personal best time for 10 miles, I started to prepare for the Swinderby and London marathons with some warm up races. The first was a half marathon at Brentwood, when I finished in 79 minutes and was the first Over 40. Next up was the Bungay Marathon, where my aim was to have a fast training run and finish in around 3 hours. However on the second of two laps, I felt good and finished in 2 hours 55 and 19th overall. I was therefore confident of retaining my RAF veterans title at the Swinderby Marathon, and setting a new personal best marathon time. I had no problem getting time off work, and as I had done before traveled to Swinderby the day before for a good night's rest at the Sergeants Mess. My aim was to run under 2 hours 40, but I faded just a little after a good 20 miles. When I spotted somebody ahead of me in the closing miles that I thought may have been another Over 40 runner, I rallied and overtook him to finish in 2 hours 40 minutes and 56 seconds. This was not only a personal best, but more than enough to retain my veteran title. At the time of the Swinderby Marathon, I had started a very foolish habit of smoking an occasional cigarette. I suppose it was therefore natural to assume that after running my all time best ever marathon, that I could get away with this. So very soon after finishing the race

I went for a relaxing warm bath whilst I waited for the prize giving. Of course it was one of those special occasions when a cigarette was called for, so having managed to scrounge one the night before in anticipation of my success, I now greatly enjoyed the moment as I lay in the bath smoking the cigarette, before getting changed and heading off back to the gym to collect my trophy and plaudits.

Twelve days later, I ran in the London Marathon for the first time. On this occasion I was running for my club, The Vale Of Aylesbury AC. We all traveled down to the start at Greenwich on a coach along with members of a jogging club from Tring, who had managed to get entries to the marathon.

Even though we had an early start, this did not stop me from an even earlier start to the day to enable me to have a 4 mile warm up run around Weston Turville, followed by an early breakfast. My preparation technique for marathons was somewhat unusual at that time, but the marathon held no fears for me, and my only concerns were how fast I could run one. This time I tried once again to beat 2 hours 40, and it looked like I might do so, but in the later stages, I started to fade a little and had to settle for 2 hours 44, which was my second all time best time. At around the two thirds point, in the midst of all the thousands of runners, a Paul Offermans from my first athletic club in Germany appeared at my side. We had a brief conversation in German on the lines of 'Hello – fancy seeing you here – how is it going?'. When I told him that I was feeling tired, – *ich bin mude*, he bade me farewell and sped off! After the finish which was on Westminster Bridge that year, I went to a meeting point to rest and wait for the slower runners on the coach, who were mainly from the jogging club. Of course this was another special occasion having run two good marathons close together, and my first London marathon, in a decent time, and I was dying for a cigarette. I thought it unlikely I would find anybody to scrounge one off, but I spotted a runner who I knew, who was rolling a cigarette. I could hardly believe it as he had just run faster than I had, but he was someone who could seemingly restrict his smoking to the odd occasion as I thought I could. He readily agreed to roll one for me, and we both lounged around smoking our roll ups, and at the same time laughing and giggling at something or other, mainly because we were on a 'high' due to post race euphoria. However, we became aware that our somewhat odd behavior was being noticed by the wife of one of the joggers from Tring, who was waiting for her husband to finish. When he did appear long after our smoke, wearing his finish medal proudly round his neck, the hero was asked 'where had he been?', the obvious implication being that two drug addicts had finished long before him. We had inadvertently spoiled his day!

After my marathon successes, I had a feeling of anti climax, and started to lose interest in racing. Perhaps after 5 years of hard training and frequent races, I needed a break, but also at that time, I also had nobody to share with me in my triumphs other than perhaps some runners at The Vale of Aylesbury AC. I also started to enjoy more than an occasional cigarette, and was now struggling to stop altogether. I did have one event planned which was more of a time trial, and that was to cover 100 miles in under 36 hours. This was to gain selection for an RAF expedition to Greece later in the year, when a group of runners would run in relays, to cover what was thought to be the original marathon route of approximately 140 miles. There was an event called the Pilgrims's 100, which took place on the Spring Bank Holiday weekend, starting out at Guildford, where the participants were mainly walkers, but there were also several entrants who would run at least part of the way. After smoking what I told myself was my last cigarette before giving up altogether again, I set off with a group who were going to jog most of the course, with rest breaks for food at regular intervals, at 4 p.m. The next morning the group split up after a stop for breakfast, after which I decided to walk the remainder of the 100 miles. Unfortunately I failed to realise that I had not trained for fast walking, and I started to suffer and was slowing down dramatically, and having to take frequent rest breaks. When I reached an aid station at 88 miles, I worked out that I had 6 hours to cover the remaining 12 miles, which should have been a generous amount of time to complete the distance. However, I estimated that at the time, I was not walking at even that speed, so I would not make the time limit. I therefore did not wish to carry on and still not qualify, so I withdrew and then went to sleep whilst I waited for a back up vehicle in the morning, but not before I had scrounged a cigarette from one of the marshals! Later on the same day, I bought a whole packet of cigarettes to cheer myself up. For some time after returning to Halton, I continued to run at lunchtimes, but my enthusiasm had waned dramatically, and it was seemingly time to find some happiness in other ways.

On the work front, I was happy to continue working what was effectively my six months notice, but there was nothing challenging in my final post, and also no need to impress anybody any more. I did have two aeromed trips to afford an escape from the routine. Both were very memorable for completely different reasons. The first was a routine aeromed trip to Germany, when I was allocated the leg to Decimomannu in Sardinia, to escort a patient back to Germany and then on to Brize Norton. As the VC10 landed and was taxing at Decimomannu, the wing of the aircraft collided with the tail assembly of a stationary Phantom jet aircraft, causing some damage. When the VC 10 taxied to a halt, some of the ground servicing crew were obviously very amused by the incident, as VC 10 crews were apparently not their favourite visitors at this NATO base, as they were seen as unduly elitist, unlike the fighter pilots who they normally dealt with. The VC10 was not seriously damaged, but was not scheduled to return to Germany until the following morning, so I joined the crew at an hotel in the nearby town for an overnight stay. The VC10 crew spent hours carrying out a postmortem of events, and no doubt coming up with an explanation of why *they* were not to blame for the collision. Finally, we all went out for a slap up meal at a restaurant, where I had a most delicious main course of sea food, all paid for by the crew member who took care of such expenses. The remainder of the trip was entirely uneventful. My patient was not really a patient at all, and was simply a child with a hearing problem, who had been on a visit to her father at the NATO base, and was now returning to a special school, but required an escort for the journey. I think that there had been a possibility of another real patient, that had not materialized.

The next aeromed, turned out to be the very last one I took part in, and consisted of a trip to Ascension Island just after the end of the Falklands War, to assist with the transport back to the UK, of the many wounded servicemen. During the fighting, the wounded were treated on a hospital ship, but they were now being flown home in VC 10 aircraft which would stage at Ascension Island. Several VC 10s were employed on this mission. I was a member of a team that would take over from a team that started out the return journey at Montevideo. When I boarded the VC 10 at Ascension Island, I was initially shocked by the sight of an aircraft full of stretchers, many of which were occupied by Welsh Guardsmen, who were badly burned, when the troopship Sir Galaghad was bombed just before the disembarkation of the troops at The Falklands. Incidentally, the most well known burns casualty of the bombing, Simon Weston, was on another aircraft. In addition to the stretcher cases, there was some walking wounded, one of whom was a soldier who had lost an arm. The wounded were mostly in surprisingly good spirits, and this was no doubt helped by somebody making the decision to let the patients who smoked, continue smoking for the flight. Some had bad facial burns and needed assistance to smoke, such as continual moistening of the tip of the cigarette by saliva. This was clearly not a time to stop smoking for anybody, either the patients or indeed the aeromed crew. Unlike other aeromed flights, I assisted with nursing of some of the stretcher cases, mainly those suffering from severe burns, for the whole of the flight, other than when relieved for a meal break. This was one occasion when I certainly did not mind carrying out some basic nursing care, which was some 24 years after training.

There were problems concerning reporting of this war right from the start. Who will ever forget the bulletins broadcast nightly in a funereal tone, or the controversy regarding the *Sun* headline of 'Gotcha', after the sinking of the Argentinian ship Belgrano, which resulted in the death of 323 sailors. Problems continued after the end of the conflict, when television crews were refused permission to film the patients aboard the aircraft at Ascension Island. A row took place with the media representatives, but the RAF authorities remained adamant that no filming would be permitted on board the aeromed aircraft. From my view of the scene aboard the aircraft, this was not exactly what most people in the UK would have wanted to see, which is probably why permission was probably refused. At Ascension Island some recent UK newspapers had been brought on board the VC10, and these were circulating amongst the patients as the flight continued towards UK. Something about the war in one of the 'Red Tops' seemed to anger some of the casualties, one of whom screwed the offending article up in a ball and kicked it. I heard later that there had been some bad feeling between the British forces and the local population, partly as a result of a remark made by one of the Falklanders, who said something to the effect, that having finally got rid of the Argentinians, they now had to put up with the British Army! What started out as a 'popular' war with the liberating British forces, sailing to The Falklands to the tunes of Cliff Richard's 'Summer Holiday' with 'The Malvinas' the Argentine name for the Falklands substituted for 'Summer Holiday' and Rod Stewart's 'Sailing' had now changed, with many, (not particularly those on the aeromed flight), questioning whether it was all worth it.

It seemed that our arrival at Brize Norton would be very low key, which it was with no camera crews in evidence as the stretcher cases were off loaded into waiting ambulances for transfer to military hospitals, particularly those with specialist burns units. However as we taxied in on the runway, somebody who must have known who was on the aircraft, was seen standing just off the runway waving a huge Union Jack. It was a most memorable and moving moment, and for myself the very last time that I would be involved in any way with casualties resulting from active service. I accompanied some of the patients who would be admitted to PARAF Hospital at Wroughton, where the aeromed teams was met by the Principal Medical Officer of RAF Support Command, Air Commodore Riseley-Pritchard, with whom I had served in Aden 15 years earlier, when he was the SMO at RAF Khormaksar, and who later met me when I was aeromedically evacuated back from Libya via Cyprus the following year. I arrived back at Halton early on a Saturday evening, and went to a party, I had previously been invited to, but did not think I would be back in time to attend. My contribution to the party drinks, was a bottle of duty free whisky, much of which I consumed myself, but I remained sober such was the effect of what I witnessed earlier in the day.

In the summer of 1982, I became friendly with Paul, another recently divorced sergeant who also lived in the Sergeants Mess. We started to visit a Divorced Separated and Single, (DSS) club in Aylesbury for a weekly disco, and also a general pub disco in nearby Wendover on Fridays. We both got to know several local women in the process, and had some brief flings, during which we would go out as a foursome, sometimes to social events at the Sergeants Mess such as the Summer Ball. At work, I instigated an occasional Friday afternoon drinks session at the end of the afternoon. This was a common practice in the RAF, when work would cease a little earlier on Friday afternoon, and everyone would have a drink to celebrate the end of the working week. It was always the case that management turned a 'blind eye' to this tradition. When I was at Wattisham, a SAC working in one of the servicing sections, invited the Commanding Officer to his section's drinks, and was pleasantly surprised when the the CO turned up, and said that it was the first time he had been invited to such an occasion! The first time I organised Friday drinks, was just after my Ascension trip, when I brought back a large case of Budweiser beer which was not as common in UK at the time. To this I added some Bacardi mixed with cans of coke in a large teapot, which would give the impression of drinking tea without milk! These drinks parties were very popular amongst the mainly female staff, and occasionally if all was quiet and we had no in patients, they would extend into the evening, and were accompanied with sing-alongs to the hit records of the day.

1982 was certainly a year for sing-along records, as practically all the number ones for that year were in that category. The only exception was two more number one hits for Jam, 'A Town Called Malice' and 'Beat Surrender'. Even the year's novelty record, 'Save Your Love' by Renee and Ronato was sing-along. One of the Friday afternoon drinks favourite songs was the Tight Fit number one, 'The Lion Sleeps Tonight'. Another was Irene Cara's 'Fame' from the television series of the same name. Both would be sung with a parody of the associated dance movements, particularly in the case of 'Fame'. 'New Pop' remained very popular with Adam Ant and Boy George. On my very last day of RAF service, Culture Club reached number one with 'Do You

Really Want To Hurt Me'. This was indeed a long way indeed from Elvis Presley, who amazingly was still in the charts in 1982, and the lyrics of his 'US Male' as ' You had better not mess with' etc.

18. Demob

When I was approaching the last weeks of my service, I found myself in charge of the RMC more than usual, as the Flight Sergeant thought it best to take annual leave whilst he still had somebody he could trust to deputise for him, after he had finally got everything 'sorted out' and running smoothly to his liking. My remaining final major task was to do an inventory check of all the non medical equipment in the RMC. This included relatively inexpensive items such as bedding, cutlery and crockery. Having ascertained what the actual totals were, I could then arrange for some deficiencies to be 'written off' as representing what was known as 'fair wear and tear'. Other deficiencies could be off set against surpluses of similar items. For example there was many different types of chairs, and it was rare for correct total for each type to be found on a inventory check. This left only items that could not be located, and may have been loaned out unrecorded to another section but never returned. I was able to remedy any such deficiencies after a visit to the main stores, and a chat to the Barrack Warden, a civilian with huge power with whom I was of course friendly with, and who had the authority to 'scrap' missing items. Soon I had replenished minor items such as missing sheets, and crockery, and had the inventory ready to hand over to the Flight Sergeant on his return form leave.

As I was entitled to a civilian resettlement course, I opted for a course held at Aldershot which would prepare students for a Civil Service entry examination, which would be taken at the end of the course. The course was seemingly designed for servicemen and women who had not had very much experience of official letter writing etc, and it was therefore relatively easy for me to pass the examination at the end of the course. This was also the case with others on the course, but the course plus exam were seemingly insepa-rable. I stayed in the Sergeants Mess at a Army Barracks, which consisted of accommodation and the usual bar, and was practically deserted during the week. During the two week course, I travelled back to Halton not only at weekends, but also on Wednesdays to break up an otherwise boring week.

After my resettlement course, I returned to Halton to complete all the formalities of my discharge. One of these was to formally hand over all the equipment in my charge to the Flight Sergeant. As I might have expected, this was not a simple process, and further visits to the Barrack Warden had to be made, armed with whatever he needed in the shape of bandages and things such as cough medicine! The next step in the process was to 'clear' the station. This process entailed visiting various sections on the camp with a form called a 'Clearance Chit', which had to be signed before you could 'clear' and depart either to a new posting or to demob. In addition to the more obvious sections such as Accounts and the Post Office, was the clothing store to hand in uniforms now no longer needed, such as a greatcoat, but also my best uniform. After 25 years of complying more or less with orders, it did not occur to me to ask if I could keep it. Instead I just removed my para wings, aeromed wings and collar dogs for keepsakes. When the clearance procedure was completed I received a folder containing a record of my service and qualifications, plus a copy of an extract from the Official Secrets Act I was required to sign. In addition I was given a notice to say that if I intended to visit any 'Communist' countries, which were listed on the notice, I should consult the Ministry of Defence first. This was a mandatory requirement. The list included 'The Soviet Occupied Zone of Germany' and included travel to West Berlin. I have never been advised since then, that I can now proceed to any of the countries such as Poland that are no longer 'communist' without asking first! I later received a valedictory letter from the Air Officer Commanding Training Units of Support Command, thanking me for my valuable contribution and wishing me well for the future.

There remained two social functions to mark the end of my service career. The first was the traditional farewell drinks with the staff of RMC after normal work had ended on my final working day. This lasted for a good few hours. I then started my twenty eight days demob leave, officially known as Terminal Leave, after which I would became a civilian once again after twenty five years and six months. The second occasion was a formal dinner in the Sergeants Mess some weeks later, which meant that I had to hire a Dinner Suit, and also purchase miniature medals for the occasion. It was a memorable evening and well worth the expense.

Postscript

The author subsequently had a successful career in the Lord Chancellor's Department of the Civil Service and has now retired back to his native Yorkshire with Joan. nowadays when he travels in an aircraft, he is content to wait until it has landed and has no desire to jump out ever again! He is still an active runner and competes for Scarborough Athletic Club.

1960 ~ RAF Bahrain

1960 ~ RAF Bahrain. Xmas in a Billet Bar.

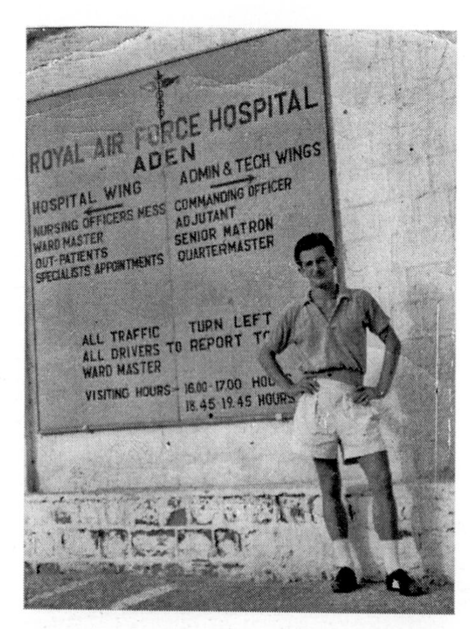

1960 RAF Hospital Aden (became Steamer Point when Khormaksar Beach Hospital was built)

1960 ~ On Safari in Tsavo National Park Kenya

RAF Henlow during the 'big freeze' 1961.
Nothing much to do at the time.

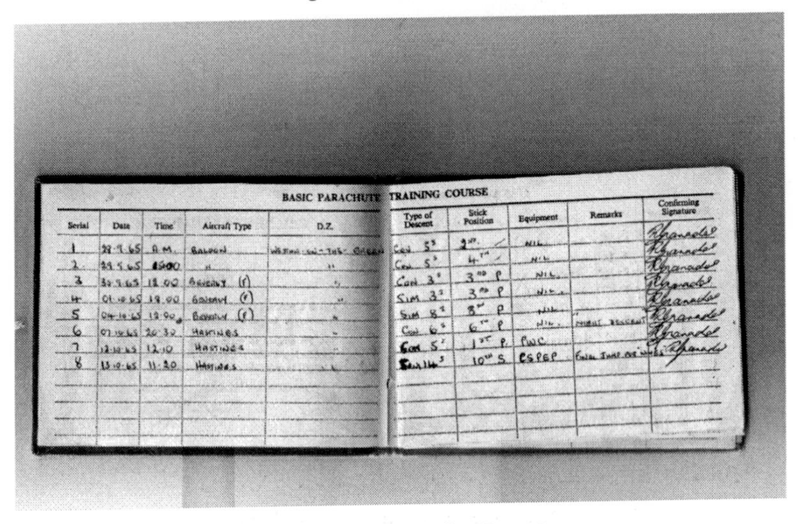

BASIC PARACHUTE TRAINING COURSE

Serial	Date	Time	Aircraft Type	D.Z.	Type of Descent	Stick Position	Equipment	Remarks	Confirming Signature
1	28.9.65	A.M.	BALLOON	WESTON-ON-THE-GREEN	CON 5^3	2ND	NIL		[illegible]
2	29.9.65	1500	"	"	CON 5^3	4TH	NIL		[illegible]
3	30.9.65	18.00	BEVERLY (F)	"	CON 3^3	3RD P	NIL		[illegible]
4	01.10.65	19.00	BEVERLY (F)	"	SIM 3^3	3RD P	NIL		[illegible]
5	04.10.65	19.00	BEVERLY (F)	"	SIM 8^3	8TH P	NIL		[illegible]
6	07.10.65	20.30	HASTINGS	"	CON 6^3	6TH P	NIL	NIGHT DESCENT	[illegible]
7	12.10.65	12.10	HASTINGS	"	CON 5^2	1ST P	PWC		[illegible]
8	13.10.65	11.30	HASTINGS	"	[illegible]	10TH S	CSPEP	FINAL JUMP FOR WINGS	[illegible]

Parachute Log Book – Page 1

1966. Aden. Preparing to jump with an airborne stretcher (Author nearest camera, bottom right)

1966 At Little Aden Ranges.

1971 RAF Akrotiri. Meeting the AOC in C.

1970 On exercise in Turkey with the Para Rescue Team

1972. Final and 100th Parachute Jump celebrations.

Page 2 Original Card issued 29-[illegible]-68 (6 Previous Contests 1961/68 P) | E.R. THOMPSON. M.P. Page 3

Date (1)	Competition Opponent (2)	No. of rounds (3)	Result (4)	M.O.'s Remarks, Recommendations, and Signature (5)
No medical suspensions			[illegible]	30.9.66.
12 OCT 66	[illegible] INTER STATION / KING	2	RSB. LOST	[illegible]
31-10-66	Wakefield v LCA Playle	3×2	Lost Pts	[illegible]
9-1-67	S Parfitt [illegible]	3×2	WON PTS	[illegible]
22/2/67	[illegible] v SAC HARVEY	3×2	LOST PTS	
13 Dec 67	Special v SAC Donovan	3×2	Lost pts	[illegible]
7 OCT 68	[illegible] v James	3×2	WON RSB (3)	[illegible]
[illegible]	[illegible]	3×2	WON RSB (3)	[illegible]
[illegible].11.68	WAKEFIELDS v LAC MORAN	3×2	WON Points	[illegible]
5 Nov 68	WAKEFIELD v MERCER	3×2	WON Points	
6.11.68	WAKEFIELDS v L/CPL PRESTON	3×2	WON PTS	[illegible]
2 DEC 68	ICN 'B' v WALK OVER	3×2	WON WALK OVER	[illegible]
2 DEC 68	ICN 'B' v MERCER	3×2	LOST PTS	[illegible]
21.1.69	INTER COMD/OPEN CHAMPIONSHIPS	3×[illegible]	LOST RSB (3)	
14.1.71	RAF CHAMPS - CPL [illegible]	3×3	LOST RSB (2)	
28.4.71	CS. RAF [illegible] v SAC Grey	3×2 +3	Won Points	[illegible]
Re-registered September 1971			[illegible]	17/9/71
11/1/72	RAF CHAMPS v CPL P. [illegible]	3×3	LOST KO 3rd	Suspended (4 days) [illegible]
6/10/72	v T. HYSLOP [illegible]	3×2	LOST KO 1st	
24-10-72	CONINGSBY v COOPER	3×2	WON RSB (2)	

Page one of Boxing Record Book

1980. GB One in the USA. San Antonio Road Race

1980. RAF Swinderby. First of two team wins and three first RAF Veteran Champion awards.

1980 RAF Belize

2002. Meeting Her Majesty just before my final retirement at the Royal Courts of Justice.

2002 Reunion of 2 Field Squadron at RAF Honington